Small Comrades

STUDIES IN THE HISTORY OF EDUCATION
EDWARD R. BEAUCHAMP, *Series Editor*

Small Comrades

Revolutionizing Childhood in Soviet Russia, 1917–1932

Lisa A. Kirschenbaum

RoutledgeFalmer
New York   London

A volume in the *Studies in the History of Education* series

Published in 2001 by

RoutledgeFalmer
29 West 35th Street
New York, NY 10001

Published in Great Britain by

RoutledgeFalmer
11 New Fetter Lane
London EC4P 4EE

RoutledgeFalmer is an imprint of the Taylor & Francis Group.

Library of Congress Cataloging-in-Publication Data
Kirschenbaum, Lisa A.
      Small comrades : revolutionizing childhood in
      Soviet Russia, 1917–1932 / Lisa A. Kirschenbaum.
          p.   cm. — (RoutledgeFalmer studies in the history of education)
      Includes bibliographical references (p.) and index.
      ISBN 0-8153-3944-5 (alk. paper) —
      ISBN 0-8153-3945-3 (pbk. : alk. paper)
      1. Early childhood education—Russia—History—20th century.
      2. Education—Aims and objectives—Russia—History—20th century.
      3. Communism and education—Russia—History.
      4. Children—Russia—Social Conditions—20th century.
      I. Title.   II. Series.
  LA833.K57   2000
  372.947—dc21   00-055341

Contents

List of Tables

Acknowledgments

M y profound thanks go to the many people who carefully read the manuscript and offered suggestions for improving it. This book began as a Ph.D. dissertation at the University of California, Berkeley, where Victoria Bonnell encouraged me to follow into the Soviet period my interest in the question of how radicals raised their children. My adviser Reginald Zelnik provided and continues to provide a rare combination of frank criticism and encouragement. Nicholas Riasanovsky read the manuscript with amazing care, and helped me to think about broadening its horizons. Richard Stites and Jeffrey Brooks were among my earliest and most helpful critical readers. Lynn Mally and Isabel Tirado suggested many important additions and helped me to rethink the overall shape of the book. Susan Gans provided all sorts of moral support along with a careful review of my use of statistics. I thank Remy Squires at the Hoover Institution Archives for his help with the illustrations. I owe a large debt to the librarians and archivists at the Hoover Institute, the library of the University of California, Berkeley, the Library of Congress, the National Archives, the Lenin Library, the Central State Archive of the RSFSR, and the Academy of Pedagogical Sciences. Finally, I wish to recognize my mother, my earliest and most enthusiastic reader. This book is dedicated to her and the rest of my family.

Series Preface

R outledgeFalmer's Studies in the History of Education series includes not only volumes on the history of American and Western education, but also on the history of the development of education in non-Western societies. A major goal of this series is to provide new interpretations of educational history that are based on the best recent scholarship; each volume will provide an original analysis and interpretation of the topic under consideration. A wide variety of methodological approaches from the traditional to the innovative are used. In addition, the series especially welcomes studies that focus not only on schools, but also on education as defined by Harvard historian Bernard Bailyn: "the transmission of culture across generations."

The major criteria for inclusion are (a) a manuscript of the highest quality, and (b) a topic of importance to understanding the field. The editor is open to readers' suggestions and looks forward to a long-term dialogue with them on the future direction of the series.

Edward R. Beauchamp

Introduction

Real and Imagined Children

W hen children appear in accounts of the early years of Soviet power, they often figure as problems that complicated, and perhaps undermined, efforts to liberate women, remake the family, and revolutionize everyday life. Bolsheviks—along with other Russian Marxists, populists, and European socialists—generally had long assumed that revolution would open the way to a reconfiguration of the family. The anticipated modification of the family was associated with the successful resolution of the "woman question," or, in Marxist terms, the emancipation of women from the onerous double shift imposed by capitalism. Making revolution an everyday reality for women seemed to require immediate and practical answers to the concrete and irreducible question of who cares for children—along with the questions of who washes the linen and who prepares the soup. The solution embraced by socialists was usually some form of socialized housekeeping and child care.[1] Even in the best of circumstances, what might be called the "child question" complicated the resolution of the woman question. In revolutionary Russia, where the regime faced the daunting task of getting swarms of abandoned and homeless children (*besprizorniki*) off the streets, the magnitude of the child question accounts, at least in part, for the failure of efforts to emancipate women from domestic labor.

Yet even as "problem" children threatened to derail or at least postpone efforts to revolutionize everyday life, the Bolsheviks continued to represent the rising generation as the vanguard of cultural change. In his study of abandoned children, Alan Ball notes that children's homes were understood not only as the best means of dealing with the immediate crisis, but also as ideal hothouses "in which to nurture the country's flowers." Acknowledging the often bitter realities of urban homelessness, the "visionaries" among the Bolsheviks pictured the children of the streets as "embryonic" collectivists, the independent, adaptable, resourceful, and bold constructors of the revolutionary future.[2] While children seemed particularly vulnerable to the social dislocations bred of war and revolution, they also appeared to be potent agents of revolutionary change. As Lynn Mally has pointed out, "the fate of proletarian children sparked more interest" among Bolsheviks than the "status of women": "Women embodied all the problems of the past, but children were the hope of the future." Children were the "real revolutionaries."[3]

The coupling of efforts to rescue children from the streets with the tendency to represent children as the agents and emblems of revolution suggests the importance of the heuristic distinction often made in studies of childhood between "flesh and blood human beings of a certain age" and the "cultural construction of ideas to do with childhood."[4] The distinction is particularly useful in sorting out the complex interaction of ideology and practice that accompanied efforts to re-envision and remake everyday life. Similar categories have been fruitfully applied in studies of attempts to revolutionize family and gender. Lynn Hunt's exploration of the French revolutionaries' "creative efforts to reimagine the political world" in terms of family relations distinguishes the family "as some kind of modal social experience" from "the family as an imaginative construct of power relations." Elizabeth Wood's study of gender and politics in revolutionary Russia argues that although "[t]he history of the woman question in Russia has usually been written as if it were about real women . . . it is really about myths," and she makes a compelling case for understanding the rhetoric of women's emancipation as primarily a way of talking about social transformation and as "only partially about women themselves."[5] Similarly separating myths of childhood from children themselves makes it possible to analyze how "childhood" functioned as a means of imagining revolutionary transformation.

At the same time, it is important to keep in mind that, at least in the Soviet case, revolutionaries in power tended to conflate (or confuse) the "real" children who had to be fed, clothed, and educated and the metaphorical children who stood as icons of the revolution's future.[6] Conceiving of their revolution as scientific rather than utopian, and of themselves as engineers rather than visionaries, the Bolsheviks often presented their images of children and childhood as mirrors of reality rather than myths or metaphors. The fusion of the real and the imagined is particularly clear in the Soviet approach to young children, which merged self-consciously "scientific" understandings of children's needs, capacities, and interests with the vision of children as "real revolutionaries."

This study takes as its point of departure the notion that children in the new Soviet state embodied both pressing practical problems and revolutionary dreams. It traces the shifting and contested meanings of childhood in revolutionary Russia as well as the consequences of the child's status as the personification of the whole enterprise of cultural revolution for teachers, parents, and children themselves. The examination of the Soviet regime's policy toward preschool children has allowed me to explore the role of the first socialist generation in Bolshevik conceptions of revolutionary transformation without losing sight of the tragic conditions facing so many families, and especially children, in the early years of Soviet power.

The book focuses on children between the ages of three and seven because by the early twentieth century those ages were taken by Russian experts as marking the boundaries of a relatively new and fluid, but undeniably important, "stage" of childhood. Such "stages" remain a pervasive conventional means of conceptualizing childhood. Indeed, many studies of school and child care limit themselves to children of a specific age without problematizing the construction of age thresholds for various sorts of institutions.[7] In the field of Soviet history, studies of women and family provide valuable accounts of activists' efforts to establish nurseries that cared for children from birth until three years of age and of the impact of rising numbers of *besprizorniki* on plans for socializing child-rearing. Histories of Soviet education begin when children entered the schoolroom at age seven, although they often emphasize secondary and university students.[8] Thus preschool children are handled by default as a separate category, largely outside the purview both of studies focused on issues of child care and of histories of education. Chapter 1 traces the ways in which the "preschool age," variously defined, became linked to "a specific social structural space for children"[9] in both Russia and the West. Here I would like to emphasize that the focus on a specific age group is not based on the assumption that at all times and places children of a given chronological age have identical, predictable needs, and therefore that Soviet policies and practices can be judged against some universal standard of child care. Instead, the focus on preschoolers, or what sociologists have called the "middle years" of childhood, stems from a recognition that educators and health workers constructed preschoolers as a distinct category—one that has received comparatively little scholarly attention.[10]

Appropriating and transforming the knowledge of pre-Revolutionary experts in pedagogy and public health, Bolshevik efforts to revolutionize the "formative" years of childhood occurred on the level of "scientific" discourse and in the institutional context of the kindergarten. A central argument of the book is that while the "scientific" language of preschool experts took real children as its referent, it also provided a means of articulating and contesting the methods and meanings of revolution in everyday life. Only partly about flesh-and-blood children, debates on childhood and the kindergarten suggested ways of putting revolutionary visions into practice under often catastrophic conditions.

While this study draws in significant ways on the work that has been done on Soviet schooling and has much to say about the concerns of histories of education—the development of institutions and curricula—it also attends to the wider context of the relationship between the family and the state and to Bolshevik visions of childhood. Well before October 1917, the Russian kindergarten, even more than its Western counterparts, had a broader and more radical mission than the school. In the Russian context, the "kindergarten" (*detskii sad*) connoted not only age-appropriate "upbringing" (*vospitanie*) that was often explicitly modeled on that provided by half-day public kindergartens in the United States, but also full-day care for children of American "nursery school" (ages three and four), kindergarten (age five), and early school (ages six and seven) age. As Chapter 1 details, the kindergarten's Russian advocates aimed to "raise" children rather than merely to "educate" them and to play a critical role in remaking the child's relationship with his or her parents.

The Bolsheviks construed the kindergarten not as an "infant school" but as a vital component of a more general effort to revolutionize childhood and refashion everyday life. Although kindergartens, like schools, fell under the jurisdiction of the Commissariat of Enlightenment, and although teachers sometimes promoted kindergartens as good preparation for school, preschools offer an important and unique vantage point for an examination of the evolution of Bolshevik attitudes toward the family. Taking their lead from the contemporary linkage of family and women's oppression, many studies of Bolshevik family policy have focused on adults and have emphasized, as Wood points out, "the apparent failure of the Bolshevik leadership to put an end to women's inequality."[11] Explanations of the Soviet state's eventual support of the patriarchal family have been structured around assessments of the nature of the Bolshevik commitment to emancipation and of the constraints imposed by material shortages and traditional attitudes.[12] Revisiting this terrain from the point of view of policies toward children can offer new perspectives on the fate of the promises, plans, and visions of the Bolshevik Revolution.

This book illuminates the ways in which the revolutionary and the traditional, the visionary and the practical, the imaginary and the real often overlapped and complicated one another in the field of family policy. It suggests less a linear "retreat" than the production of complex amalgams of programs that promised to liberate, enlighten, modernize, indoctrinate, and discipline the oppressed masses. Paying attention to children opens questions about how the "practical" decision to postpone fully socialized child care, usually understood as a critical blow to the project of women's emancipation, coexisted with highly "impractical" efforts to revolutionize the whole texture of family life by revolutionizing the kindergarten curriculum (Chapter 6). Likewise, the Stalinist "Thermidor" can be understood as a paradoxical mix of support for traditional gender and generational hierarchies with images of defiant, revolutionary youth (Chapter 7).

Despite the clear and acknowledged debts of Bolshevik children's policies to Western educational theorists and to the Western tradition of philanthropic kindergartens for the children of the poor, efforts to revolutionize childhood were among the most reviled of Soviet experiments in the realm of culture. They can still elicit strong negative reactions. As Chapter 2 details, opponents of the Revolution proffered the wide gap between the Bolshevik rhetoric of children's liberation and the brutal circumstances in which so many children lived as evidence of the regime's illegitimacy — ignoring the fact that the circumstances deplored often predated the Revolution.[13] Here it is worth emphasizing that the vision of children as vulnerable, innocent, dependent, and weak that animated so much of the anti-Bolshevik rhetoric at the time remains a component of current Western notions of childhood, and indeed is a key element in current political contests over "family values."[14] Finding "scientific" grounds for imagining children as independent, rational, and powerful agents of revolution, the Bolsheviks rejected some of the most cherished, naturalized, and emotionally charged Western visions of childhood. That the Bolsheviks' views of the "nature" and "needs" of children can still seem shocking, or at least cutting-edge, underscores the importance of exploring social constructions of childhood as well as the affective power of conventional images.[15]

Approaching childhood as constructed both by institutions and by the language and practice of pedagogy, this study attends both to debates on whether the kindergarten ought to shore up, regulate, or replace the parent–child relationship and to contests over "how people (that is, largely children) ought best to be."[16] Because tsarist Russia had relatively few kindergartens, Chapter 1 focuses mainly on outlining the powers of cultural and individual transformation attributed to kindergartens and to young children by socialists and nonsocialists in Russia and the West in the years between the invention of the kindergarten in mid-nineteenth-century Germany and the Bolshevik Revolution. The chapter examines the pedagogical and political contexts shaping the Russian reception of the kindergarten.

In the first years after October 1917, the new state built preschool institutions at a rapid pace. Throughout the Civil War (1918–1921), it was the kindergarten's potential as an institutional substitute for the family that recommended it to revolutionaries. Chapter 2 focuses on the combination of practical planning and revolutionary dreaming that led policymakers at the Commissariat of Enlightenment to define upbringing (*vospitanie*), rather than famine relief or social welfare, as the primary task of preschool institutions. Chapter 3 examines the relationship of the kindergarten to the anticipated "withering away" of the family and explores Bolshevik conceptions of ideal parent–child relationships and the social "family." Chapter 4 details the broad range of preschool programs initially tolerated by the Bolsheviks and the ways in which preschool experts worked to lend "scientific" weight to revolutionary images of childhood.

By the late 1920s, the Bolsheviks were questioning both the possibility and the wisdom of speeding the withering away of the family. The budget cutbacks mandated by the New Economic Policy in 1921 had an immediate and devastating impact on kindergartens. It soon became clear that far from replacing parents, kindergartens would have to rely on their active material and financial support. Chapter 5 charts the withering away of the kindergarten in the early 1920s and the concomitant debates on the possibility of reeducating parents and remaking the life of the child at home in the face of a profound lack of resources. Chapter 6 examines the move away from defining the kindergarten in terms of its role in "liberating" children from the family and toward emphasizing the power of explicitly "socialist" pedagogy to revolutionize families and children, who were now imagined as almost infinitely malleable. Implementing for the first time a standard preschool curriculum, the Commissariat of Enlightenment provided a new "script" for childhood along with a new, "proletarian" science of child study.

Chapter 7 details the construction of the emblematic child of the years of the First Five-Year Plan (1928–1932). Stalinist childhood appears less as a clear break with previous images of revolutionary childhood than as an often paradoxical reworking of earlier institutional arrangements and conceptions of the nature and needs of children. With the First Five-Year Plan came a renewed interest in building kindergartens, now aimed not at replacing the family, but at remaking children and, through them, parents, in the image of the Stalinist state. The child remained the revolutionary par excellence, now trained to defy parental authority in the name of the patriarchal state.

Standing at the intersection of the family, society, and the state, the kindergarten can tell us much about adults. More difficult to tease out of the sources is an understanding of the lives of children. Did debates on the nature of childhood touch the children enrolled in kindergartens? How did the first socialist generation remember its childhood and identify itself? Answering such questions is risky. The "script" of childhood provided by the regime structured teachers' observations of their pupils and, in less transparent ways, adults' recollections of their revolutionary childhoods. Working on the assumption that cultural representations and self-definitions are not entirely separable in any case, the postscript offers at least tentative answers to the questions that motivated this study: What did children make of the Revolution? What did the Revolution make of them?

part one

The Kindergarten and the Revolutionary Tradition in Russia

1

Pedagogy and Politics

From the 1850s until well into the twentieth century, Russian radicals—educators and noneducators alike—often framed criticisms of authoritarian social structures, and articulated alternatives, in the language of education. As Svetlana Boym has noted, "Pedagogy in general is one of the most important revolutionary and postrevolutionary disciplines."[1] The linkage of pedagogical and social critique was hardly unique to Russia. It can be traced back at least to Rousseau, whose *Emile* (1762) can be read not only as an "educational manual" but also more broadly as the author's "positive statement about the highest possibilities of society and the way to live a good life within it."[2]

Part of the power and appeal of the language of pedagogy was its ability to make the visionary appear practical. The system of education proposed in *Emile* may well be "manifestly impossible for most men and virtually impossible for any man." Rousseau himself never implemented it in his own household, preferring to abandon his children to the foundling hospital. Still, other educators took *Emile* as a guide to practice and raised their children according to Rousseau's prescriptions, often with disappointing results.[3] A similar sense that the "manifestly impossible" might be doable is visible in Boym's example from the Soviet Union in the mid 1920s. Training the "former homeless hooligan-*besprizornik*" to be a conscientious constructor of communism entailed a fundamental, but seemingly not a "fantastic," transformation. The prosaic methods of the "scientifically" organized schoolroom promised the reliable production of new and self-disciplined citizens. Before the Revolution, a rather different, although still "scientific," pedagogy provided blueprints for putting visions of the future into practice in the present.

This chapter argues that the kindergarten proved a particularly attractive arena in which to envision and try to enact individual and cultural transformations. The kindergarten's appeal was due in part to its institutional newness and flexibility, in part to its assumptions about the "nature" of early childhood, and in part to its location at the intersection of the public and private spheres. Invented in the mid-nineteenth century, the kindergarten quickly spread beyond Germany. By the early twentieth century, "kindergarten" could denote a variety of institutions and pedagogical practices.[4] Common to all was the conviction that "early childhood" constituted a discrete and formative stage of a child's development. That conviction, coupled with the kindergarten's intervention in the private sphere, recommended it as an institution capable of remaking individuals, the family, and even public life.

In Russia, as elsewhere, both the political and the pedagogical contexts shaped the reception of the kindergarten. Russian educators drew on the complex and sometimes contradictory legacy of Western educational theory and practice to create and (more often) theorize institutions that promised to emancipate both women and children from the constraints of the traditional family and to turn children into "small comrades." The radicalism of the 1860s provided the immediate setting for the appropriation and modification of the kindergarten in Russia. By the eve of the Revolution, the Russian kindergarten was animated by a tension between the desire to liberate both women and children and the perceived need to regulate the life of the child and to train women to be modern mothers.

A New Place for Young Children

Located between the home and the school, the kindergarten provided an institutional structure for the construction of early childhood as a unique and uniquely important stage of life. In 1837, Friedrich Froebel (1782–1852) organized an "institution for fostering small children" (*Anstalt fur Kleinkinderpflege*) that he envisioned as a place where children would receive the "care of a skilled, intelligent gardener" and where mothers would be educated to meet the needs of children (ages four to six) who had outgrown the nursery but were not yet ready for school. He dubbed the new institution a "kindergarten" (child garden), a name that provided the "perfect romantic metaphor" for an institution that intended, as Froebel expressed it in 1840, to cultivate "the noblest of all growing things, men (that is children, the germs and shoots of humanity) . . . in accordance with the laws of their own being, of God and of Nature."[5] A new place for young children organized around a rigid sequence of activities and games, the Froebelian kindergarten established early childhood as a discrete "stage" with its own "script."[6]

On the level of pedagogy, the kindergarten represented an important innovation that ultimately offered a template for school reform. Froebel's practice owed much to Rousseau's insistence that early formal learning and literacy deformed the "natural" development of children. It also drew on Swiss educator Johann Pestalozzi's "object teaching," a system that downplayed books and provided children with concrete things to explore, touch, and manipulate on their own. Froebel spent two years at Pestalozzi's model school (1808–1810), and found his mentor's methods compelling but too "mechanical."[7]

What most clearly set Froebel's program apart from that of Pestalozzi was its emphasis on tailoring concrete experiences to match the "stages" of the young child's mental, physical, and spiritual development. Froebel explicitly rejected the passive obedience and discipline of the school along with its emphasis on academic achievement. He set about devising a curriculum that allowed children to learn through guided play and that introduced city children to the delights of country life. In the kindergarten, children undertook a series of sequenced activities with increasingly complex geometrical objects that Froebel called "occupations" and "gifts." They also participated in structured games and undertook handwork modeled on peasant crafts such as sewing and weaving. Froebel himself wrote stories, songs, and poems that he viewed as appropriate to the world of the young child—often saccharine evocations of rural life that have been characterized as "children's kitsch."[8] For all his rhetoric of organic development, Froebel's program arguably owed more to a nostalgia for an imagined preindustrial idyll of childhood than to a "scientific" understanding of young children. Many of his kindergarten "occupations" were later rejected as requiring fine motor skills that preschoolers lack.[9] Still, the insistence on play, on learning by doing, and on creating a developmentally appropriate and nurturing environment for the child constituted a significant departure from pedagogy in the schools.

The kindergarten's origins outside the established school system helped to make it a center of pedagogical reform. In the schools, reformers had to contend with deeply entrenched practices—relying on rote memorization, enforcing quiet, assigning grades—that had the support of many teachers and parents. Even the physical space of the traditional schoolroom worked against reform. In British infant schools (for children ages three to seven), the "gallery," fixed tiers of desks, hampered the introduction of kindergarten methods.[10] By contrast, the kindergarten was by definition a relatively unstructured "garden room," where rows of desks gave way to a circle of chairs and the interests of children always came first. Specially trained teachers created a space for young children outside the school and the home, but it was still linked to the life of the family via efforts to educate mothers. By the late nineteenth century, the kindergarten stood among the most radical experiments in child-centered education. American progressives like John Dewey and Francis Parker proposed its hands-on, socially oriented approach as a model for schools of the future.[11]

The construction of early childhood as a critical stage of individual development also facilitated the association of the work of the kindergarten with reform or even revolution. Kindergarten teachers viewed their charges as, in Froebel's phrase, "the germs and shoots of humanity" or, in the more "scientific" language of American psychologist Stanley Hall, as at a "nascent period" of life.[12] At this critical moment, kindergartens encouraged a "spirit of independence and curiosity" that schoolteachers who valued passivity and quiet sometimes deemed "troublesome."[13] If one granted the assumption that these early experiences carried enormous developmental importance, then the kindergarten raised the possibility (or the specter, depending on the point of view) of nurturing assertive, independent, "troublesome" citizens.

For many of its advocates, the kindergarten functioned as a sort of laboratory for building a model society. Removing child-rearing from the private sphere of the family, the kindergarten offered a place to instill public values in young children. Historian Ann Taylor Allen notes that "the kindergarten movement in Germany was originally created by the liberals of 1848 as a center of education in the public virtues that would help to produce a new generation of citizens." In both Germany and the United States, kindergarten teachers "described their classrooms as microcosmic models for a new ideal of citizenship that reconciled individual freedom with public responsibility."[14] Taking the kindergartens' subversive potential seriously, the Prussian government banned them between 1851 and 1860.[15]

The kindergarten's location at the intersection of the public and private spheres opened fundamental questions about the role of women in public life and about the need for public intervention in the life of the family. Steeped in nostalgia for the peasant mother's "natural" connection to her children, Froebel sought to restore the "primordial union" of womanhood and motherhood that he believed had been severed by industrial society. In the kindergarten he offered the somewhat paradoxical solution of taking children and mothers out of the home and of training women to fulfill their "natural" roles.[16] Making mothering public and important work, the kindergarten can be understood as what historians Seth Koven and Sonya Michel identify as a "maternalist" movement that "extolled the private virtues of domesticity while simultaneously legitimating women's public relationships to politics and the state, to community, workplace, and the marketplace." From the maternalist point of view, motherhood was seen "as empowering, not as a condition of dependence or weakness."[17]

While some European socialists embraced maternalist rhetoric,[18] others associated "the kindergarten with the socialist critique of the bourgeois family" and viewed public child care less as a means of expanding the reach of women's special virtues than as an "important social service supporting a new status for both women and children in the socialist society of the future."[19] The two positions were potentially, but not necessarily, irreconcilable, and socialists could be heard advocating both the application of "womanly" virtues to a wider sphere as well as the emancipation of women from traditional constraints. In either case, socialists often paid more attention to the act of removing the young child from the family than to what went on in the kindergarten itself. German socialist Wilhelm Liebknecht's only objection to Froebel's kindergarten was that it took in only the children of "the rich and richest classes."[20] Opponents of public child care also tended to ignore the curriculum, focusing instead on maintaining the integrity of the family. The program of "babies' rooms" (for children ages three to five) in British infant schools resembled that of the school more than the kindergarten. Nonetheless, opponents of the babies' room worried that even in a relatively disciplined environment public child nurture meant "opening the way to socialism."[21]

If the kindergarten could potentially subvert or replace the family, it could also function as a means of "policing families" and of regulating the lives of children. In the West, the kindergarten participated in the late nineteenth-century "medicalization and moralization" of child care that is often associated with charitable and public institutions for the children of the poor, especially nurseries or crèches for nursing infants and toddlers.[22] Supporters of free kindergartens and nursery schools in the United States promoted early public surveillance of and intervention in the life of the child and the family as a means of rectifying the "problematic habits of the poor" and of giving immigrant children "at the earliest possible moment habits and ideas that will develop good American citizenship."[23] Such appeals helped to establish the kindergarten as part of American public school systems by the early twentieth century. When health and hygiene became central concerns of the kindergarten (as in Russia), the distinction between the kindergarten and the nursery or crèche temporarily receded. In Britain, preschool pioneer Margaret McMillan lobbied for "the national medical inspection of schoolchildren" as the best means of rescuing the children of the poor.[24] Children entering London's free crèches were required to bathe and change into clean clothes supplied by the institution. Both before and after the Revolution, many Russian kindergartens implemented similar policies. As Anna Davin notes, "Mothers who considered they kept their children neat and clean anyway would find these procedures insulting; some would also have seen the emphasis on baths and (later) fresh air as cranky and even dangerous."[25] However "insulting," such rituals emphasized the child's entry into a new space structured by "scientific" norms and devoted to enforcing, at a most impressionable moment, habits of cleanliness, if not citizenship.

Between the 1840s and the early twentieth century, there was no single, unified, unchanging "kindergarten." Rather, part of the allure of the kindergarten for reformers seems to have been the fact that its form and content were frequently contested and reworked. It remained situated between the public and private spheres, but the contours of that position shifted over time. In the

United States, where the kindergarten movement achieved some of its most notable successes, the move away from Froebel's program to more flexible, "scientific" activities and from charitable to public institutions was hardly linear or preordained. The fundamental assumption that early childhood constituted a formative stage persisted. Yet the conception of the relationship between the family, the young child, and the state embedded in the kindergarten changed as the kindergarten entered the public schools. Moreover, the resulting U.S. norm of a half-day institution for five-year-olds must be understood as one variant of the kindergarten idea. The Russian *detskii sad* (a translation of kindergarten/ child garden) grew out of similar assumptions about the child's "nature," but took in a broader range of children than U.S. kindergartens did and also combined efforts to educate parents and lighten the burden of child care that had affinities with institutions that North Americans would have identified as nursery schools or day cares. As will be discussed later, the situation poses problems of translation and complicates comparative analysis. It also underscores the usefulness of conceptualizing the kindergarten as both a pedagogical innovation and a space constructed between the home and the school, between the private and the public.

The Reception of the Kindergarten in Russia

The kindergarten arrived in Russia in the late 1850s at a rare moment of wide-ranging, relatively open public discussion of political and cultural reform. The "cultural politics" of the 1860s, "which called into question traditional forms of social life and were expressed through the medium of everyday life—in clothes, speech, and social conduct,"[26] had an important impact on the reception of the kindergarten, with its claims to raise children in new and improved ways. It is not my purpose here to offer a comprehensive review of the wide variety of kindergarten programs and methods adopted and advocated by educators in pre-Revolutionary Russia.[27] Rather, I would like to argue that the Russian pedagogical and political contexts— specifically the tradition of modifying Western pedagogical innovations for Russian use, the state's suspicions of private initiatives in popular education, and the linkage of social transformation with the transformation of everyday life—endowed the Froebelian definition of early childhood as a discrete and critical stage of development with radical implications largely absent or muted in the West. If in Germany and later the United States the kindergarten was associated with a liberal insistence on individual rights and civic responsibility, in autocratic Russia it became linked to a more radical vision of individual emancipation from the authoritarian constraints of school and family and the creation of a free community of equals—

both within and beyond the kindergarten. The Russian kindergarten presents if not a special case then at least a "heightened and intensified version"[28] of the kindergarten's challenge to established relationships between families, children, and the state.

Almost from the first, Russian advocates of the kindergarten idea questioned and substantially modified Froebel's program. The German émigrés and Russians trained in Germany who organized some of the empire's first private kindergartens in the late 1850s and early 1860s often remained faithful to Froebel's program. However, few of the kindergartens founded in the 1860s and 1870s in Petersburg, Moscow, and a number of other cities adhered strictly to Froebel. In the period of reaction that followed the assassination of Alexander II in 1881, few kindergartens opened. In the 1880s, the state supported private initiatives to establish traditional shelters (priiuty) for indigent children, rather than kindergartens. The second wave of private kindergartens and philanthropic kindergartens for the children of the urban poor that appeared in Russia at the end of the nineteenth century displayed even less deference to Froebel than had the mid-century kindergartens.[29]

Sofia Liugebil', the wife of a professor of Greek at St. Petersburg University, opened one of the capital's first kindergartens in 1863, with scarcely a nod to German models. The kindergarten operated until 1869, when financial shortfalls forced her to close it.[30] In her memoir of the 1860s, Elizaveta Vodovozova (1844–1923), a graduate of the Smolny Institute for aristocratic girls, who went on to become an important pioneer of early childhood education in Russia, described Liugebil's kindergarten as a loving, but hardly structured, place. The teacher kissed away her charges' tears, and the professor playfully threatened to eat up the delighted children, and then led them in imitating animal sounds. Clearly enjoying themselves, the children begged to stay when their mothers and nannies arrived to claim them. Reflecting on her visit, Vodovozova mused that "it's difficult to say whether Madam Liugebil' implemented any sort of method in her kindergarten."[31]

Although drawn to these "wonderfully good, loving, warm-hearted people," Vodovozova did not fully endorse what she saw. She told the friend who had joined her at the kindergarten that "it is impossible to bring everything to the altar of love. . . . You have to do something to broaden the children's intellectual horizons."[32] Still, in her widely influential book on early childhood education, published in seven editions between 1871 and 1913, Vodovozova advised parents to jettison or supplement freely Froebel's strictly ordered "gifts," and provided detailed descriptions of alternative toys and activities. She also included Russian folk stories as well as words and music for Russian folk songs to replace translations of Froebel's cloying originals.[33] Vodovozova and her husband, Vasilii Vodovozov, also an educator, deemed Froebel's system too rigid, too German, and too sentimental.[34] More critical was Leo Tolstoy, who, busy with his own educational experiments in the early 1860s, dismissed Froebel's kindergarten as "one of the most monstrous excrescences of the new pedagogy."[35] Even the Froebelist societies organized in Petersburg, Kiev, and other cities in the 1870s harbored factions hostile to a strict application of Froebel's program.[36]

What Vodovozova and other Russian educators valued in Froebel was the overarching commitment to engaging children's imaginations, along with the simplicity of his "gifts." Vodovozova concluded that Froebel's primary achievement was his demonstration of the pedagogical potential of everyday objects that were accessible to rich and poor alike.[37] Vodovozov and Konstantin Ushinskii, a prominent educator who had been forced to resign his post at Smolny when his modernizing reforms produced accusations of atheism and political radicalism, applauded Froebel's recognition of the educational value of "worthless" objects. Simple shapes that a child's fancy could turn into any number of things promised, they argued, not only a "natural" means of developing curiosity and creativity but also of breaking down artificial barriers of class.[38]

Replacing Froebel's stories with Russian folk tales and using his simple "gifts" to forge links between the privileged children in the kindergarten and the common people, Russian kindergarten advocates drew on contemporary thinking about the schools. Whether or not one accepts the notion of a "Russian tradition in education" reaching back to Peter the Great,[39] it seems clear that kindergartners in the 1860s shared school reformers' willingness to borrow from the West, along with their commitment to adapting Western programs to Russian conditions. By the 1860s, Ushinskii's work had helped make the principle of *narodnost'*, a concept that encompassed both a respect for Russian nationality and an idealization of the Russian common people (*narod*), central to thinking about Russian schools. He placed the "native word" (*rodnoe slovo*), rather than Latin and Greek or modern European languages, at the center of the school curriculum. Casting his advocacy of Russian language in populist terms, Ushinskii celebrated the vernacular speech of the peasants, who "created the poetry which saved us from the amusing, childish babble in which we imitated foreigners."[40] This pedagogical context helps account for the Russian kindergartners' eagerness to find Russian substitutes for Froebel's "mother songs" and to give children objects that suggested the unadorned toys of the *narod*. The connection was especially pronounced in the cases of Vodovozova and Vodovozov, who had personal ties with Ushinskii.[41]

At the same time, as Ushinskii's paean to peasant wisdom suggests, ostensibly scientific pedagogical debates provided a means of participating in broader discussions of cultural transformation. After all, one could advocate the study of Russian language without picturing the peasant as the savior of a corrupt elite. The rhetoric of pedagogy, and, I would argue, of kindergarten pedagogy in particular, provided not simply an Aesopian language but a means of concretizing the concepts of freedom and community central to radical visions of the future. Much as discussions of the "woman question" were, as Elizabeth Wood argues, "only partially about women themselves" and primarily about social transformation in general,[42] the radicals' interest in educational reform can be understood as going beyond a concern with the shape of the school day. The work of radical critics Nikolai Chernyshevskii and Nikolai Dobroliubov, the peasant school established by Tolstoy at Iasnaia Poliana, and the theory and practice of Russian kindergartens proposed various sorts of educational reform as the precondition and prefiguration of change beyond the classroom.

Like the woman who constituted the ostensible subject of the "woman question," the "rising generation" at the center of discussions of education and child-rearing was as much myth as reality. Education became politicized partly because the concept of the "young generation" had acquired political meanings. In the context of the cultural politics of the 1860s, "youth" constituted a key marker of revolutionary consciousness. The people who embraced the new radical spirit—grounded in realism, reason, and natural science—identified themselves, and were identified by others, in generational terms as rebellious "children."[43] The locus classicus of the formulation is the nihilist disdain for the "men of the forties" immortalized in Ivan Turgenev's 1862 novel *Fathers and Children* (*Otsy i deti*, often translated as *Fathers and Sons*). While Turgenev's representation of the nihilist Bazarov, who dissects frogs and attempts to deflate what he regards as the sentimental illusions of the "fathers," may not have been altogether flattering, his generational imagery was immediately adopted by the young radicals themselves. Radical literary critic Dmitrii Pisarev recognized Bazarov as a reflection, only slightly distorted by the novelists' age, of the young generation.[44]

For radicals, the destruction of traditional generational hierarchies functioned not only as a means of conceptualizing revolutionary change, but also as a critical step toward realizing it. Chernyshevskii's novel *What Is To Be Done?* (1863), still widely known in radical circles when Lenin wrote his own "What Is To Be Done?" in 1902, represented radical social transformation as the work of a rising generation of "new people" struggling to reject artificial, irrational, and oppressive personal relationships, and thereby to reconstruct society. In the novel, Vera Pavlovna's fictitious marriage is more than a means of escaping an unappealing match arranged by her father. Her act of defiance and independence begins her transformation into a person of a new sort and can be understood both as a metaphor for the radicals' attack on all patriarchal authority and as a first successful skirmish.[45]

While such visions did not provide clear guidance for those working to remake the classroom, the cultural context of the 1860s helps to explain the anti-authoritarian rhetoric so frequently attached to Russian experiments in child-centered pedagogy. In her memoir, Vodovozova noted that young radicals tended to understand "upbringing by means of fear, punishment, threats, and the rod" that "produced only slaves" as the linchpin of autocracy.[46] Both Chernyshevskii, who had taught Russian literature for two years at the Saratov Gymnasium, and Dobroliubov, who had studied at the Pedagogical Institute in St. Petersburg, linked the power of the old regime and the older generation to the authoritarian educational system. Of the two, Dobroliubov wrote more extensively and systematically on educational issues.[47] In a well-known essay "On the Meaning of Authority in Education" (1857), Dobroliubov condemned the arrogant assumption that the teacher stands "above an entire generation." He doubted that the educational system as currently constituted offered anything of value to the rising generation, since the older generation that ran it "cannot foresee or even understand the demands of the new age and considers them absurd." He underscored the need to replace a system of education that demanded the pupil's "absolute obedience" (*bezuslovnoe provinovenie*) with a program of freedom for children.[48]

The school Leo Tolstoy created for peasant children at his country estate Iasnaia Poliana in many ways epitomized the reform era's anti-authoritarian pedagogy. Tolstoy envisioned the school as a "pedagogical laboratory." It operated from 1859 to 1862, and the journal *Iasnaia Poliana* published in the last year of the school's existence brought the novelist's experiments wide publicity. Viewing any systematic educational theory as an artificial and unhappy imposition on pupils, Tolstoy organized his program around the observed interests of the children themselves. His permissiveness extended even to allowing his charges the freedom to skip class when they desired. Tolstoy deemed the mischievousness and "external disorder" that might result from granting children complete freedom for creative improvisation as "useful and necessary, however uncomfortable for the teacher."[49] The true enemy, according to Tolstoy, was not disorder but compulsion, authoritarianism, and externally imposed discipline.

The rhetoric of the Russian kindergarten movement shared with the radical critics and with Tolstoy a mistrust, if not a disdain, for the authority of teachers and parents. Petr Kapterev, who trained kindergarten teachers at the Petersburg Froebelist Courses from 1874 to 1898, characterized the 1860s as an "epoch of liberation" that called forth a generation of "teacher-radicals," who viewed the child's lack of freedom in the classroom as the "root evil" in current educational systems.[50] The kindergarten offered a promising place to extirpate this evil, since it provided a less structured environment than the school as well as a place where young children were temporarily free from their parents' control. In the early 1880s Ushinskii and Vodovozov reminded teachers and parents that they must respect the freedom of preschool-age children. They urged adults to avoid "repressing children." "To upset or prohibit children's games without good cause" they deemed "cruelty" (*zhestokost'*).[51] Their rather strong language highlights the difficulty of distinguishing "scientific" objections to Froebel's rigid program from principled opposition to the exercise of arbitrary adult authority over the young child.

At the same time, radicals tolerated adult guidance of the child in the name of inculcating respect for science or a sense of social responsibility. The activities that replaced Froebel's occupations in Russian kindergartens often reflected the radicals' cultural politics and were not necessarily free or unstructured. Vodovozova remembered that in accord with the "opinion of the times," makeshift kindergartens organized by female radicals in the early 1860s emphasized natural science and "acquaintance with the *narod* and working people in general." She described kindergartens where children undertook one of the defining activities of the young radicals — the dissection of frogs and rabbits. To introduce young children to the "people," teachers took their charges to tinsmiths', blacksmiths' and cobblers' workshops. Older children made visits to factories. Here Vodovozova had to draw the line. She concluded that such efforts to familiarize children with the plight of workers often stirred up intense emotions and did more harm than good.[52]

However, Vodovozova did not dispute the larger assumption that it was possible and desirable to remake and "free" children by exposing them to a carefully selected and ideologically charged range of experiences. She had nothing but praise for a friend's efforts to ground her daughter Zina in natural science. The seven-year-old had boxes filled with natural objects — stones, leaves, oats, shells — that she had learned to identify. The apparently rote memorization of dry facts, a simplification of Pestalozzi's "object teaching," was the sort of exercise that progressive educators usually abhorred. However, Vodovozova concluded that the child's knowledge and appreciation of the natural world compared favorably to her own childhood ignorance of nature — especially since Vodovozova had grown up in the country, while Zina was a city girl. That the child valued simple natural objects and did not envy the toys of wealthier peers (as Vodovozova remembered herself doing) was regarded by Vodovozova as an indication of the possibility of raising a truly new young generation.[53]

The state's suspiciousness of educational experiments and its commitment to traditional pedagogy worked to reinforce the association of pedagogical reform and social change. The tsarist regime never instituted a system of compulsory primary education, let alone a network of public kindergartens. Until the Revolution the Orthodox Church continued to run a large proportion of Russian schools. Even in the schools administered by the Ministry of Education and local governments (*zemstva*), religion remained the centerpiece of primary instruction.[54] Moreover, instructional methods were old-fashioned and teacher-directed. As

Jeffrey Brooks describes it, the village priest "usually lectured all three levels of the one-room schools together so that the second- and third-year pupils heard the same lectures as the year before." Pedagogical innovations, particularly when they involved allowing children latitude to challenge their elders, were viewed as a political threat. According to Brooks, in the last years of the tsarist regime, when schools began to adopt more secular curricula, observers noted, with considerable alarm in the wake of the 1905 revolution, a "growing rivalry and strife between generations," as literate young men challenged the authority of their less-educated elders. For the regime and its supporters, educational re-form and the increasingly science-minded, self-reliant young people it produced embodied a potential threat of enormous proportions.[55]

The conviction that the reform of early childhood education could serve as the germ of changes beyond the classroom constituted a central legacy of the mid-century Russian kindergartens to later pedagogical theory and practice. Russian educators were not alone in connecting the kindergarten to profound individual and social transformations. The kindergarten's position between the life of the family and public life invited such connections. However, in Russia the insistence on the power of the kindergarten to both liberate and enlighten the rising generation tended to go further than in Western Europe or the United States. Froebel's program, with its series of ordered gifts and occupations, had managed to honor the interests and capacities of children without abandoning the adult desire for order. Even the "most radically open-ended approach to kindergartening" in the United States, the so-called "free play curriculum" in-troduced in the Santa Barbara public schools at the turn of the century, called only for two unstructured "recesses" that tempered, but did not replace, activi-ties directed by the teacher.[56] By contrast, the rhetoric of the Russian kinder-garten movement tended to be more anti-authoritarian, a trend that became more marked by the turn of the century. Like their Western counterparts, Russ-ian educators viewed the kindergarten as an educational reform with broad in-dividual and social implications. Yet while Western educators often character-ized the kindergarten as a place to raise future citizens, Russian educators represented it as a place where the young generation would experience a wholly new, enlightened, and liberated way of life.

Free Upbringing

Anti-authoritarian rhetoric coupled with a commitment to enlightenment con-tinued to constitute key components of Russian thinking about the kindergarten into the twentieth century. On the eve of the Revolution, an approach known as "free upbringing" (*svobodnoe vospitanie*) stood as the most influential theory of the kindergarten in Russia. Konstantin Venttsel' (1857–1947), an academic rather than a kindergarten teacher, was the primary theorist of free upbringing. Rejecting the possibility of establishing a method that would work with all children, Venttsel' proposed a sort of anti-method that, at least in theory, required the near total subordination of teachers to each pupil's creative impulses. Yet much like its precursors in the mid-nineteenth century, the free kindergarten also aspired to nurture children's allegedly natural instincts for labor and to create a model community of equals.

Much like Tolstoy at Iasnaia Poliana, advocates of free upbringing insisted that the immediate interests of children be the primary determinant of the curriculum. Venttsel' argued that the kindergarten's program must be as varied and spontaneous as children themselves. In his *The Theory of Free Upbringing and the Ideal Kindergarten* (1915), Venttsel' emphasized that "every child proposes its own particular system of upbringing (there are as many systems of upbringing as there are children)." The "system," therefore, could not be prepared in advance, but had to be "discovered" anew in each individual case, and could never be "established definitively." An acute awareness of the needs and capacities of each child constituted the teacher's primary qualification. "To love the kind, good child is not a great accomplishment," wrote Venttsel', "but to love the nasty and spoiled—that is where the true calling of the educator [*vospitatel'*] is revealed." In the free classroom, the teacher ideally functioned not as a guide but as a sympathetic and ceaseless observer.[57]

Free upbringing's insistence on the need to follow, rather than try to direct, the child's inclinations grew out of a vision of the child as an innate creator. Venttsel' juxtaposed two understandings of the nature of children and the opposed methods of upbringing associated with each. His language, equating teacher-directed pedagogy with brute force and suggesting the illegitimacy of any restrictions on children, is worth quoting at length.

Under the first approach [to upbringing] the educator is declared the creator, and the child becomes like a block of marble, out of which a fine statue must be created. With the aid of a hammer and chisel, the sculptor ruthlessly [*bezzhalostno*] cuts, chops, and beats the marble. Fragments of marble are broken off, and little by little the stone block takes on the form desired by the sculptor. By contrast, the second way of understanding the word "upbringing" [*vospitanie*] emphasizes that the child is not lifeless material, not a block of marble, but instead that there are latent creative, formative sources within the child itself. And the creativity of the artist-educator must set out not to shape the child's individual personality into the form which [the teacher] imagines to be ideal and fine, but to awaken the creative forces slumbering with the child itself, in order to liberate [these forces] from all restrictions, from all reductions in their range, in order to give them the opportunity to shape that which is ideal and fine in a given individuality [*individual'nost'*].[58]

Venttsel's sympathies clearly lay with the second approach, and he rejected any force, "crude or hidden," in the raising of children.

Taking respect for the child's unique inclinations and capacities as the only legitimate starting point for education, Venttsel' viewed the authority of parents as well as teachers with suspicion. He pictured the "contemporary family" as a sort of microcosm of autocracy:

> The contemporary family is in general an unfree family, and in particular it is the family of the unfree child. In the contemporary family, the child is the slave, and the parents are slavemasters. In the contemporary family only the parents', not the children's, rights are realized. In the family as it is equal rights do not exist: the parents are almost always the ruling party.[59]

Since freedom in the classroom would mean little if parents continued to limit children's freedom, Venttsel' emphasized that the "theory of free upbringing presupposes a new family and in any case it presupposes an effort within the old family to reconstruct itself on new foundations."[60] He hoped that once parents understood that the "natural basis of the family union must be mutual love and respect" they would renounce their power and allow children to voice their feelings, "even when parents do not like that expression," and to share in family decisions.[61] Echoing the anti-authoritarian rhetoric of mid-century educational reformers, Venttsel' linked educational reform and the liberation of the rising generation. His educational system required that the "principle of the absolute power of the current over the future generation . . . be shaken."[62]

For advocates of free upbringing, the liberation of children from the tyranny of parents and teachers constituted the first step in the larger process of the spontaneous emergence of self-governing communes. The zealous encouragement of creativity and self-expression could produce permissive, sometimes almost anarchic, kindergartens. But the creation of small, cooperative communities constituted the ultimate goal. Venttsel' admitted that "at first glance, the theory of free upbringing may appear to be an expression of the most extreme individualism." But far from an atomistic institution, the free kindergarten aimed to help each child become conscious of the "natural and fundamental solidarity that exists between him and humanity, between him and the world."[63]

Venttsel' envisioned a kindergarten community that united boys and girls in productive labor and self-government. "Free physical productive labor" constituted a vital means of linking individuals together in useful tasks, even when it seemed to require some infringement on the child's freedoms. Venttsel' recommended that a large proportion of the kindergartner's day be devoted to "socially necessary work" such as housekeeping, preparing breakfast, washing dishes, and making items for use in the kindergarten, like toys or chairs. The model children's institution would have a series of workshops and a garden, perhaps even a working farm. Venttsel' did not specify how this work would be organized, and he avoided any detailed explanation of how such tasks could be squared with the insistence on full freedom for children. He apparently counted on children's "social instincts" to interest them in labor activities and implicitly rejected the assumption that children preferred fun to useful activity.[64] Venttsel' valued children's meetings as a forum for including pupils in the organization of their kindergartens. Additionally, he insisted on coeducation as a means of achieving "healthy, normal, natural" relations between the sexes. Viewing a cooperative community as the "normal" state of affairs, Venttsel' did not need to address the objection that placing children in coed groups, organizing a meeting, or training children to cultivate plants required adult intervention, some imposition of adult ideas on the "free" world of the child.[65]

Venttsel' posited a remarkable overlap of the teacher's "natural" and "rational" ideas and the child's own desires that was no doubt difficult to achieve in practice. His program made no allowances for pupils whose impulses ran to the disruptive rather than the productive. Stanislav Shatskii, a progressive educator sympathetic to calls for free activity, visited Venttsel's Home of the Free Child in 1906 and left disappointed. He found the children "insolent and indifferent. . . . Here disorder rules."[66]

Venttsel's writings tended to ignore such practical considerations. He focused less on the difficulties of granting freedom to real, often unruly preschoolers than on the kindergarten as an ideal, albeit small, society that would ultimately facilitate larger social transformations. Venttsel' envisioned his Home of the Free Child as a "small pedagogical *obshchina* [community] made up of children, instructors, and parents . . . which attempts to implement as fully as possible the ideas of free brotherhood and equality."[67] As noted earlier, Venttsel' believed that the organization of such a community required a simultaneous grant of equal rights to the child at home. World War I's "economic and moral jolt to family life" added compelling reasons for making the kindergarten part of a children's home that could become a child-centered community in advance of the remaking of family life.[68] Venttsel' also imagined that the free kindergarten would provide a model for the reform of the family. "The family of the future," Venttsel' predicted, "will be a free cooperative of children and parents in the work of spiritual and moral perfection. Not only will parents raise their children, but children will raise their parents." Attributing the current hostilities between parents and children to parents' unjust displays of authority, Venttsel' argued that if parents, like teachers, would "renounce their power" and "stop being slavemasters" then generational conflict would disappear.[69] The reformed and harmonious family, in turn, would both facilitate and anticipate changes in the wider society. Venttsel' described "contemporary society," in sharp contrast to the ideal free kindergarten and the "new" family, as "a society based on force and coercion." He asserted, "Only thanks to the family of the future will it be possible to develop on earth that true, creative community that, based on creativity, nourishes, supports, and develops the creativity of every personality who makes up society."[70]

Other educators, who were more concerned with actual preschoolers than with ideal communities, softened Venttsel's animosity toward structure, authority, and efforts to mold the child more generally. Such was the case at one of the best-known kindergartens based on the principles of *svobodnoe vospitanie* founded by Maria Khrisanfovna Sventitskaia (1855–1932) in the Arbat district of Moscow. Her kindergarten is of particular interest because it continued to exist in the same location and to follow the same precepts in the years after the Bolsheviks came to power and made it a public institution.

In a 1912 brochure designed to attract pupils, Sventitskaia described a kindergarten in which the rational leadership of a trained kindergarten teacher replaced the haphazard care often provided by families. She directed her criticism less at authority in general than at untrained parents, who, however unwittingly, prevented their children from realizing their full potential. Animated by the principles of free upbringing, her kindergarten aimed to "develop and strengthen" the child's "natural abilities" and "social instincts." She asked parents to recognize that "egoism is sometimes fostered by the family" and that, by contrast, "a society of peers and rational instructors" can create "a small *comrade*, a member of the whole children's family, the future social person." Sventitskaia rejected efforts to teach preschoolers to read, draw, or speak a foreign language as unduly didactic and disciplined. But outside of these tasks, the teacher took an active part in planning and guiding kindergarten activities. While the schedule allotted one hour to self-generated games, which, Sventitskaia noted, provided teachers with "rich observational material," it also allowed teachers to organize games, singing, and physical exercise based upon their own assessment of what was best for children.[71] Sventitskaia removed some of the stigma of repression from efforts to guide, rather than simply observe, young children.

As recast by educators like Sventitskaia, the practice of free upbringing had much in common with the child-centered pedagogy of Western kindergartens and of other, more structured Russian kindergartens. Even the opponents of *svobodnoe vospitanie* took as their point of departure sensitive responses to the interests and inclinations of children. The most serious challenge to free upbringing as the dominant approach to the kindergarten in Russia came from the program developed by Elizaveta Ivanovna Tikheeva (1866–1944) in St. Petersburg. Originally an elementary school teacher, Tikheeva opened a kindergarten in Petersburg in 1913. A year later, a visit to Maria Montessori's *Casa dei Bambini* in Rome helped convince Tikheeva of the need for a systematic and structured approach to young children.[72]

Where Tikheeva differed most obviously from the proponents of *svobodnoe vospitanie* was in her insistence that preschool children, or, more specifically, seven-year-olds (the oldest preschoolers in the Russian system), be taught to read and count. Sventitskaia rejected such a program out of hand as intolerably didactic and unfree, despite the fact that banishing reading and arithmetic from the kindergarten simply put off the inevitable for an additional year. By contrast, Tikheeva argued that her observations demonstrated that by age seven, children were ready, and often eager, to sit still and learn to read and write their native language and to study arithmetic. Moreover, Tikheeva envisioned the introduction of basic literacy and mathematical skills as occurring without the tedious drills and rigid discipline of the traditional schoolroom. Instead, organized lessons complemented other, less structured, activities. The precise mix and methods would emerge out of scientific research. Even the most radical advocates of free upbringing had to agree with Tikheeva's exhortation to "study children!"[73] That kindergartens ought to nurture the pupil's individual talents both sides took as a given. What they could not agree on was how to reconcile efforts to enlighten the child with respect for the child's impulses and inclinations. However, the rhetoric of free upbringing that dominated Russian discussions of the kindergarten at the beginning of the twentieth century often obscured the potential conflicts between a commitment to liberating children and a desire to teach them.

The Kindergarten and the "Woman Question"

Russian radicals understood children's emancipation and women's liberation in much the same terms. In both cases they connected educational reform with efforts to end the "tyranny of the family." The debate on what was known as the "woman question" had, in fact, begun as a discussion of the need to reform women's education. In a signal essay published in 1856, Nikolai Pirogov, a doctor and educator who had trained female nurses for the Crimean War and who had been favorably impressed by their service on the front lines, argued the need to improve women's education. He charged that girls' schools turned out dolls, gracious housewives competent in French and music and little else. The conviction that new methods of education could emancipate women remained central to the evolving and expanding debate on the woman question.[74]

The question of how "new women" might be raised from earliest childhood, while not at the forefront of discussions of women's emancipation, did engage women involved in the kindergarten movement. Elizaveta Vodovozova described the efforts of two sisters to raise a child to be science-minded, socially conscious, and unhampered by gender stereotypes that confined women to the home. The child's Aunt Vera, the more radical of the two sisters, feared that playing with dolls would foster coquetry and an empty-headed love of clothes. However, neither sister wished to thwart what they seemed to view as the girl's natural desire to care for something, so they decided to give the child a primitive wooden doll that she could nurture but not dress up. Vera pointedly rejected the assertion that "to doll yourself up" is female nature. "If woman's nature is so empty and insignificant," Vera responded, "if her thoughts are primarily directed toward frivolity, then this nature needs to be changed for the better."[75] Perhaps nothing better sums up the radicals' faith in education as a tool of cultural transformation than Vera's conviction that it could alter "nature."

A commitment to women's liberation did not necessarily entail a rejection of woman's "unique" virtues. It was the frivolous, not the nurturing, aspects of women's "nature" that the radical Vera rejected. While male radicals called for equal rights for women, they continued to put woman on a moral pedestal, lauding her maternal instincts and natural capacity for loving self-sacrifice. In an 1861 article, critic Dmitrii Pisarev charged man "as the only active members of society" with the task of rousing the woman who loved him to struggle against her childhood convictions, the oppressive power of the family, and the prejudices of fashionable society in order to liberate herself. He suggested that women, once emancipated, would possess a "freshness and strength" that men could never match. Pisarev located the source of women's "future rich development" in the "love of mothers, sisters, lovers, and wives [that] pours bright rays of happiness and poetry on our gray lives" and in women's "lack of moral economy and reasonableness." Similarly, Dobroliubov could find no male peer for the morally activated new woman. He took as the new ideal Elena in Turgenev's *On the Eve* (1859), who was steeped in traditional values despite her courageous improprieties.[76] For the radicals, the most traditional of womanly virtues became essential forces for social transformation.

Such sentiments appeared in pedagogical literature in the form of "scientific" demonstrations of woman's unique talents and recognition of the social importance of women's child-rearing skills. As in the West, the kindergarten movement in Russia adopted maternalist rhetoric that pictured the organization of public child care as a means of empowering mothers. Ushinskii and Vodovozov began their advice manual for teachers and parents with the aphorism that "the first education of the child is naturally the mother's responsibility." They found fathers "always by nature too harsh, too impatient" to care for young children.[77]

Educators tended to propose purely biological explanations of gender differences. Kapterev provided detailed analysis of scientific experiments that he concluded demonstrated unequivocally the dangers of intensive mental activity for women and the suitability of a maternal role.[78] While such conclusions may sound limiting, many women took their recognized maternal abilities as the basis for public activity. Vodovozova described the appeal of kindergarten teaching for an unmarried woman who loved children and wanted to do socially useful work.[79] Evgeniia Konradi, a feminist best known for her work to open higher education to women, became involved in the kindergarten movement in the 1860s and 1870s. She considered women's work in child care—at home and in the kindergarten—to be the foundation of women's public role.[80]

Women organized kindergartens in the 1860s and 1870s not only to raise their children in new ways and to turn mothering into public work, but also to allow themselves time to pursue interests outside the home.[81] However, it was not until the late 1880s and 1890s that kindergartens became linked to efforts to provide day care for working mothers. The rapid growth of industry and the recruitment of women into the factory labor force spurred the organization of charitable all-day kindergartens or day care centers (*ochag* or *dlinnyi detskii sad*) in the working-class districts of Russia's cities. The "long kindergarten" provided day care for children and classes in child care for mothers. In Russian philanthropic kindergartens children received supervision, food, and occasionally free medical care. Many institutions operated from six in the morning until eight or nine at night. The educational component was often negligible. Children spent from six to eight hours per day in classrooms that often lacked materials and trained personnel—one teacher might be responsible for up to fifty pupils. When a Sunday kindergarten organized in 1897 became a daily kindergarten the following year, its organizers found that none of them had the requisite pedagogical experience to organize "systematic activities," although they slowly implemented an eclectic program that began with efforts to teach children prayers.[82]

The Russian *detskii sad* could designate both care-taking and more purely educational institutions. In other words, Russian kindergartens often resembled contemporary nursery schools in the United States and the charitable and public nurseries established in many Western nations and in Russia.[83] The situation stands in marked contrast to the clear distinction usually made in both Western Europe and the United States between kindergartens on the one hand and day cares or nurseries on the other. In the West, care-taking institutions, in contrast to kindergartens, often lacked an educational component or emphasized the most traditional sorts of religious education.[84] The kindergartens attached to Russian factories further blurred the line between the kindergarten and other institutions for young children by sometimes accommodating children of "pre-

preschool" age (newborn to age three) along with the preschoolers. Such institutional variability inevitably complicates comparative analysis, not to mention translation. Organizers used *ochag* (hearth) and *dlinnyi detskii sad* (long kindergarten) interchangeably to designate full-day institutions for preschoolers, whether or not they included an educational component. I have translated *ochag* as "day care" or "full-day kindergarten" because these terms provide a clearer picture of the nature of these institutions than does the more literal "hearth." However, it is worth emphasizing that these terms are not meant to imply equivalencies between Russian and Western institutions.

Educational theorists who valued the kindergarten as a place to raise children in new ways viewed the narrow emphasis on nutrition and supervision with disdain. Tikheeva emphasized that the kindergarten must be "an educational rather than a philanthropic institution."[85] But among teachers accustomed to understanding schools in social context, full stomachs and decent hygiene were at least as important to the "harmonious development of the human personality" as correct toys. That full-day care-taking institutions were called kindergartens by their organizers suggests a tendency to value the kindergarten's social role as much as its educational role, a tendency that owed much to the roots of the Russian kindergarten in radical movements and in efforts to resolve the woman question.

Regulating Families

Russian organizers of philanthropic and public institutions for the children of the working class shared with their peers abroad deep misgivings about the child-rearing practices of uneducated mothers. Russian kindergartens often operated on the assumption that many parents, especially, but not only, peasants and workers, were dangerously lacking in the resources and skills necessary to raise children. Even educators who did not regard parents as "slavemasters" questioned the ability of mothers to raise their children properly. According to Tikheeva, the kindergarten relied not only on the material contributions of parents but also on their desire to raise their children well. "Unfortunately," she concluded, "at this time such a desire belongs almost to the sphere of utopia. Our family is inert, oppressed by routine; it is ill-informed on questions of child-rearing or strangled by indigence and adversity."[86]

Research on the family echoed Tikheeva's pessimistic conclusions. Child mortality rates in prerevolutionary Russia were among the highest in Europe. In 1912 in Moscow, nearly 29 of every 100 children died within the first year of life. The blame, of course, did not belong entirely to parents; "poor living conditions and nutrition," Tikheeva's "indigence and adversity," was cited as the prime cause of

Russia's high child mortality rates.[87] But observers did not always make clear distinctions between the effects of poverty and bad parenting. A 1914 survey of 254 "working families" revealed that parents left their preschoolers in the care of older children, relatives, or landladies. Nurseries took in less than 1 percent of children with working mothers. Educators and doctors concluded that such improvised arrangements produced both physical and emotional damage. Children whose mothers worked not only suffered higher mortality rates, but they also "absolutely did not know maternal love and tenderness."[88]

Poverty no doubt made the provision of adequate child care difficult. Nonetheless, descriptions of poor conditions often shaded into attacks on the cultural backwardness and low moral tone of the family. Tikheeva offered no suggestions for overcoming "indigence and adversity," stressing instead parent education. Even in the context of a brochure inviting parents to enroll their children in a kindergarten that charged 80 rubles per year, in advance, "returned under no circumstances," one finds hostility to the family. Sventitskaia noted that families as currently constituted often interfered with the healthy development of the child. Here "health" connoted moral as well as physical well-being.[89]

Such accusations were not tantamount to a call for the destruction of the family. What was required was attention to the advice of experts. Tikheeva recommended that parents incapable of providing "rational upbringing in the bosom of the family" visit the kindergarten and learn from specialists. Since the "education of fathers and mothers . . . is a matter of utmost importance, without which the rational upbringing of children is inconceivable," kindergarten teachers had no choice but to teach both children and parents.[90] Sventitskaia likewise advised parents to take an active interest in the life of the kindergarten, attending open houses and informing teachers about their child's home life.

In a published account of a philanthropic kindergarten established in 1897, E. P. Kalacheva described how the kindergarten gathered information on the children it served and worked to overcome their "material and spiritual" deficits. Kalacheva emphasized that she "believe[d] in the child's receptivity to good, ascribing the majority of sins weighing on their little heads to the account of adults, who spoil, less through cruelty than through irrational treatment, the good beginning of noble qualities in the child's nature."[91] Home visits allowed women working at the kindergartens to collect information on poor families, which Kalacheva divided into three categories: families in which the relative health and hard work of the parents allowed a marginal existence, those in which a drunken father squandered money on vodka, and those in which a mother struggled alone to support her children. She deemed insufficient the uncoordinated efforts of nurseries, kindergartens, and schools to collect information on poor families and called for a "central bureau" to keep records on families that would provide the basis for rational decisions about what each family needed.[92]

Despite such appeals, the tsarist state never lent its support to efforts to investigate and educate parents. The dislocations of World War I added urgency to efforts to establish protective institutions, but privately funded kindergartens accommodated only a small number of children.[93] Charitable societies were most active in Moscow, where for the 1916–1917 school year they supported a total of forty kindergartens serving somewhat less than 2 percent of the preschool-age population—2,000 children out of a total of 103,000.[94] Such small enrollments can be explained by both the lack of public funds and restrictions on the dissemination of information about preschool education.[95]

Whereas Western governments often supported the professional regulation of working-class families, the tsarist state tended to view such interventions with suspicion. In her study of Russian doctors' efforts to decrease child mortality by setting up nurseries and educating poor mothers in modern child care techniques, Nancy Frieden argues that Russia should be considered a "special case." She emphasizes that Russian physicians confronted a culturally "backward" nation, where "preventive measures such as improved sanitation and water supply, and hygiene education" that "worked well in the West" had little chance of succeeding. That an inadequate number of health workers faced the challenge of reforming the child care practices of a largely illiterate, predominately peasant population certainly complicated Russian medical reform efforts. At the same time, the tendency of Russian teachers and physicians to represent "women as negligent mothers, witch doctors, untrained midwives, and bearers of old wives' tales,"[96] while perhaps extreme, was hardly unique to "backward" Russia. Educators and health workers in Western Europe and the United States also expressed hostility to the "backward" practices of poor women.[97] However, unlike their colleagues in the West, Russian physicians and teachers confronted a state "jealous of its monopoly on tutelage" that "obstructed attempts by the cultural elite to exercise its own kind of influence on the social body."[98] The tsarist state's reluctance to delegate disciplinary authority complicated the Russian kindergarten's relationship to the regulatory impulse central to so many Western kindergartens.

Socialism and the Kindergarten

It was the Russian Marxists who saw the revolutionary potential in the full-day kindergarten. While organizations like the *Obshchestva popecheniia o detiakh* (Society for the Care of Children) attempted to provide food and adequate supervision for the children of working mothers, socialists who gave the matter any thought promoted public child care as a critical step toward the emancipation of women and a means of modernizing and revolutionizing the family.[99] It was an article of faith among socialists that the family was useless, often harmful, and in any case disappearing; guided by superstition and limited by poverty, it oppressed both women and children.[100] By contrast, a kindergarten grounded in apparently universal scientific principles and run by professionals would aid working mothers while raising happier and healthier children.

The commitment to full-day care for the children of working mothers—rather than a "proletarian" curriculum—distinguished socialist from bourgeois kindergartens. Even Nadezhda Krupskaia (Lenin's wife), who wrote extensively on educational issues in the years before the Revolution, failed to articulate a specifically socialist kindergarten program. While her articles on primary and secondary schools focused on curricula and methods, she discussed the kindergarten largely in terms of its care-taking functions.

Coming to the kindergarten via the Marxist critique of the family, Krupskaia emphasized that even the most conscientious working mother could not raise her children properly. In the pamphlet "The Woman Worker" (1901), she began with a sketch of the impossible burden borne by the working mother. Her story echoed in important respects the descriptions of the working-class family found in the literature on philanthropic kindergartens. "Arriving tired from the factory, she must attend to the laundry, the sewing, and the housework; she must feed and bathe the children. Occasionally she spends the entire night without a break caring for a sick child." The whereabouts of the father are obscure. Krupskaia implicitly rejects the possibility of men taking greater responsibility for child care and leaves the reader with the impression that every working mother is essentially a single mother. Overwhelmed by her dual burden and without access to a trained professional, the working mother in Krupskaia's tale gladly takes the advice of a neighbor to quiet the child with a drop of opium, without any understanding of the potential harm. Overwork coupled with ignorance produced unfit mothers.[101] As Krupskaia presented the situation, even the most caring mother could do little for her child during the work day. Factory women had no choice but to leave their children in the hands of an old neighbor woman or, when the children got a bit older, without any supervision at all. "The children," she reported, "are practically raised on the street." Such upbringing undermined the health of body and mind. Hungry, dirty, and cold, the children of the streets grew up with "drunkenness, debauchery, and fighting."[102]

In her work on child care, Krupskaia emphasized the socialists' efforts to meet the immediate needs of working women rather than their desire to preside over the elimination of traditional familial relationships. Socialists offered socialized child-rearing as the best means of improving the lives of mothers and their children. Leaving their children in the hands of skilled kindergarten teachers allowed mothers to concentrate on their work and saved children from the streets. Krupskaia dismissed as "utter nonsense" the bourgeoisie's indignant charge that "those awful socialists . . . want to destroy the family, to take children away from their parents." "Public upbringing" (*obshchestvennoe vospitanie*) simply meant that "the burden of supporting children will be lifted from parents and that society will guarantee to the child not only the means of existence but also everything necessary to his full and multifaceted development."[103] Krupskaia implied that parents would continue to play a role in their children's upbringing. The kindergarten would simply reduce the working woman's child care worries while producing the docile, orderly, hardworking children that she imagined most mothers desired.

However, in other writings, Krupskaia made it clear that the family itself might be inimical to the "full and multifaceted development" of the child. One telling shortcoming was the inability of even poor families to instill in their children a love of labor. Krupskaia concluded that "often the family not only fails to promote but suppresses the child's social instincts." She also condemned the family for imposing artificial gender distinctions. In an article published in the journal *Svobodnoe vospitanie* in 1910, Krupskaia raised the issue of the husband's responsibility for housework that she had ignored in her brief for socialized child care. She reproached both the working man and the "intelligent" men for sleeping while their wives tended to the sewing late into the night; women, she contended, were no more made for housework than slaves were made for slavery. The family taught such "unfair" arrangements not only by example but also by actively discouraging boys' willingness to help with the housework.[104] If the family was not only an inadequate caretaker but also a poor source of what Krupskaia apparently construed as proper values, then preserving it made little sense. Krupskaia assured mothers that "in the public kindergarten, children are able to spend their time extremely usefully and more cheerfully than at home."[105]

Interestingly, Krupskaia seemed to believe that current kindergarten practices could inculcate the necessary new values. She described with approval Western programs in which— despite appearances to the contrary— activities followed a strict plan. The children planted flowers, washed vegetables and dishes, sang, sewed, drew, and played games. "Each game, each activity teaches something, and most importantly, the child gets accustomed to order, to work, gets accustomed to not arguing with comrades and to giving in without caprice and tears." Krupskaia also had kind words for free upbringing. In fact, much of Krupskaia's prerevolutionary pedagogical writing— mostly on school-age children—appeared in the journal *Svobodnoe vospitanie* (Free Upbringing). While her 1901 description of a prototypical kindergarten emphasized the kindergarten's ability to teach children to work together, in 1914 she uncritically reported an educational congress's resolution on the right of every child to "preschool education in the sense of the harmonious development of his personality on the basis of free upbringing."[106] Like most progressive educators, she trusted that scientific research would suggest how to reconcile order and freedom in the kindergarten.

Beginning in the 1860s, the kindergarten in Russia was associated with efforts to transform childhood, the family, and society. By the time the Bolsheviks came to power, Venttsel's conception of free upbringing shaped the programs of the majority of private kindergartens in Russia. Believing that only children accustomed to independence could successfully reform a state system grounded in compulsion, proponents of free upbringing took Froebel's insistence on child-centered pedagogy to extremes and renounced, at least in theory, all but the most essential interventions in children's activities. In practice, "freedom" for children often went hand in hand with the inculcation of new values. The full-day kindergartens organized in working-class districts were a long way from both Froebel's and Venttsel's ideals. Yet purely care-taking institutions could be considered kindergartens in Russia, where the kindergarten had long been associated with, if not defined by, efforts to resolve the woman question.

Given the radicals' appropriation of the kindergarten idea, it comes as no great surprise that the tsarist state never established any public kindergartens. Indeed, in the late 1860s, the Ministry of Education emerged as one of the most consistently reactionary centers in the government. Apparently suspecting that educational reform might, as the radicals hoped, have effects beyond the classroom, the ministry opposed innovations at all levels. In the primary and secondary schools, the state implemented curricula that emphasized religion and ancient languages; it simply ignored kindergartens. Liberal-minded educators bemoaned their lack of influence on educational policy. "The participation of society in the organization of popular education," Kapterev declared, "is both unavoidable and necessary."[107] However, their pleas were never heeded, and in 1917, the newly minted bureaucrats charged with organizing Soviet kindergartens found not even a scrap of paper relating to preschool education in the old tsarist ministry.[108]

Under the circumstances, it seemed possible that current programs could be made to serve revolutionary ends. The assumption that biological "laws" of physical and intellectual development transcended distinctions of class allowed socialists to embrace programs worked out in existing kindergartens. Moreover, the emphasis on physical labor and collective tasks that characterized so many kindergartens had much to recommend them. Who could argue with Sventitskaia's view of the preschool child as a "small comrade"? Nonsocialist programs further acknowledged that an end to parental domination was the precondition of any effort to improve childhood. If socialists were uncomfortable with the potential chaos of *svobodnoe vospitanie*, so were other progressive educators. Socialists and nonsocialists shared a vision of the child as the author of the future, who had to be both liberated from the weight of the past and molded by the ideals of the revolution. Only when the Bolsheviks began to organize a system of public kindergartens did the contradictions and complications of the pre-Revolutionary legacy become evident.

part two

The Children of October and the Civil War

2

"Save the Children"

The first years of Soviet power were tragic ones for children. Both World War I and the Civil War removed, often permanently, the primary male breadwinner from countless families. The easing of divorce laws added to the number of households run by single women. Mothers compelled to work outside the home frequently left their children without supervision during the course of the work day. The food shortages that plagued urban areas throughout the Civil War and culminated in the massive famine of 1921 further undermined parents' ability to care for their children. The resulting flood of homeless and neglected children (*besprizorniki*) that crowded Russia's cities constituted one of the most visible, heartbreaking, and intractable problems facing the new regime.[1]

For children, the crises bred of war, revolution, and civil war often proved fatal. Russia's already high child mortality rates grew grimmer. According to one estimate, half of all newborns in 1918 died within the first year of life. In the famine year of 1921, 90–95 percent of children under the age of three and nearly one-third of their older siblings perished.[2]

For the Bolsheviks, the necessity of immediate measures to save the lives of the revolution's heirs could never be separated from the political and ideological dimensions of the crisis. They saw in the upheaval both an urgent human problem and a prelude to profound and imminent cultural transformation. With the old order conspicuously crashing down on all sides, the Civil War period was, in Richard Stites's phrase, "a moment of expectant utopia."[3] In this spirit, educators understood state intervention to save hungry and abandoned children as the first step in a larger effort to bring enlightened care to all children.

Welfare or Enlightenment

The specter of neglected and starving children created broad consensus among parents and government officials on the need for immediate state action. There was less agreement on whether relief efforts ought to preempt programs designed to remake childhood. Given the magnitude of the emergency, it is somewhat surprising that the debate took place at all. Under the circumstances, establishing even a rudimentary system of relief for children would have constituted a tremendous achievement. Yet the debate did take place and, even more startling from a purely materialist point of view, resulted in the decision to link relief efforts to a sweeping plan of cultural enlightenment.

Officials at the Commissariats of Social Welfare and Public Health (Narkomsobes and Narkomzdrav), whose work necessarily brought them face to face with the human cost of the crisis, tended to emphasize immediate needs over the long-term goal of rooting out "backward" practices. Commissar of Social Welfare Aleksandra Kollontai vividly recalled heartrending appeals from the mothers of starving children. The women who made their way to Kollontai's office were "firm, tough" working mothers, but "in the face of children's hunger and malnutrition, the maternal heart lost its strength of character, and the will to struggle weakened."[4] With a nod to the socialist dictum that "the family is more and more losing its meaning, and that the raising of children is becoming more and more the responsibility of the state," Narkomsobes warned that for the present, programs had to be confined to the children most at risk. A detailed list of the target population included orphans, "illegitimate" children (regardless of the fact that the legal category no longer existed), abandoned children, victims of child abuse, and children of alcoholics, prostitutes, and prisoners. Kollontai looked forward to the "raising of children in children's colonies and children's dormitories." But the crisis prevented her from doing more than urging women to set up central children's kitchens. She offered mothers appealing for aid the advice that "it is easier to feed 200 children from a central pot than from 200 separate bowls."[5]

Emphasizing the children's homes' role in relief operations, the Commissariat of Social Welfare proposed that it take primary responsibility for their administration. Although both the Commissariat of Enlightenment (Narkompros) and the Commissariat of Public Health would continue to play a part in overseeing various aspects of the children's homes, Narkomsobes would take the leading role. Assuming that the dream of raising *all* children in state-run institutions had to be deferred, officials at Narkomsobes connected the home to a panoply of other social welfare measures ranging from a reform of family law to the establishment of juvenile prisons.[6] Workers at Narkomzdrav, where immediate threats to children's health likewise took center stage, reached similar conclusions.[7]

Educators agreed that children's institutions had to make relief and the provision of full-day care a priority. The 1919 handbook of preschool education asked rhetorically who would care for children when both parents worked outside the home. "There can be only one answer: the preschool institution, the

kindergarten, nursery, day care [ochag], playground." The Preschool Department of Narkompros insisted that kindergartens feed their students; "otherwise
children will starve." It proposed covering up to half the cost of meals in
kindergartens and day cares.[8] Instructions for establishing kindergartens emphasized the advantages to the working mother of the full-day variety and
called for institutions to provide regular medical checkups and hot meals.[9] An
exhaustive list of essentials to be furnished by kindergartens constituted a
prominent part of the keynote address at the First All-Russian Congress of
Preschool Education in 1919 and testified to the importance of the kindergarten's relief mission.[10]

Along with public health and welfare workers, educators assumed, not un-
reasonably, that parents desired and needed programs focused on food relief
and day care. The half-day kindergarten, operating only a few hours a day and
"leaving children the rest of the day without supervision and almost without
food," failed to satisfy parents.[11] According to the 1919 handbook of preschool
education, "the present demand is for institutions that substitute for the family
during the parents' work day" and offer a "fuller, happier" life to children.[12]
Vera Lebedeva, the head of the Commissariat of Public Health's Department of
Maternal and Child Welfare, argued that full-day institutions allowed women
both to work and to be mothers. The ochag aimed "to help the members of the
family who work outside the home . . . and therefore are forced to leave children without supervision, running through the streets or through the corridors
of factory buildings."[13] Common sense, if not elaborate surveys, suggested that
parents were more interested in reliable day care than preschool education.

Nonetheless, officials at the Commissariat of Enlightenment tended to view
the provision of emergency aid and supervision less as an end in itself than as an
effective means of introducing parents to the broader benefits of the kindergarten. Before the Revolution, few working-class children attended kindergartens. Apparently, in 1917 all of Petrograd's kindergartens charged 7–15
rubles a month—putting them beyond the reach of the average working
woman, whose monthly income was between 25 and 40 rubles.[14] In Moscow,
where a wide variety of charitable societies had organized free kindergartens,
parents were somewhat more familiar with the newfangled institutions. Outside
the capitals, few kindergartens of any description existed,[15] and educators faced
the daunting task of persuading parents to enroll their children.

Educators recognized that the promise of food and adequate supervision
could induce skeptical or merely uninformed parents to send their children to
kindergartens. Nothing was more encouraging to preschool teachers than a
kindergartner's complaint that his father made him attend the kindergarten giving way to the child's realization that he loved going.[16] Ideally, parents would
grow to appreciate the kindergarten's educational offerings. A delegate at a

1920 preschool conference related that parents initially lured by hot meals slowly came to see the kindergarten as more than a feeding station. An "educated American woman" built a broader program that included a blind eighty-three-year-old peasant with a gift for story-telling; the old peasant probably further reassured parents that, at minimum, the kindergarten could do no serious harm.[17] That the delegate felt this "success" merited attention suggests that teachers were accustomed to rather unimpressive results. However, within the government, Narkompros's definition of preschools and other children's institutions as agencies of enlightenment rather than welfare had appeal. In 1919, the Commissariat of Enlightenment won control over children's homes established by the Commissariat of Social Welfare.[18]

The change in management did not seem to coincide with any clear shift in parents' priorities. The urban food shortages of 1919 and 1920, rather than Narkompros's goal of facilitating the child's physical and spiritual development, prompted parents to clamor for spaces in rural children's colonies. The applications of parents seeking to enroll their children underscore the colonies' essential role in relief efforts. One father "having absolutely no prospects for the long-term support" of his family, hoped to send his thirteen-year-old son and six-year-old daughter along with his wife "who could do necessary housework" to one of Narkompros's winter colonies.[19] That pupils would have the opportunity to play outdoors, to draw, and to work with clay, sand, hammer, and nails still mattered less to parents than the promised meals.

Scarcity in the Schools

The Preschool Department insisted on the primacy of the kindergarten's educational mission in the face not only of parents appealing for famine relief but also of profound shortages of everything imaginable. Educators were not, it seems, being very "realistic." Yet they went out of their way to be systematic and "scientific"; moreover, they openly admitted their failures. Well aware of the daunting obstacles, officials at Narkompros apparently refused to grant that difficult conditions necessarily ruled out the creation of educationally sound kindergartens. Simultaneously (and paradoxically) a high ideological and low budgetary priority, the efforts to educate young children illustrate the difficulty of characterizing Soviet policy as straightforwardly motivated by either practical considerations or revolutionary commitments.

With no tsarist network of public kindergartens on which to build, preschool teachers had to start almost from scratch. Only in Moscow did educators find much of an institutional foundation for their work, and even there, only about 2 percent of preschool-age children attended kindergartens. In January 1917, the charitable *Obshchestva popecheniia o detiakh* funded nineteen day care centers that together accommodated 655 children. In the summer of 1917, the same society organized thirty-four playgrounds for 4,559 children and assisted in the organization of fifty-one more.[20] After October, Narkompros took over many of these institutions along with some of the private kindergartens, notably Sventitskaia's.[21] Putting the best possible spin on the lack of trained teachers and the dearth of functioning kindergartens, the Preschool Department gloated that it did not have to "waste time on destruction."[22] Still, it was difficult to deny that preschool teachers had little to work with and, to make matters worse, stood near the bottom of Narkompros's budgetary priorities.[23]

The effort to build kindergartens was driven largely by the policymakers at Narkompros. The Preschool Department began by instructing localities to establish preschool subdepartments. In 1918, the department circulated questionnaires in an effort to determine how work was progressing. Within those *gubernii* (provinces) responding, 104 *uezdy* (counties) had set up subdepartments, and an equal number had not. If demand for kindergartens existed in these areas, the means of building them usually did not. The reasons proffered for the failure to set up the required bureaucratic infrastructure underlined the paucity of the department's resources. Lack of trained personnel and supplies headed the list. Only one *guberniia* listed "war" as the excuse. When asked to describe their immediate needs, organizers suggested instructors, teaching materials, money, and adequate buildings; a large number simply answered "everything."[24]

Even with these constraints, local administrations managed to set up some institutions. In 1918, Moscow *guberniia* led the way with twenty-three kindergartens, eight day cares (*ochagi*), and thirteen summer playgrounds. A year later it boasted a total of 279 institutions. The city itself (apart from the *guberniia*) reported five kindergartens, thirteen colonies, and fifty-one playgrounds. By October 1919, the number of institutions of all types in Moscow reached 203. Petrograd had no preschool subdepartment in 1918, but a year later it reported 106 institutions in the city and 180 in the *guberniia* outside the city. Other areas reported slower, but still remarkable, increases. Few, however, matched the sanguine predictions made a year earlier. Workers in Kaluga, with no institutions in 1918, optimistically anticipated eighty-five; sixty actually existed in 1919.[25]

Where numbers are available, the percentage of the preschool-age population served by new institutions remained low (Table 1). In 1919, 10 percent of Moscow's 88,384 potential kindergartners (15,000 less than the 1917 figure) attended some type of preschool. In the *guberniia* as a whole, institutions accommodated only 4.5 percent of the preschool-age population. In general, the percentage in the cities ranged from 5 to 12 percent. All numbers reflected tremendous increases since 1918.

Table 1 Percentage of Preschool-Age Children
Served by Institutions of All Types, Fall 1919

	Preschool-Age Population	Children in Institutions	Number of Institutions	Percentage of Children Served
City				
Moscow	88,384	9,059	203	10
Petrograd	[34,860]*	6,975	106	2
Samara	13,499	0	0	0
Tula	13,252	1081	19	8.2
Nizhnii-Novgorod	11,547	1660	20	13.9
Total for 20 reporting population	249,631	27,156	464	10.9
Total for 26 cities		33,706	518	
Guberniia				
Moscow	297,340	13,366	279	4.5
Petrograd	N/A	14,948	188	N/A
Samara	325,647	2,850	57	0.5
Tula	219,695	5,058	49	2.3
Novgorod	103,209	7,415	60	7.2
Total for 22 reporting population	4,026,810	103,632	1,913	2.5
Total for 31 *gubernii*		155,443	2,615	

* The population was calculated from the statistics provided in the source.

Source: "Obzor polozheniia doshkol'nogo vospitaniia po dannym otchetov na 1 okt. 1919," *Narodnoe prosveshchenie* Nos. 16–17 (Nov.-Dec. 1920), Tables 4 and 8.

While the department's statistics indicate sustained growth, they remain silent on what criteria, if any, preschools had to meet before being included in the tabulation (Table 2). With most areas in 1918 reporting at most two or three specialists, it seems safe to conclude that the majority of teachers had little training or experience. Did an untrained young woman "supervising" forty or fifty preschoolers constitute a playground? Did institutions included in the inventory meet some minimum standards of pedagogy and health? The figures suggest no answers. The 1919 statistics published in *Narodnoe prosveshchenie* do not even distinguish between the various types of institutions: half-day and full-day kindergartens, loosely organized playgrounds, temporary summer playgrounds and colonies, and children's homes. Moreover, it is not always clear at what point in the school year figures were collected. The failure to specify which institutions were being included makes comparing figures from different surveys problematic at best. Anecdotal evidence from conferences of preschool teachers generally correlates with the published figures and suggests less a widespread practice of inflating numbers than a lack of agreement on what exactly should be counted.[26]

When the figures are read against instructions for building kindergartens, the increases become less impressive. Aware of the material difficulties of organizing

Table 2   Preschool Institutions of All Types in the Russian Soviet Federal Socialist Republic, 1917–1921

Year	Number of Institutions of All Types	Children Served by All Institutions
pre-October 1917	40–50 (kindergartens and *ochagi*)	N/A
1917	247	17,290
1918	2,436	146,160
1919	2,615	178,013
1920	3,286	191,360
November 1921*	7,784	350,000

Source: TsGA RSFSR f. 1575, op. 7, d. 14, l. 105. The 1919 figures are from Table 1.

* Later sources that exclude playgrounds and may be from another point in the school year report much lower figures for 1921. The number of pupils is reported as 245,527, and the number of kindergartens and *ochagi* as 4,723 in *Kul'turnoe stroitel'stvo Soiuza Sovetskikh Sotsialisticheskikh Respublik* (Leningrad: Gosudarstvennoe izdatel'stvo, 1927), diagram 15. The number of pupils is reported as 221,400 in *Narodnoe prosveshchenie v RSFSR v tsifrakh za 15 let sovetskoi vlasti* (Moscow-Leningrad: Gosudarstvennoe uchebno-pedagogicheskoe izdatel'stvo, 1932), 16.

institutions—especially, but not exclusively, in the provinces—the Preschool Department decided to build a few experimental-model (*opytno–pokazatel'nyi*) kindergartens and a large number of "primitive" kindergartens (*sad primitiv*). The primitive kindergartens provided supervision but lacked trained teachers and adequate materials; however, they were supposed to meet some vaguely defined minimums of pedagogy and hygiene. The department hoped to build one model kindergarten for each *guberniia*, or at worst one for every two or three *gubernii*. In addition, each province was supposed to have a minimum of four "primitive" *ochagi* and two "primitive" kindergartens.[27] Most of the institutions in the statistics undoubtedly fell into the "temporary, transitional" *sad primitiv* category.

Actually, it is not at all clear that any model institutions existed in the Civil War years. The distinction between model and primitive may be better understood as a reflection of the department's wishful thinking than as a picture of the kindergartens it managed. Even the model kindergarten run by the department's own Preschool Institute in Moscow, the 1919 handbook of preschool education admitted with regret, was not much of a model, as it lacked toys, furniture, teaching materials, "etc., etc."[28] Such meager resources notwithstanding, officials repeatedly insisted that kindergartens provide each group of forty to fifty children with four to five bright, airy, clean rooms and individual beds.[29] With seemingly infinite optimism, the department produced exhaustive checklists of kindergarten supplies—sand, clay, paper, pencils, crayons, blocks, wood, scissors, boxes, pictures, dolls, simple toys—at a time when preschools in Moscow, where conditions were best, reported shortages of beds, shoes, and linens.[30]

The department's conventions of reporting raw numbers and of formulating remarkably concrete, albeit largely impractical, plans produced the impression of the steady expansion of truly educational institutions. But effective as the department's publications might have been in legitimizing the emphasis on enlightenment, they could not wish away the painful realities faced by teachers in the field. A 1920 questionnaire sent to Moscow children's homes revealed some uncertainty that even minimum standards of health and hygiene could be maintained. The department inquired not only whether each institution had running water but also whether it worked. In questions perhaps designed less to elicit truthful answers than to remind teachers of what was expected of them, the department asked instructors to rate various areas of the home as "dirty" or "clean."[31] Inspections in 1921 in Moscow rated conditions "unsatisfactory" or "especially bad" in over three-quarters of the 213 kindergartens and over two-thirds of the 183 children's homes surveyed. Nearly all lacked fuel and adequate buildings. While food supplies were generally adequate, sick and poorly clothed children abounded.[32] "Primitive" may have been the most polite way of describing prevailing conditions.

Undersupplied institutions not only endangered children but also put tremendous pressure on the country's small cadre of preschool teachers. Instructors at a kindergarten in Kursk related that they wasted much time making teaching materials themselves.[33] Teachers at children's homes (*detskii dom*) often had the added responsibility of housework. In Moscow, their work days ranged from six to ten hours, with at most one day off per week. Food for teachers depended entirely on the local situation.[34] It is not surprising that a chronic teacher shortage persisted throughout the 1920s, even after the Preschool Department introduced three-month courses in hopes of training new recruits more quickly, if not more thoroughly.[35]

Some teachers questioned the wisdom of persuading parents to send their children to poorly supplied and understaffed institutions. Students and teachers at a 1920 teacher-training course were appalled to find overworked children at a summer colony visited by the class. Responsible for a large portion of the housework, the colony's preschoolers often could not finish their assigned tasks and cried frequently during the day. The woman who ran the colony, apparently also an instructor at the teaching-training courses, defended the arrangement on the grounds that people had to learn that they could not always expect to finish their work. She further explained that the class's observation had come on an "exceptional day," when a teacher's illness upset the housework schedule and relations between the teachers and the colony's technical personnel were particularly strained.[36] The visit turned out to be an educational one, but probably not of the sort anticipated by the organizers.

Teachers conceded the existence of painful and alarming failures. A delegate from Petrograd to the 1920 Scientific Congress related a story that she had not witnessed personally but had heard from what she deemed reliable sources. Comrade Efrusi recounted how teachers at a Petrograd kindergarten, hoping to spare their pupils the ravages of famine, "eloquently" persuaded the children's parents to send them to a colony in a region with bread. After only a short stay, teachers hastily returned the children to the city. Mothers and fathers meeting the train at the station saw that all the children's eyes were bandaged; it turned out that the entire group had been blinded by gonorrhea. The facts as she recounted them seem improbable, yet even those delegates who defended efforts to place as many children as possible in institutions did not question the authenticity of Efrusi's admittedly second-hand story.[37]

However, a recognition of the system's failures did not necessarily dampen enthusiasm for it. The most wretched conditions could be explained as aberrations; one delegate argued on the basis of undisclosed sources that conditions in kindergartens generally surpassed those in children's homes and colonies and that, in any event, research proved that more illness could be traced to families than to institutions. Another delegate, who began by affirming that he did "not doubt these horrors," explained that "teachers do not meet basic demands of hygiene because they do not understand them." He seemed to have more confidence in the ability of teachers than of parents to learn. Comrade Orlova, a teacher from Moscow, suggested, with a measure of condescension, that the worst cases were limited to Petrograd. She further pointed out that such situations were by no means unique to Soviet Russia; even in well-supplied bourgeois institutions one could find similar problems.

Saving Children from the Past

Orlova's comparison points to the political significance of Soviet efforts to save children. For revolutionaries, saving children meant safeguarding the communist future that they embodied. It was possible to measure the revolution's success in terms of the conditions not only of the working class and of women, but also of children. It was among youngsters that the cultural revolution would have its fullest impact. The fate of the Revolution was linked, if not practically then metaphorically, to the state of its children.

The regime's enemies exploited this linkage, finding few more potent expressions of the perceived communist threat to civilized values than lurid tales of disrupted families and starving children. The account of the remarkable evacuation of eight hundred children from Petrograd, through Siberia to Vladivostok, across the Pacific to San Francisco, and then through the Panama Canal to New York, amounted to an indictment of the Revolution as a whole.[38] If, as Commissar of Enlightenment Anatol Lunacharskii declared, the Revolution had been made in the name of the rising generation, then it was reasonable to measure its success in terms of the lives of children. Boris Sokolov's 1921 diatribe *Save the Children!* juxtaposes a review of the horrendous conditions in Soviet institutions with the Bolshevik desire, as expressed by Zlata Lilina (Grigori Zinoviev's wife), to raise a "generation of communists" in state-run kindergartens and schools. For Sokolov, the failure of these plans had less to do with a gross imbalance of ambitions and resources—as Trotsky would later contend in *The Revolution Betrayed*—than with the "wicked irony" that the Bolsheviks, in their haste, clumsiness, and desire for publicity, transformed the best and purest ideas into "extraordinarily noxious fruit." Sokolov presented the failure to provide material and spiritual nourishment for children as a synecdoche for the entire Bolshevik effort to remake culture.[39]

The Bolsheviks took a longer view. They recognized the seriousness of immediate threats to children, but were unwilling to allow such concerns to undermine the commitment to a revolution in everyday life. Pamphlets and posters advertised improvements that existed for the present only on paper. In her overview of programs for women and children in the Soviet Union, Vera Lebedeva of the Commissariat of Public Health conceded that the Bolsheviks had done little more than lay a foundation for future work. Nonetheless, she offered detailed sketches of institutions and services that remained a long way from realization.[40] Bolshevik propaganda emphasized legal reforms that guaranteed the health and welfare of all children, inviting parents to envision a city of the future equipped with kindergartens, homes for pregnant women, and well-stocked public kitchens.

The mood, and its limits, is captured in Fedor Gladkov's novel *Cement* (1925), in which the view of a children's home nestled in a mountain gorge against "the sea, intensely blue and flecked with dazzling sparks" inspires Gleb's most lyrical effusions of the future. He "felt wings unfolding in his soul. . . . This is Workers' Russia; this is us; the new world of which mankind has dreamed throughout the centuries." The image is reinforced, rather ironically, by the hungry, ragged children singing in "deafening, discordant voices" the "Children's International": "Arise ye children of the future!/The builders of a brighter world!" For Dasha, the Revolution is first and foremost for children. Upbraiding the teachers, who have appropriated the home's best furniture and pictures for their private quarters, Dasha lectures, "For us — nothing, but for them — everything. Even if we have to cut ourselves to pieces, even if we have to die, we must give them everything."[41]

Focusing on goals far beyond famine relief, Soviet accounts argued that the immediate dangers facing children should not be allowed to obscure the deeper menaces of superstition and backwardness that threatened to remain after the crisis passed.[42] The Bolsheviks aimed to save children not only from famine but also, more fundamentally, from old practices, from the older generation itself. From this perspective, food shortages constituted a transitory phenomenon, and scarcity became a poor excuse for deferring efforts to raise cultural levels. This uncoupling of the practical and the revolutionary may have made it easier to accept, or ignore, the paradoxical policy of allocating few resources to a task of allegedly monumental importance.

Parental Incompetence

Bolshevik solicitousness about the needs of working families was highly ambiguous. The insistence on full-day kindergartens grew out of a desire to help parents through the emergency created by the Civil War and, as Lebedeva expressed it, to allow women to be both workers and mothers. At the same time, the Bolsheviks assumed that the average mother, ignorant of modern methods of child care, often did her children more harm than good. Here Bolshevik assumptions had much in common with those made by the organizers of philanthropic kindergartens in the West. But unlike kindergartens in the West, Soviet kindergartens initially aimed to replace, or substantially supplement, rather than simply educate parents. Reservations about parents' child-rearing practices constituted the most salient constant in Soviet preschool policy at least through the early 1930s. The tendency to define parents as both victims of circumstance and as enemies of progress precluded a purely "pragmatic" approach to providing relief for families.

From a Marxist perspective, war and revolution merely dealt the death blow to a family structure long in decline. On this point, Marxist logic coincided with the "scientific" observations of doctors and teachers, who had documented the failings of family upbringing well before the October Revolution. Luiza Shleger, a preschool teacher trained before the Revolution and less hostile to the family than many, nonetheless warned that "science tells us that this [preschool] age is awfully complicated," too complicated for mothers to handle alone. An article in *Narodnoe prosveshchenie* summed up the situation more bluntly: "[P]reschool education is usually seen as only a matter of feeding and clothing, and even this most parents do not do well."[43]

Home visits and conversations with mothers revealed profoundly difficult circumstances, which educators concluded inevitably impinged on parents' ability to care for their children. A typical study of the parents of one hundred preschoolers in Moscow in 1927 found that 42 percent of the children came from families living in economic circumstances below "normal" levels. Only 25 percent of the families enjoyed "normal" living conditions (two rooms), while 75 percent lived in a single room.[44] Such close quarters meant that most children shared a bed with parents or a sibling.[45] A study of thirty-eight parents of three- and four-year-olds revealed that only 30.5 percent of the fathers and 33.3 percent of the mothers considered themselves healthy; the doctors doing the study concluded that the real figures were undoubtedly lower. Cramped living conditions and a meatless diet of *shchi*, kasha, and potatoes produced equally unhealthy children. Nineteen of thirty-eight children in the study had suffered pneumonia by age five; seventeen had had measles.[46]

Studies of the family circumstances of their charges ostensibly aided preschool teachers in "correcting deficiencies" and tailoring programs to children's needs.[47] But such studies also reinforced a general disdain for parents' child-rearing skills. From the experts' point of view, shortages of food, clothing, shoes, and other essentials did not fully explain or excuse parental failures. Children needed not only bread but also "scientific feeding." An early statement of the aims of the day care noted that it must provide "correct nutrition, to fill out the incorrect, irregular, and unhealthy feeding at home." Scarcity merely exacerbated problems produced by ignorance.[48]

Educators and health workers viewed the kindergarten as the antidote to the poverty and negligence so many children suffered at home. Lilina, one of the most ardent advocates of stripping the family of its child-rearing functions, described the status of preschool children before the Revolution in bleak detail; "squeezed in crowded, unhealthful apartments—kennels without light or sun—most workers' children are left shut up at home."[49] Health workers employed similar terms after the Revolution. In the city, the child did not get enough fresh air, and the din produced by several families sharing a tiny apartment made it impossible for the preschooler to get the necessary eleven to twelve hours' sleep. Doctors warned that the situation would not improve until mothers learned the health risks of leaving their children in dark, stuffy rooms.[50] The handbook of preschool education asserted that even a rudimentary kindergarten, where teachers at least understood the necessity of fresh air and individual beds, "was healthier than the godforsaken holes and dirty backyards in which our children must huddle."[51]

Researchers often understood filth and noise not as the by-products of overcrowded, dilapidated apartments but as a sign of the parents' benightedness. While educators might sympathize with parents' inability to move their families to more spacious quarters, they had little patience for parents who failed to keep their single-room apartments clean. A picture offered by investigators as typical of what they found highlights the concern for cleanliness. Lena S. lived with her mother, older brother, and sister in a small dirty room off a dirty, dark cold hallway. She slept with her mother and brother on a narrow bed "covered with dirty rags." The entire room was caked with soot from the metal stove. Sleeping in such conditions, investigators concluded, made children particularly prone to illness.[52] Where spotlessness signified enlightenment, parents' shortcomings were obvious to the most casual observer.

As in studies conducted before the Revolution, condemnations of the physical environment of the home slid into attacks on its moral tone. Researchers warned that in overcrowded apartments "swearing, curses, indecent songs, cynical conversations in which sex organs and the sex act take an honored place . . . sound continuously in the child's ears." The child witnesses "scenes of open debauchery"—a mother's prostitution, a father's alcoholism.[53] One study found that of the fathers present at home, 44.7 percent were alcoholics.[54] The "Little Star" day care in Iaroslavl reported that "the majority of children do not have a father or he does not live in the family and has been replaced by 'Uncle Misha' or 'Uncle Nikolai.'" And because most families shared a single room, "all intimate life goes on in front of the children."[55] Doctors and educators agreed that such circumstances inevitably produced coarse, cruel, shameless children. A model questionnaire for students entering preschool institutions reflected these concerns. In addition to questions about childhood development and diseases, doctors were supposed to inquire about any early manifestations of sexual feeling in masturbation or obscene conduct.[56] The professional literature described the home—dirty, overcrowded, uncultured—as a dangerous place for children.

Researchers characterized parents themselves as, above all, ignorant of the true "nature of the child." Lacking the kindergarten teacher's scientific knowledge of early childhood development, parents did not begin to provide children with vital preschool experiences.[57] The cultural deprivation of their charges alarmed teachers. The report of five playgrounds in Moscow noted that only a handful of the 150 children enrolled—including eight-year-olds—could name colors. The children did not know which city they lived in, and most had never left it to experience the forest or plowed fields.[58]

Teachers lamented the family's inability to provide creative outlets for children. One study found that only eighteen of one hundred parents gave their children the opportunity to engage in the "concentrated and quiet solitary play" deemed essential to proper development. In some homes, visiting teachers observed that children had no toys at all.[59] Teachers were not eager to trust often illiterate mothers (56.3 percent in one study) with the task of education.[60] Doctors confirmed that working-class children suffered from "weak intellectual development." The only thing family upbringing seemed capable of developing in the child was "fear before God," not exactly a ringing endorsement as far as the Bolsheviks were concerned.[61]

The reduction of the family to its role in religious education is telling. What troubled the Bolsheviks most about family upbringing was its ability to undermine "socialist values." The exact nature of such values is not entirely clear. Dora Abramovna Lazurkina, the head of the Preschool Department of Narkompros, an old Bolshevik who participated in the October seizure of power, charged parents with narrowing their children's "social horizons." "If we consider that the family must raise not an egoist but a citizen in the full sense of the word, then it appears completely bankrupt."[62] She did not expand on what a "citizen in the full sense of the word" might be, and there appears to be nothing uniquely socialist in the distinction between "citizens" and "egoists." Advocates of free upbringing had leveled similar charges against the family before the Revolution.

Lazurkina's formulation can be read as expressing in general terms the Bolsheviks' doubts about the ability or willingness of parents, including working-class parents, to prepare their children for the communist future. The family's tendency to look inward and the lack of explicit political education at home were treated as inseparable problems. Kollontai was unwilling to entrust the early education of "the future of communist Russia" to parents. She believed that "if we can raise [children] in our spirit, no enemy is terrifying. The future is ours."[63] Similarly, Narkompros's "practical" instructions on the organization of children's homes advised that since "socialism requires socialists, . . . it is necessary to put children from the tenderest age into such circumstances as quicken the process of communism."[64] Families could not be counted upon to raise children in a rather vaguely defined "socialist spirit."

Explanations of *why* parents could not raise their children in the proper spirit leave far less to the imagination. Parents' tendency to spoil children quite simply destroyed their allegedly natural propensity for socialism. In an article published at the time of the first preschool congress in 1919, Lazurkina suggested that family upbringing failed because it could not nurture the individual creativity that comes only from working with others. Sounding very much like a pre-Revolutionary advocate of free upbringing, Lazurkina explained that "the child, living in familial circumstances, is always the center of attention and . . . unwillingly becomes a person with poorly developed social instincts."[65] Lilina presented the same case in more biting language. "Out of love for her child, a mother overfeeds him; out of love for her child she encourages his caprices and harmful pranks. . . . [O]ut of love for the child the family turns him into an egoistical being, accustoming him to see himself as the center of the universe."[66] Family love was not "rational" love, and even "ideal" parents ended up distorting their children's development.

The clearest practical manifestation of the family's "egoism" was its tendency to raise children in isolation. In one study, only four of thirteen children played on a regular basis with children other than their brothers and sisters. The family precluded the child from experiencing solidarity with other children.[67] Such findings led one educator to conclude that the "deepest, cardinal difference between traditional family upbringing and public upbringing, which encompasses the fact that the mother is an untrained educator [*vospitatel'nitsa*], is the antisocial development of children" that produces youngsters capable of breaking their playmates' toys.[68]

The picture of the child at the center of the universe is difficult to reconcile with the numerous reminders that the "majority of children grow up without supervision."[69] On the one hand, children "are deprived of maternal caresses and solicitude."[70] On the other, they are deformed by a surfeit of irrational love. As an educational institution, the family committed two seemingly mutually exclusive errors: It left children unsupervised in "dirty backyards" *and* it overindulged them.

One way out of the conundrum was to distinguish between proletarian and bourgeois families—a solution perhaps obvious but rarely employed. It could easily be argued that whereas the working-class mother left her children without supervision, the "intelligentsia" mother spoiled and pampered hers. Public kindergartens could solve the "social problems of the working mass" and remedy the egoism of the bourgeois family.[71] However, few commentators made the distinction, as it carried the unfortunate suggestion that the working class would have little need for the kindergarten's educational program.

If instead, as Lazurkina contended, the inward-looking, egotistical family was not a class phenomenon, then preschool institutions gained importance. At the preschool congress, she argued that because the family—regardless of class—evaluates everything only from the point of view of its own interests, it bred a narrow, self-centered outlook in children.[72] And it was egoism that she viewed as incompatible with socialism. No mythical "proletarian family" could rival public kindergartens, day cares, or children's homes as sites for raising children devoted to the life of the collective.

Educational theory largely ruled out the possibility of rectifying mistakes made by parents. Russian preschool workers, like progressive doctors and teachers everywhere, began with the proposition that the preschool years laid the foundation for all that followed. By the time children entered school at age seven, the pattern of their future development was seen as substantially set.[73] This vision of the child's formative years made it clear that parents could effectively undermine efforts to raise, in Lilina's phrase, a "generation of communists." The struggle to "save" children from the arbitrary authority and backward practices of their parents and to raise them as healthy, happy, and rational communists stood at the core of the revolutionary transformation. Remaking childhood became as much a "practical" necessity as providing famine relief.

3

The Family as Fiction

In the Marxist script of revolution, the withering away of the family occurs late in the fourth act. The disappearance of the family, whose presumably oppressive structure was understood as modeling and mirroring society at large, presaged the dawn of a natural and just community of equals. Expectations fueled by the Marxist view of history encouraged the Bolsheviks to see the Civil War's blow to family life as the painful, but necessary, prelude to the new world. Dismal realities that rendered even modest programs unworkable also made the most extravagant plans appear possible.[1]

What precisely would supplant the family remained open to debate. Bolshevik policymakers at the Commissariat of Enlightenment, educational experts at the Preschool Department, and kindergarten teachers who attended conferences or contributed to pedagogical publications proposed a multiplicity of visions of the future of the family and the child. In speeches, articles, directives, and school reports the kindergarten figured as both a catalyst of cultural transformation and as a precocious, fully functional outpost of emerging socialist society. Differing assessments of the family's proximity to its prophesied extinction; of the meaning of parental, especially maternal, rights; and of the degree to which shortages of teachers and material could be overcome produced a wide variety of answers to the fundamental question of when socialized child-rearing could (or should) replace parents entirely.

Not all educators, not even all Bolsheviks, agreed with the head of the Preschool Department Dora Lazurkina's contention that by 1918 the family had become a "fiction." Lazurkina argued that since the family had ceased to function, if not yet to exist, establishing public institutions to raise all children constituted an immediate necessity.[2] For others, the family was a different sort of "fiction"—a pliant reality that could be remade or remake itself. The family was pictured as capable of abandoning its egoism and of providing both a germ and a model of the new way of life. Still other educators viewed the family and the maternal instinct as immutable, or nearly so.

In a sense, the question of whether or not the family could be immediately replaced or revolutionized was a question without much "practical" significance. Scarcity ultimately doomed efforts to provide fully socialized child care. Nevertheless, the debate on the relationship of parents, children, and the state was a critical one. On one level, it suggests that "common sense" and a "pragmatic" weighing of resources and goals were never entirely separable from ideological concerns. Moreover, the alternatives articulated during the Civil War remained key points of reference in the evolution of policy toward families and children. The debate also provides a unique view of efforts to conceptualize and realize social and cultural transformation. In the discourse of teachers and public health workers, as in more frankly political contexts, "family" functioned as a means of imagining the revolutionary future, and the child as both revolutionary icon and agent.

The Case for Children's Homes

The Preschool Department's official line, as expressed by its head Lazurkina, was that the family was, by early 1918, a thing of the past. In her keynote address to the First All-Russian Congress of Preschool Education, Lazurkina argued, following the logic of Engels' "The Origin of the Family, Private Property, and the State," that the double shift imposed on women by capitalism had destroyed the family. Krupskaia, focusing less on supervision and more on education, reached essentially the same conclusion; since the family did a poor job of raising creative, productive children, the state had to build kindergartens to accommodate all children, whether or not their mothers worked.[3] Preschool Department publications claimed, on the basis of undisclosed evidence, that even the full-day kindergarten did not "satisfy children, parents, or teachers." By contrast, the children's home (*detskii dom*), which raised children entirely outside the family, relieved overburdened parents of child care worries, afforded teachers the opportunity to affect every aspect of children's lives, and allowed children to live their "natural life" all day long.[4]

Even as they attested to inauspicious conditions, accounts from the field often imitated the department's formulations on the disappearance of the family and the need to raise all children in public institutions. The report of a Moscow *detskii dom* facing closure affirmed that the home's goal was "to create the necessary conditions for the normal development of children, to replace the individual family," and to "raise citizens." Two photographs included with the report make one wonder how such a mission could be accomplished. The pictures show some fifty, generally unsmiling, rather scruffy children seated on the crooked steps of the home. The building itself has peeling paint and a door hanging off its frame. Two tired looking young women and a young man in uniform apparently made up the teaching staff.[5] Nonetheless, the report never argues that scanty resources require the abandonment of the grandiose end.

The annual review of the enormous Third International Children's Town in Moscow similarly began with the declaration that "all care for children in Soviet Russia is the responsibility of neither parents nor the family but of the state." The children's town (*detskii gorodok*) served between five hundred and one thousand children from age three to seventeen. It consisted of six children's homes, two schools, two kindergartens, an infirmary, and a hospital. As of the 1919–20 report, it took only the orphans and "half orphans," children missing one parent, produced in such large numbers by the war. But, its director emphasized, it was not an orphanage. The institution approached children as individuals, with love and tenderness, and only the current crisis precluded the enrollment of children with parents.[6] Such reports reflected if not the opinions of the teachers then at least their perception of a stand that would conform to the line articulated by prominent policymakers.

For teachers in the field, finding the "correct" position was no doubt complicated by the fact that the messages emanating from Moscow were decidedly mixed. While officials like Lazurkina called for the immediate socialization of child-rearing, prominent non-Bolshevik educators associated with the Preschool Department emphasized the vital role of the family during a period of "transition." In its official pronouncements, the Preschool Department denied that meager resources dictated that the children's home remain a vision of the distant future. "There is no doubt," Lazurkina asserted at a 1920 conference, "that at the present time, of all preschool institutions, the most desirable is the home, even though it is more difficult to establish. . . . [I]t must be opened to the extent possible."[7] The students at a teacher training course the same year learned that "the ideal institution, where the best upbringing is possible, must be the children's home where children live full time in a rural environment."[8] At the same time, many participants at the department's conferences and congresses along with well-respected nonparty specialists like Tikheeva, Sventitskaia, and Luiza Shleger insisted that the failure of existing institutions to meet this pastoral ideal required a more charitable assessment of the family's role.

While only a small number of the teachers trying to make sense of these mixed signals were likely to be party members, there was a higher percentage of Bolsheviks in the preschools and especially in the children's homes than in the schools. Only 7.5 percent of preschool teachers for the 1923–1924 school year were party members. The percentage among workers in the children's homes was higher, 10.2 percent. Low as these figures are, they become more impressive when compared to the 2.5 percent of schoolteachers who were party members in the same year.[9] That the almost exclusively female cadre of preschool teachers had a higher proportion of party members than the more gender-balanced pool of schoolteachers is especially striking, since as late as 1922, only 8 percent of party members were female.[10] The 1923–1924 figures for party membership among teachers in children's homes are not very far behind the figures published in 1932 to demonstrate the "growth of party affiliation among pedagogical cadres," when 11.8 percent of preschool teachers were members or candidate members of the party or Komsomol (it is not clear whether the 1923–1924 statistics include candidates or Komsomols). However, by 1932 the schools boasted more Bolsheviks (19.7 percent) than the preschools; teachers at children's homes were no longer included in the tabulation.[11]

The early ability of preschools and children's homes to attract percentages (not, of course, numbers) of party members not found in the schools until 1927 can be understood as a result of the kindergarten's ties to the Revolution. Since few kindergartens existed before the October Revolution, the absolute number of preschool teachers was quite small. The total number of preschool teachers was just over half the number of party members in the schools. Additionally, as products of the Revolution, kindergartens lacked a large contingent of older, experienced teachers (Table 3). Over 64 percent of the teachers in preschools and nearly 57 percent in children's homes in 1923–1924 had begun their careers "in revolutionary times," to borrow the phrase employed by Narkompros statisticians. The corresponding figure in the schools was 38.2 percent. Many of these new teachers were young. Of preschool teachers in 1925–1926, 40 percent were under 25, and nearly 70 percent were under 30 years old.[12] The rapidly growing network of children's institutions may have provided more opportunities than did the schools for newly trained teachers. It is also possible that the young teachers who chose to work in preschools or children's homes did so out of a genuine commitment to the revolutionary mission of these institutions. More self-consciously than their peers in the schools, teachers in preschools and children's homes may have felt themselves to be building and living the future.

Granting some measure of sincerity to teachers' claims that they viewed their institutions as the leading edge of cultural transformation helps to explain the persistence of utopian visions in the face of appalling material constraints. It is possible to read reports to the center both as calculated efforts to impress policymakers in Moscow and as testaments to revolutionary optimism and idealism. Throughout the Civil War, orphans flooded children's institutions. A 1920 survey of eighteen preschool homes revealed that nearly 80 percent of the 1,044 children enrolled were orphans or half orphans, mostly with missing fathers. In the average home of fifty-eight children, usually only five or six had both parents. Even Lazurkina had to concede that the *detskii dom* in most cases did not replace biological families but "compensated" children for their lost parents.[13] Teachers knew firsthand how meager that compensation could be. State institutions often proved unable to provide basic necessities or sanitary environments, let alone toys, blocks, dolls, and sandboxes. Turning on its head the assertion that even a

Table 3 Teachers' Length of Service, 1923–1924 (percentage of teachers in each cohort)

Type of Institution	Number of Teachers	Percentage reporting	*Length of Service in Years*					
			1–3	3–5	5–10	10–15	5–25	Over 25
School	174,596	92.7	20.1	18.1	28.1	17.1	11.7	4.9
Preschool	2,238	91.7	31.1	33.2	22.4	9	3.5	0.8
Children's home	15,333	100	29.5	27.4	25.5	10.7	5.3	1.1

Source: Narkompros, *Statisticheskii ezhegodnik: sostoianie narodnogo obrazovaniia v RSFSR za 1923–24 god.* (Moscow: Izdatel'stvo "Doloi negramotnost'," 1925), 40, 328. Number of school teachers from Narkompros, *Narodnoe prosveshchenie v RSFSR v tsifrakh za 15 let sovetskoi vlasti (kratkii statisticheskii sbornik)*, (Moscow-Leningrad: Gosudarstvennoe uchebno-pedagogicheskoe izdatel'stvo, 1932), Table 22.

rudimentary kindergarten was better for children than the family, a delegate to a congress on children's health argued that "even in the worst family, children are almost always happy, but in our institutions, children laugh too little."[14] At the same time, the conviction that the family was defunct or at best on the verge of collapse fostered the belief that children's homes were not only possible but also absolutely necessary.

Institutional Families

Ironically, "family" emerged as one of the most powerful and prevalent ways of imagining both the state institutions that would raise children under socialism and socialist society as a whole. In describing and designing the collectives that were supposed to replace parents, policymakers turned to the vocabulary of family. More broadly, the family metaphor made it possible to imagine the communist future as built on the mutual care and loving ties that were commonly associated with "family" but that had been, from the socialist point of view, corrupted by their restriction to the narrow, egotistical family hearth.[15] One did not have to be a Bolshevik to accept the distinction between the family as "distorted" by capitalism and the true, loving, natural, but not necessarily biological, family that would emerge (or perhaps be restored) under communism. Such rhetoric attached the sentiment or even sentimentality of "family" to hopefully modern and scientific, but potentially cold, forbidding, and bureaucratic institutions. The language of "family" naturalized the drastic modification of personal relations and public life.

Among educators and educational policymakers, the need to endow the kindergarten with a "family" atmosphere and to build children's "homes" rather than orphanages constituted a constant refrain. The section of the 1919 preschool handbook detailing the furniture appropriate to the kindergarten advised teachers to avoid a bureaucratic, institutional look. "In general, all opinion concurs that the set-up of the kindergarten must, as far as possible, resemble that of the family"—somewhat strange advice from a department that had few kind words for parents' child-rearing skills.[16] In teacher training courses, the highest praise went to kindergartens where "the connection between students and teachers makes itself felt" and where, in contrast to observed families, children washed their hands frequently.[17] A model-experimental children's home received praise for its "cozy and familial" atmosphere.[18] A successful playground operated like a "big happy family."[19]

Teachers, almost exclusively women, were assigned the roles of rational mothers. Such associations had long been a common feature of the kindergarten movement's "maternalist" rhetoric. What made the association revolutionary in the Soviet context was the suggestion that teacher-mothers might supplant biological mothers. A delegate to a conference on preschool methods related, "When I go to a kindergarten, I don't pay attention to the kinds of drawings hanging up or to the character of the physical surroundings, I look at the faces of the children, I see how they approach the teacher, . . . what kind of smiles they have, what sort of facial expressions." Even an inexperienced teacher might be capable of becoming not a "surrogate," but the center of a truly loving family.[20] Some educators suggested that teachers live at the preschool in order to enhance its "family" character.[21]

Ideally, the child would come to see the preschool as its true home. An early statement of the aims of day cares asserted that "the *ochag* is their home, its is the place where they feel *at home* [*u sebia*]." Accordingly, the only punishment the kindergarten need mete out, and only in the most extreme cases, would be a one or two day suspension; "children become attached to the day care and are bored without it." More than an unfeeling institution, "the day care is a family."[22]

The preferred form of the children's home was the "family" or mixed-age home that served children ranging in age from three to sixteen or seventeen. Echoing the department's rhetoric, the central children's home in Viatka reported in 1923 that it paid particular attention to organizing the "life of the children as in a large family." Teachers explained to the six- and seven-year-olds that as the oldest members of the kindergarten "family" they had a responsibility to care for the younger children.[23] The Third International Children's Town in Moscow set up mixed-age houses, and Sventitskaia, whose kindergarten became part of the children's town, defended them on the grounds that without the example of older children, "preschoolers are less likely to develop independence and initiative." She argued that separation by age was "unnatural" and that children ought to live in mixed-age groups as they did in families.[24] Such "family" houses were seen as "closer to life" and as facilitating collective labor, with older children assisting their younger comrades.[25]

The positive valuation of "family" in this context suggested at least the possibility of a more sympathetic attitude toward traditional families. This potentiality—coupled with the fact that war, famine, and, later, the New Economic Policy's budget cuts largely limited enrollment in children's homes to orphans[26]—allowed educators who did not share the hope that the traditional family would be stripped of all its child-rearing functions to support Bolshevik policy even as they publicly articulated alternative approaches. In a practical guide for new teachers published in 1923, Tikheeva praised children's homes that mixed preschoolers with school-age youngsters. She further suggested that only when teachers lived in the home could a truly family situation be created. Regardless of teachers' opposition, Tikheeva argued, their children had to be treated exactly the same as the others, "sleeping in the general bedrooms, eating the same things." However, she emphasized, contrary to the official line, that it was best to reserve children's homes for orphans; the ideal institution for children with parents was the kindergarten. According to Tikheeva, "tearing children from mother and family in the first years of life must be recognized as undesirable and harmful." She used the Bolsheviks' insistence on imitating a "family" atmosphere in state institutions to suggest the superiority and necessity of the genuine article.[27]

Some Bolshevik educators expressed discomfort with the use of the adjective "family" to denote the desired type of state institutions, but they seemed unable to find a more compelling way of conceptualizing socialized child-rearing or the socialist future in general. Anna Elizarova, Lenin's sister, averred that her advocacy of "family" homes was purely descriptive and carried no deep significance. At the same time, she concluded, without defining her terms, that "all our communes—for children and for adults—ought to be such a family, in the best sense of the word."[28] At the Third All-Russian Conference of preschool teachers in 1920, Lazurkina tried to move away from the word "family" entirely, and talked of "mixed" homes. The department preferred such homes "not because the form of the old family is the ideal social unit" but because children ought to be exposed to life in all its variety.[29] Despite such reservations, the term "family home" remained common. On the questionnaire sent by Narkompros to Moscow children's homes in 1920, the adjective "mixed" referred not to the practice of mixing children of various ages but to the homes' ethnic makeup.[30]

"Family" had undeniable resonance for revolutionaries working to imagine and to enact socialism. Even as she protested efforts to attribute meaning to her word choice, Elizarova characterized not just children's homes but "all our communes" as families. Lauding the Family Code of 1918 that aimed to undermine the patriarchal structure of the traditional family, Zinaida Tettenborn explained that "the new family rights stand on the border between the old world and that shining new world where all society will be one family."[31] This vision of the future offered assurances that once women and children were liberated — from the tyranny of husbands and housework, parents and teachers — new and more satisfying social forms would emerge naturally and automatically. The "big happy family" model of communism emphasized the organic and spontaneous melding of free individuals into a collective on the basis of shared ideals and interests. Lenin had envisioned this sort of "natural" society in *State and Revolution*. While, as Jane Burbank argues, in the wake of crises in foreign and domestic affairs, he may have rejected the "image of a people released into self-directed community," this image retained its appeal and its potency for many Bolsheviks and for many reform-minded teachers.[32]

A Mother's Natural Love

The family imagery could suppress — or confuse — the degree to which the Bolsheviks proposed ultimately to sever, or at least modify radically, traditional relationships, most notably the bond between mother and child. While only the assumption that parents were a bad influence on children could make the prospect of parent-free upbringing appear unreservedly liberating, characterizing public upbringing in familiar, old-fashioned terms might allay the fears of parents. The family model of future social organization suggested that deeply felt ties of kinship would be redeployed rather than destroyed.

Teachers who opposed the construction of institutional families contended that the Bolsheviks dangerously underestimated the resiliency and power of traditional family bonds and the maternal instinct. For many teachers, the family was not a fiction that could be co-opted and rewritten by the Bolsheviks. Rejecting a Marxist perspective entirely, some educators characterized the family as "natural" and largely immutable. At a 1920 conference on teaching methods, one teacher began by categorically disagreeing "with the opinion of comrade Lazurkina that the family has been destroyed." Granting that changing "economic circumstances" might make the family less isolated, the delegate concluded that the family as a basic unit of society "never will be destroyed."[33] Other teachers characterized the family as endangered without sharing the Marxists' belief that its destruction was an unavoidable consummation devoutly to be wished. In response to Lazurkina's address at the First All-Russian Congress of Preschool Education, one delegate agreed that the working-class family had ceased to function, but added that "if we say the family doesn't exist, that doesn't mean this is a good thing."[34]

The image of the maternal instinct as eternal and universal constituted a key figure in opposition to plans for socialized child care. A teacher at the methods conference reminded her colleagues that in many cases an ignorant but instinctive mother did a better job than an unfeeling, if well-educated, teacher.[35] A delegate responding to Lazurkina's keynote address urged teachers and policymakers to respect the "rights of the mother and her role in the life of the child. A mother undoubtedly gives more warmth and light to her child than the most perfect public organization taking upon itself the task of its upbringing."[36] Advocates of family upbringing insisted that the family constituted a permanent fact of social organization and that mothering was an instinct, impervious to culture and independent of social structure.

Advocates of institutional families granted the power of maternal instinct and predicted not so much that it would wither away as that it would find a broader field of application. The official journal of the Commissariat of Enlightenment could concede that "not every mother can be a teacher, but almost every one has a natural love for her child."[37] In a less subtle effort to quiet parents' fears, Narkompros adamantly denied that it intended to "snatch children from their mothers."[38] But a change in family relationships remained part of the revolutionary agenda.

Kollontai imagined that socialized child care would expand the scope of family affections. Defining motherhood as a social responsibility, she doubted that women increasingly involved in public life would spend much time caring for their children. At a congress of public health workers in 1920, she argued that "to the extent that women are drawn into the construction of communism, that instinct which is the guide of the whole of women's lives— the maternal instinct— will not strengthen but weaken." With creative and rewarding participation in life beyond the nuclear family, women would direct their nurturing instincts toward the larger social family. "Maternal feeling" would no longer lead mothers to dote exclusively on their own children, but to reach out to "all the children of their working sisters and brothers."[39] In a similar vein, Nikolai Bukharin and Evgenii Preobrazhenskii in the *ABC of Communism* pictured the new communist world as a place where parents no longer used possessive pronouns to refer to their offspring.[40]

The Bolsheviks seemed to be predicting no less than a wholesale transformation of what they themselves accepted as human *nature*. Taking as axiomatic the grounding of a mother's love in instinct and biology, Soviet policymakers looked forward to its transmogrification. The formulation bespeaks tremendous optimism in the power of the Revolution fundamentally to remake the world; it also opened the way to conceptualizing a period of "transition." To anyone with even a passing familiarity with Darwin, it would have been clear that the process of reforging instincts was likely to be a relatively long one. While estimates of the length of the transition could fluctuate wildly, the act of situating the family *anywhere* along the spectrum that ended in the communist social family worked to reinforce the assumption that the "withering away" of the nuclear family and the broadening of the maternal instinct described a real and inevitable phenomenon. Somewhat paradoxically, the notion of a transitional period also opened a space for voicing a multiplicity of alternatives to the official line that the family was a "fiction."

If the concept of a period of transition deflected questions about the Marxist script itself, it allowed policymakers to debate its staging and pacing. Luiza Karlovna Shleger, among the most prominent of Moscow's pre-Revolutionary preschool teachers and a founding member of the Preschool Department, attempted to strike a balance between the recognition that the family appeared to be falling apart and the conviction that it still had a substantial role to play in the transition to public upbringing. At a 1919 teachers' conference, she refused to "look ahead a hundred years, when the family perhaps will be destroyed; we now live in a fixed time when the family exists, and we say that the family can be neither artificially created nor destroyed."[41] But she also got caught up in, or at least propounded, official optimism about the imminence of revolutionary transformation. As an instructor at a teacher-training course the same year, Shleger took a position closer to Lazurkina's and argued that "the family as a result of contemporary circumstances is being destroyed, and therefore kindergartens are spreading as social units, replacing the child's family."[42] Whatever the time frame, the eventual elimination of the family was taken as a given.

For the Bolsheviks, the right of parents to control the upbringing of their children during the period of transition was open to constant renegotiation. Commissar of Enlightenment Lunacharskii stressed the transcendence of the child's rights and transferred to teachers emotions usually associated with parents. In his view, "the child is the object of state upbringing and has the sacred right to an equal, loving, and educational relationship with its pedagogue." He conceded that the mother had a right to "follow the development of her child," but not to "wallow" in it.[43] Preschool workers reported taking precautions to prevent mothers from influencing their children too deeply. At one kindergarten teachers claimed that they checked up on the family before the child was allowed to spend a vacation at home in an effort to prevent parents from undermining the work of the kindergarten.[44] By contrast, Kollontai, who also looked forward to raising all children in public settings, seemed to privilege maternal rights; "whenever a mother desires—the children are always with her."[45] An article in the Commissariat of Enlightenment's journal *Narodnoe prosveshchenie* went further and affirmed that, for the present, parents would retain their rights to raise their children.[46] Neither Bolshevik policymakers nor nonparty educators articulated a unified vision of the "transition" to socialized child-rearing.

The Kindergarten as Vanguard

As long as the family retained much of its responsibility for child care, the first task of the kindergarten was to garner the support of parents. But even as kindergarten teachers worked to win parents' trust, they assigned themselves and their pupils a crucial role in speeding and shaping the transformation and eventual elimination of the family. So pervasive was the conviction that parents were ignorant of modern child-rearing methods that even educators sympathetic to family upbringing looked forward to making the kindergarten a center of parent education. Indeed, this was the case in most philanthropic kindergartens in the West as well. However, more than their colleagues in the West, Soviet teachers assumed that kindergartners themselves would prove staunch allies in the effort to remake parents. The preschool aimed to turn children raised even part-time in the kindergarten into the vanguards of cultural transformation in their own homes. By helping to build kindergartens, parents essentially raised their own gravediggers.

Even teachers who expressed reservations about fully socialized child care did not doubt that parents had much to learn from teachers. The Preschool Department's section of experts, which included Sventitskaia, Tikheeva, and Shleger, resolved in 1920 that "public preschool education must be a right and not an obligation for children who can be raised by parents." The old adversaries Sventitskaia and Tikheeva agreed that "the interests of the child demand the participation of the family in the preschool age."[47] However, even as they created the impression that the family's role in child-rearing might be permanent, the experts affirmed that "social upbringing" had to take place "alongside the family—through the family." These experts imagined that the family would welcome the kindergarten teacher's advice. Shleger maintained that, at least for the present, "the kindergarten does not take upon itself the task of replacing or displacing the family. The task of the kindergarten is to supplement the family, i.e., what the child does not receive at home he ought to receive at the kindergarten." She envisioned the teacher as "a member of the family, its desired guest."[48] As an instructor at a teacher-training course, Shleger defined the kindergarten as "the assistant of the family, which is the first social organization."[49] Such formulations suggested that parents would cooperate with the professionals' efforts to rationalize family upbringing.

Elsewhere the kindergarten acted less as the family's "assistant" than as its mentor. Teachers and health workers expected that parents would follow the advice of the professionals, especially in the spheres of health and hygiene. Visiting nurses from the Commissariat of Public Health observed the home lives of preschool children, made suggestions, and followed up to see that they were carried out. Narkomzdrav organized child care exhibitions as a means of persuading parents to adopt more modern techniques of child care.[50] The posters at an exhibition in Saratov in 1927 made clear that parents had much to learn. Drawings showed children telling their mothers "we must take walks every day," "don't wash me in the tub you wash laundry in," and that they ought not eat from the same dish as the family dog. A poster at the entrance that proclaimed "through the kindergarten to a new way of life" suggested that such seemingly small adjustments might add up to a great deal.[51]

Meetings with parents organized by kindergartens also aimed to teach parents "correct" methods of child care. Envisioned primarily as a means of "providing rational advice on education, nutrition, and hygiene," such sessions tended to be rather one-sided.[52] The commissariat's questionnaires asked not about meetings *with* parents but about lectures *to* parents.[53] The parent meeting was primarily a "means of propagandizing the preschool idea among the broad mass of the population."[54]

Although few kindergartens included the minutes of parent meetings in their reports to Narkompros, an account from the Griboedovskii home for the 1920–1921 school year made it clear that teachers set the agenda. The first two meetings focused on purely organizational matters—the selection of a chair and secretary. The rather sketchy report of the third meeting explained that those present "worked out the function and rights of parents." Before the meeting, parents apparently had "entered into pedagogical work with a consultative vote." During the session, parents were notified that their role did not extend beyond "responding to the call of the kindergarten." Here the family was clearly the assistant of the kindergarten. A planned fourth meeting failed to materialize.[55]

Teachers expected that helping to organize kindergartens would transform parents. Lazurkina suggested that the "material and technical" difficulties of opening preschool institutions could be overcome by drawing the parents into preschool work.[56] Expressing the same hope, posters at the Saratov exhibition portrayed a "peasant woman building a playground" and a "working woman opening an evening room." The consequences of this active support were suggested by Kollontai, who argued that involvement in building day cares would speed the transformation of women workers into communists. Even modest neighborhood children's kitchens "can become wonderful nurseries for raising the spirit of collectivism in mothers themselves."[57] The Women's Department (Zhenotdel) was seen as the natural ally of the Preschool Department in the effort to liberate women by drawing them into work outside the home.[58]

Whatever effect they had on parents, kindergarten teachers predicted that they would be able to have an indelible impact on their pupils. In reports of the kindergarten's effects on family life, children themselves emerged as the true agents of change. On the basis of long-term work in four rural preschools, one teacher concluded that the "new life" [*novyi byt*] of the kindergarten did, slowly, penetrate the family. She considered the increasingly frequent arrival of her pupils in clean clothes, with clean hands and noses and carrying clean handkerchiefs a "big achievement." Such work, she advised other teachers, required efforts to befriend peasant families and "get a feel for the questions that interest" them. Even more important was teaching children how to wash themselves because they could be counted on to teach their older siblings as well as their mothers and grandmothers. Experience apparently demonstrated that children not only explained to their parents "why it is necessary that each person eat from a separate bowl" but also "demand[ed] to wash their hands before eating."[59] A little older, the same children would be ready to teach their parents that insecticide—not prayer—could kill cabbage worms.[60]

Teachers hoped to make the few hours per day the child spent in the kindergarten more meaningful and more powerfully formative than all the time passed with parents. Students at a 1919 teacher-training course were instructed "to fight and fight earnestly" the belief that kindergartens were simply feeding points, "so that the life of the child at home will be an extension of his life in the kindergarten."[61] Teachers looked for ways to allow children to take the kindergarten's spirit home. One educator suggested teaching children songs that, when sung at home, would remind children of "their kindergarten and their comrades."[62] Such efforts suggested an abiding faith not only in the power of education to produce cultural transformation but also in the ability of young people to overcome allegedly pernicious lessons learned at home and become "real revolutionaries."

In arguing for or against children's homes, educators entered a larger debate on the meanings and process of revolution. Long before the October Revolution, most preschool educators agreed that the kindergarten could provide the germ of a new way of life. After the Revolution, the visible and often painful dissolution of the old order accentuated the shortcomings of family upbringing and fueled the most extravagant and impractical dreams of cultural transformation. The "practical" opponents of the immediate socialization of child-rearing emphasized the state's lack of resources and maternal rights and feelings, but they proposed their own utopian vision—children raised in revolutionary environments, even for only a portion of the day, would become the vanguard of cultural transformation. For the less "practical," the disappearance of the traditional family marked the end not only of adult authority but of the entire cultural legacy disavowed by the revolutionaries. The children's home became a first crucial step on the road to communism, the "happy family" of the future in miniature. In both cases, educational rhetoric elided the distinction between practical problem solving and revolutionary dreaming.

4

The Nature of Childhood

During the Civil War, the conception of the Revolution as a moment of liberation may have been in the ascendent, but it remained contested. The Bolsheviks' "glorification" of the proletariat's fighting spirit and Promethean possibilities coexisted with an abiding "suspicion" of the working class's ability to make revolution on its own.[1] Temporarily swamped by the first wave of revolutionary euphoria, an emphasis on enlightenment, active leadership, and discipline remained deeply embedded in the Bolshevik ethos. Even at its most libertarian, Bolshevism combined an optimistic faith in the revolutionary power of the oppressed and proletarian contempt for bourgeois niceties with the intelligentsia's desire to "civilize" Russia. The impulses to liberate, enlighten, and discipline structured a grid of revolutionary options, desires, and images that coexisted in all sorts of awkward and improbable combinations.[2]

Lenin gave voice to all of these impulses. On the eve of the October Revolution, his confidence in the proletariat and in the "spontaneous nature" of the revolutionary process found expression in the prediction in *State and Revolution* that the task of running post-Revolutionary society could be entrusted to "any literate person" possessing "knowledge of the four rules of arithmetic" and capable of "issuing appropriate receipts." In the post-Revolutionary world envisioned by Lenin in 1917, the rising generation would acquire the "habits" of communism naturally and inevitably.[3] Three years later, with world revolution an increasingly remote possibility and with the economy in ruins, Lenin pictured revolution as a far less automatic process. Speaking to the third Komsomol congress in October 1920, he enjoined young people to "learn" (*uchit'sia*), to prepare themselves for the difficult task of modernizing the economy, to reign in their disdain for the achievements of pre-Revolutionary culture and science, and to respect their revolutionary elders.[4]

Putting this tension between revolutionary emancipation and revolutionary discipline at the center of an analysis of the debate on the best way to raise the children of October makes it possible to see the "scientific" language of educators as articulating competing approaches to revolutionary transformation under inauspicious circumstances. The linkage between visions of children and revolution is especially clear in discussions of kindergarten curriculum. Kindergarten teachers had long touted their institutions as pedagogically and socially "revolutionary" and had envisioned "revolution" alternately, and sometimes simultaneously, as a process of liberating children from the authority of teachers and parents and of cultivating "modern" values and habits. After the October Revolution, even non-Bolshevik kindergarten teachers found much that was appealing and familiar in the plans promulgated by the Commissariat of Enlightenment. While schoolteachers resisted innovations that constituted an unqualified attack on pre-Revolutionary pedagogy — on teacher-directed methods, rigid distinctions between disciplines, memorization, and formal grading — preschool teachers understood the emphasis on making school fun, active, and relevant to the life of the child as a vindication of the kindergarten and its revolutionary mission.[5] The meaning of that revolutionary mission and the best way of realizing it, rather than a defense of traditional practices, shaped discussion within the Preschool Department and among teachers gathered at conferences or training classes. The contest over the nature of childhood was in significant and telling ways a battle over the nature of revolution.

The Life of the Kindergarten

The heated curricular debates of the Civil War period offer oblique glimpses of the experiences of both teachers and children. At the same time, the sometimes sharp pedagogical disagreements suggest not only that kindergartens could vary a great deal but also that accounts of classroom practice often carried polemical and political intent. Teachers' descriptions of their classrooms never function as snapshots of the life of the kindergarten. Nonetheless, it seems both possible and useful to suggest the contours of a day at the kindergarten and to draw some conclusions about the experiences of both teachers and children. What emerges from teachers' accounts is a striking consensus regarding the tensions and compromises that characterized and shaped the Civil War preschool classroom. How these tensions got resolved varied tremendously, but we can suggest a range of conceivable alternatives — if not a single somehow "typical" day, then a matrix of possibilities from which a series of "average" days might be imagined.[6] However incomplete or tentative, a narrative account of a day in the life of the kindergarten may be the best means of visualizing the lives of children and of contextualizing the contest over the meaning of childhood for the Revolution.

For most kindergartners, whether they live with their parents or at the children's home to which the kindergarten is attached, the day begins in much the same way—with the obligatory hand-washing followed by breakfast. At the children's homes, children rise at eight or eight thirty, and by nine or nine thirty are washed and ready to make their way to the dining room. There they might meet the nonresident pupils, who have already donned their smocks and washed their hands. Breakfast consists of tea with sugar or milk or maybe both along with bread, perhaps with a slice of cheese. Under the supervision of the "nurse" (*niania*), the children "on duty" for the day (*dezhurnye*) distribute the sugar and bread, and the older ones might also help to clear the table and wash dishes after the meal. The teachers' day also begins with tea, possibly in a separate dining room.

The serious tasks of washing and eating having been taken care of, the remainder of the morning is devoted to all sorts of activities, usually chosen by the children themselves. The hour or so after breakfast is usually the least structured part of the day. In some kindergartens, especially those in which the seven-year-olds learn to read during this time, teachers divide the children into three groups according to age. In others, the children separate themselves into groups according to their interests. In one corner of the kindergarten's large activity room, a number of children are drawing; others busy themselves cutting and pasting, while others—assuming materials are available—work with clay or building blocks. A few of the older children organize some kind of game that involves a great deal of commotion. One little girl, oblivious to the activity around her, focuses on constructing a doll bed. At the same time, a few children have gone out into the corridor and are arguing about something or simply whispering together rather than taking up any sort of work.

For teachers, the chief practical problem becomes how to encourage creative and exuberant tumult, while reigning in unproductive or "antisocial" activity. Some teachers interrupt the morning's free activity with a half hour of storytelling. Where only two teachers look after fifty pupils, adequate supervision is most difficult. In other kindergartens, four teachers care for only forty children, since as many as fifteen or twenty children are absent on any given day—sick or simply lacking shoes to make the trip to school.

The afternoon is generally more structured than the morning. Children store their work in their individual boxes in the activity room, and preparations for lunch begin between eleven and noon. The *dezhurnye* distribute cups, and another round of hand-washing ensues before the children sit down at the table. After lunch, all the children, or perhaps just the four- and five-year-olds, nap or observe a "quiet hour" during which there is no talking or reading. If they did not take an hour stroll before lunch, the children probably take one after napping. After the walk, it is time for a mid-afternoon snack, during which the children on duty once again pass out cups for tea. An hour of organized games and perhaps another hour walk occupies the time until dinner. In some kindergartens, non-resident pupils leave by four in the afternoon; in others they leave after dinner, at about eight in the evening. For the children who live at the home, the day ends as it began—washing up at the bathroom sink.

From morning tea until lights out, the kindergarten's staff put in a ten or eleven hour day, trying to keep forty or fifty preschoolers busy, fed, and clean. Even without factoring in the lack of adequate educational supplies—not to mention food, linens, or running water—the schedule asked a great deal of even the most dedicated teacher. But while the conditions may have been more demanding than before the Revolution, the curriculum was not significantly different. The daily routine required innovation, patience, and a sense of humor, but little or nothing explicitly socialist.

What children made of the experience is difficult to gauge. In their teachers' accounts they are alternately diligent, excited, inventive, and occasionally mischievous and disruptive. In the kindergarten, one report concluded, "the children feel very free."[7] Free activities and socialization with peers may have been the most appealing part of the program for children. On the other hand, banishing of books in the name of respecting the immediate interests of children frustrated the (probably few) pupils who arrived knowing how to read.[8] Kindergartners may have felt constrained by the new insistence on unfamiliar norms of hygiene, but as inspections made clear, it is also quite possible that the kindergartens failed to meet basic sanitary standards. Finally, it seems unlikely that preschoolers regularly associated what went on at the kindergarten with their hazy understanding of something called "revolution."

"Scientific" Pedagogy

Preschool teachers emphasized that, unlike the schools, the kindergartens inherited by the Soviet state were free from any taint of authoritarianism. A delegate at the First All-Russian Congress of Preschool Education in 1919 noted that since under the old regime only a small circle of people involved themselves in preschool work, the kindergarten was not "penetrated with the old State spirit that completely seized the school."[9] Kindergartens in general were characterized as inherently radical. A 1920 declaration on preschool education admitted that kindergartens had been designed originally for the children of the rich, but excused positive references to Froebel by noting that the Prussian state had cracked down on his kindergartens because of their socialist "tendencies."[10]

Along with the kindergarten's allegedly rebellious roots, the conception of child development as a biological given transcending class and culture provided teachers with a powerful argument for the co-optation of both foreign and pre-Revolutionary kindergarten practices. Teachers portrayed early childhood as a discrete period with "its own laws of development and an individual place in the child's life."[11] The bourgeois origins of "old pedagogues" like Froebel and Maria Montessori did not necessarily discredit their "scientific" insights.[12] In the best examples of Western preschool pedagogy, often located in the United States, Soviet teachers found "that normal regime, that normal method of development and education that ought to hold sway in the kindergarten." Only above the kindergarten level did the class basis of Western programs overshadow the universal scientific principles at the heart of preschool pedagogy. Joining the attack on traditional schools, the Preschool Department declared that "the correct sowing of the kindergarten quickly gets distorted by the repulsive path of the bourgeois school."[13] Teachers represented science, rather than class, as shaping kindergarten programs everywhere.

Russian experts, like their colleagues in the West, viewed the establishment of clean and safe environments for children as both a critical priority and a transparently scientific task. The same eagerness to overcome backwardness that made the notion of scientific upbringing so appealing produced a near mania for fixing norms of health and hygiene. At teacher-training courses, instructors emphasized that "maintenance of cleanliness" constituted one of the primary missions of the kindergarten teacher.[14] The handbook of preschool education set the precise number of wash basins and towel pegs that institutions ought to provide.[15] In descriptions of the sorts of buildings, furniture, dishes, and toys appropriate to the kindergarten, the necessity that they be "hygienic" always came first. Doctors were to be included on committees researching toys and furniture to ensure that all decisions met health standards. The Preschool Department proposed regular visits by health care personnel as a means of certifying that kindergarten teachers carried out doctors' orders.[16] Teachers apparently needed constant reminders of the scientific importance of an immaculate environment.

Among the "useful habits" acquired by children in the kindergarten, bathing emerged as among the most essential. If cleanliness was not next to communism, it was clearly next to modernity. Descriptions of kindergartens usually mentioned how often children washed. One report began with the observation that upon arriving children donned smocks and washed their hands before taking up their activities. That children washed their hands again before lunch was also deemed worthy of notice.[17] At the Narkompros "collector," a way station for *besprizorniki* awaiting permanent placement, inspectors noted the seemingly mundane fact that children washed "above the waist" and brushed their teeth before bed.[18] Schedules often included the times at which hand-washing occurred. At a teacher-training course, a discussion of a poorly run kindergarten ended with the damning observation that "the children did not wash their

Figure 1   "Cleanliness, sunlight, and fresh air guarantee the child's health" c. 1925

hands before tea."[19] Clean bodies, hands, faces, teeth, and clothes emerged as the sure signs of modern, effective child-rearing.

In a larger sense, "scientific" pedagogy referred to the process of designing educational programs on the basis of careful observation of children, especially children at play, who, acting on their own initiative, supposedly revealed their true natures.[20] The process took as a given that the school's central function was to provide an environment in which children could explore and develop their individual interests. Teachers claimed that studying children allowed them to set rational, as opposed to arbitrary and repressive, limits on the free activity of the child. Most straightforwardly, teachers had to protect children from physical dangers. Shleger considered swings hazardous to the nervous systems of small children and potentially damaging to girls' sex organs. She concluded that "we do not always have to consider the children's desires, because children often want what they do not need."[21]

Teachers also had to guard against psychic threats to the child's development. Asserting the scientific necessity of activating children's creativity, teachers rejected or modified some well-loved activities. Shleger warned future teachers that while children enjoyed singing rounds, such activity tended to foster excessive passivity.[22] Similar concerns shaped the debate on the role of fairy tales (*skazki*) in the kindergarten. Recognizing that children delighted in *skazki*, the Preschool Department published catalogs of recommended stories. One list included tales of magic, bewitched princesses, and mythical creatures ("Po shchuch'emu velen'iu," "Zakoldovannaia korolevna," "Volshebnyi kon'," "Zhar-ptitsa") and overlooked more down-to-earth stories like "Repka," about a collective effort to pull an enormous turnip out of the ground.[23] Although unreflective of the "real" world, such stories might be tolerated on the grounds that children always ended up sympathizing with the forces of good.[24] Other educators saw *skazki* as an effective means of developing "aesthetic sensibilities and fantasy."[25] Still others argued that a quiet hour of story-telling worked to deepen the bond between pupil and teacher.[26]

What worried teachers was not the magical content of the stories, but the passivity of children sitting and listening to them. While *telling* stories might be scientifically sound pedagogy, reading them to children was not. Russian educators echoed the hostility to early literacy that had also been a feature of Rousseau's educational prescriptions. On the basis of classroom observation, teachers concluded that books severed the direct tie between students and their surroundings; however, stories told in "living" language allegedly strengthened that essential relationship.[27] Such findings shaped teacher-training courses, where students learned that the child's apparent passivity belied an active interest in story-telling.[28] The same distinction between reading and telling appeared in reports from kindergartens.[29] The conclusions of "objective," scientific observation reflected progressive pedagogy's aversion to stiff, teacher-directed activities.

Preoccupied throughout the Civil War with the task of caring for *besprizorniki* and with the dream of socialized child care, Narkompros proved willing to defer to the technical experts in matters of classroom practice. The conception of pedagogy as a universal science allowed purportedly "socialist" kindergarten curricula and teacher-training courses to borrow freely from foreign and pre-Revolutionary sources. Questionnaires for preschool institutions assumed the predominance of "bourgeois" models, asking teachers to characterize their methods as grounded in Froebel, Montessori, or free upbringing. The publishing subdepartment resolved to reprint the best pre-Revolutionary children's literature for use in Soviet kindergartens that apparently did not require specifically "proletarian" stories.[30] Bibliographies of suggested readings for new teachers in the provinces included many standards such as Montessori's *House of the Child* and John Dewey's *School and Society*. Also suggested were progressive, if not especially Marxist, works such as Leshaft's *Semeinoe vospitanie*, Venttsel's *Novye puti vospitaniia i obrazovaniia detei*, and the journal *Svobodnoe vospitanie*.

Readings at a three-week teacher-training course included Rousseau's *Emile* along with works by Montessori, Dewey, and Froebel.[31] The clear assumption was that, at least in the kindergarten, "bourgeois" methods were grounded in science and thus applicable to Soviet experiments.

American examples proved alluring models of modern, scientific, child-centered pedagogy. Russian educators found particularly attractive the degree to which American kindergartens took as their point of departure not "the interests and needs of the future," but instead observations, always understood as "scientific," of the child's inclinations and capacities.[32] A laudatory review of the American system in *Narodnoe prosveshchenie* in 1919 asserted that "nowhere, finally, is the question of familiarity with the real world, with nature as the source of the child's development presented so profoundly as in this nation of wonderful and rapid transformations, experiments, and achievements." The fact that "Yankee" kindergartens emphasized the same sorts of hands-on activities favored in pre-Revolutionary Russian kindergartens became evidence of the "scientific" validity of both programs.[33]

Rather than rejecting bourgeois technical advances, socialists aspired to apply them more justly and completely than in the capitalist West. Whatever their origins, child-centered programs would find their fullest expression in the socialist state. Only socialist schools, Lazurkina and Venttsel' contended, were capable of raising truly "harmonious" and "creative personalities."[34] Pavel Blonskii, a psychologist and educator who shared few of Venttsel's assumptions, agreed that while all education had to take the "child's natural development" as "not the goal but the criteria . . . only socialism created the natural, normal conditions for the development of humanity." Blonskii made socialist and natural (*estestvennoe*) upbringing synonymous.[35] Until the mid-1920s, when Narkompros repudiated radically child-centered education and constructed a self-consciously proletarian "science" of education, the "natural laws" of child development seemed to cross class lines.

Education—like everything in the modern, enlightened, efficient socialist future—was to be above all scientific. That even Taylorist time-motion studies could be represented as liberating and revolutionary in the Soviet context gives some idea of the potent appeal of rationalizing all aspects of life.[36] On the terrain of science, it was possible to ignore, elide, or harmonize any opposition between liberation and the enforcement of often rigid norms of modern life. When Shleger argued that teachers did "not always have to consider the children's desires, because children often want what they do not need," she suggested the essential compatibility of emancipation and "scientific," albeit externally imposed, discipline. Not exactly proposing that children be forced to be free, educators implied that only when children internalized habits of cleanliness and rationality would they be truly liberated.

Freedom and the "Construction of the New Life"

Throughout the Civil War, free upbringing influenced the programs of many Soviet kindergartens. The method's pervasiveness can be attributed in part to the Bolsheviks' willingness to trust the "experts." With few viable alternatives in any case, Narkompros employed prominent pre-Revolutionary educators, most of whom were devoted to *svobodnoe vospitanie*, to train new teachers. The result was a situation in which, as one Montessori teacher complained, kindergartens based on free upbringing were virtually immune to criticism.[37]

Whatever the necessity of enlisting preschool teachers regardless of their politics, the dominance of free upbringing cannot be understood as a purely practical matter. Teachers characterized *svobodnoe vospitanie* not only as scientific but also, despite its rather un-Marxist insistence on innate capacities and individual rights, as revolutionary. The free kindergarten's emphasis on providing an environment in which children could build a creative, self-regulating community of equals was represented as a vital component of the Bolshevik effort to "liberate" children from their parents and to facilitate the spontaneous restructuring of social life. Advocates of free upbringing insisted that the shared concern for liberation, labor, and community was, if not fully homologous, then certainly more than skin deep. For those who conceived of the Revolution as a release from unnatural and dehumanizing authority, free upbringing held deep emotional appeal.

Collapsing the distinction between respecting the child's individuality and "liberating" it from what Marxists characterized as the oppressive patriarchal family, teachers suggested that free upbringing constituted the necessary pedagogical accompaniment of the withering away of the family. As an instructor at a teacher-training course, Shleger made the progressive educator's standard complaint that children in the family lacked the opportunity to engage in independent work an argument "for the emancipation of the child."[38] In its report to the center, one kindergarten explicitly linked the decision to raise "the banner of *svobodnoe vospitanie*" with the effort to free children from the fetters of the family. Liberated children, the report continued, would be capable of "destroying even the political chains that constrain us."[39] In a move designed to highlight its revolutionary pedigree, *svobodnoe vospitanie*'s long-standing hostility to parents, imagined as "slave masters," was transformed into a condemnation of the family per se.

Proponents of *svobodnoe vospitanie* insisted that it constituted the surest method of fulfilling the socialist promise, as expressed by Lenin's sister Anna Elizarova, that "our children, raised in new circumstances, can and must be happier than us."[40] Free upbringing's insistence on the powerful influence of physical surroundings on the child's future development can be read as a literal translation of Elizarova's statement into the language of pedagogy. The 1919 handbook of preschool education provided meticulously detailed lists of "supplies and materials for games and activities." The checklists probably had relatively little practical value for teachers. Only the catalog of natural and discarded objects—pine cones, acorns, chestnuts, shells, twigs, leaves, sand, snow, bobbins, ribbons, boxes—described articles that most kindergartens could realistically hope to supply. Likewise, most kindergartens did not have the resources to apply the advice that furnishings be "beautiful and simple," and never "routine."[41] Such seemingly unattainable directives underlined free upbringing's materialist outlook; the kindergarten shared the socialists' faith that new conditions would necessarily produce a happy future.

That the kindergarten offered a space where the child could assert his or her independence was taken as a further sign of its revolutionary appropriateness. Like their colleagues in Germany and the United States, Russian kindergarten teachers had long emphasized the kindergarten's potential as a place to raise new sorts of citizens. In Soviet Russia, the potent, if not necessarily Marxist, conception of children as the embodiment of the Revolution's future reinforced the significance of free upbringing's commitment to raising self-directed children. Lazurkina exhorted teachers to avoid offering excessive advice to preschoolers. Since the child, as "the future builder of life after us," would have to do "without our instructions and help . . . he must above all become accustomed to independent activity."[42] The free kindergarten was designed to do precisely that. Low storage shelves allowed pupils to gather desired materials without the teacher's assistance. In the same vein, the handbook provided precise specifications for child-sized tables and chairs that children could move around as their games and fancies dictated. "No less necessary," according to the handbook, "are low pegs and low attached taps for wash basins." Simply making available the "opportunity" for children to hang up their coats and wash themselves "without adult help" somehow made such events likely, if not inevitable.[43] By allowing, as one teacher expressed it, the "free development of [children's] inherent capabilities and developing independence, creative initiative, and social feeling," *svobodnoe vospitanie* played a "very important role in the construction of a new life."[44]

Svobodnoe vospitanie left it to children to create their own world. The task, teachers maintained, necessarily led children spontaneously to organize self-directed collectives. Teachers emphasized the popularity with the children of construction materials—especially natural materials like sand, wood, clay, and stone. The child in the kindergarten became a builder, taught by experience the value of collective work. Games provided further occasions for children to cooperate with one another. The handbook advised teachers to allow students to run games themselves so that they would "become accustomed to equal relations with their comrades. In this way, general games lay the foundation for social [*sotsial'noe*] feeling."[45] Teachers insisted that freedom in the classroom was part and parcel of the Revolution's transformation of social life.

Labor Instincts

If any component of progressive education was ripe for wholesale adoption by socialists, it was the kindergarten's array of innovative, sometimes messy, hands-on projects. Kindergarten teachers everywhere saw in such activities the most effective method of engaging children's imaginations. In Soviet Russia, teachers also understood that casting kindergarten activities as "labor" enhanced the resonance of their program for socialists.

Svobodnoe vospitanie claimed to raise precisely the "multifaceted people with conscious and organized social instincts . . . people prepared in theory and practice for any type of labor, physical or intellectual,"[46] that, according to Krupskaia, socialism both made possible and required. Even the smallest comrades in the kindergarten worked. Most kindergartens incorporated "self-service"—for example, washing and dressing oneself—as a means of fostering independence and good work habits. Many also required that the children take turns "on duty" (*dezhurstvo*) setting tables and distributing bread. For reasons both pedagogical and political, teachers went to great lengths to deny that such work ever became a burden. Children were supposed to experience collective labor as natural and joyous.

Echoing socialist formulations, preschool teachers made no distinction between creative and physical work in the kindergarten. Any activity that entailed a measure of physical exertion—play with blocks or games that involved moving furniture—qualified as work.[47] At a teacher-training course, Shleger characterized handicrafts along with more mundane and practical tasks as "labor."[48] The department's official publications envisioned children helping the cooks in the kitchen, working in the vegetable garden, washing dishes, straightening shelves, and helping younger pupils.[49] Including modeling with clay in the same category as self-service (*samoobsluzhivania*) at meals suggested that nearly everything that went on in the kindergarten fostered the child's love of labor. Conflating work and play reinforced the proposition—as essential to socialists as to progressive educators—that the impulse to create and to cooperate constituted a fundamental component of human nature.

The vision of the child as naturally interested in labor distinguished Soviet programs from the similar, but less "revolutionary," curricula of Western kindergartens. Soviet educators rejected the assumption, so prevalent in Western societies, that "children play while adults work."[50] Since free upbringing demanded that the "initiative for activities comes not from teachers but from the children themselves, the participation in general activities" had to be "voluntary." How then could children be required to clean up after themselves or to set the table? The instructions for the establishment of kindergartens and day cares that made this assertion simply added that all work "must correspond to the children's capacities and be carried out willingly and gladly."[51] That children were naturally interested in activities suited to their stage of development was taken as axiomatic. Laziness was deemed abnormal.[52]

Teachers counted on "scientific" observation to suggest precisely the sorts of labor in which children were ready and eager to participate. The science involved in such cases was not necessarily sophisticated. At a summer colony, pupils responsible for washing their own dirty linen cried frequently and proved unable to finish their assigned tasks. A visiting group of student teachers and their instructor concluded that doing laundry could be condemned on the grounds that it was beyond the children's capabilities and therefore "dangerous from both the hygienic and pedagogical point of view." They found work in the vegetable garden more acceptable, although still challenging in sandy soil without fertilizer.[53] A delegate to a 1919 conference similarly noted that she had no objection to "older children cleaning ten carrots, but fifty is already beyond their strength."[54] Lilina suggested simply presenting less appealing tasks as play. She recommended that all labor in the kindergarten—drawing, caring for plants, cleaning up—be accompanied by singing and music.[55]

What teachers and policymakers adamantly rejected was any imposition of adult authority. For progressive educators attuned to the needs of children as much as for socialists looking forward to the emergence of new types of social relations, the child's ability to discipline himself was crucial. Ideally, the *dezhurnye* would distribute cups "willingly and thoroughly" as they did at a kindergarten visited by student teachers.[56] Shleger ruled out threats or punishment as a means of maintaining order, relying instead on children to control themselves. Lilina shared the progressive educators' abhorrence of the rod; "the pedagogue knows that besides harming the child, punishment accomplishes nothing."[57] Only when adults renounced their power would children be free to work, play, and create according to their instincts.

Teachers recognized an element of the utopian in the vision of thirty or more preschoolers spontaneously working together to clean the room or tend the garden. Lazurkina cautioned student teachers that they should not expect life in the kindergarten always to go smoothly. Perfect self-discipline was possible only in "some sort of ideal colony that does not exist in life." Another instructor suggested that in practice new teachers might indeed resort to guiding, if not coercing, their charges, explaining that "by granting complete freedom, we will raise lazy people who quickly become unfree." Shleger emphasized that freedom had to be based on certain rules "because absolute freedom does not exist in the lives of children or adults." Where children had total freedom to choose their activities, she told student teachers, they could be found wandering aimlessly from room to room, fighting, and gossiping.[58] Here, perhaps, is an indirect flash of the frustrations of relying on the social instincts of children.

If not always possible in practice, self-disciplined labor remained necessary in theory as the key to the revolutionary transformation of both school and society. Shleger argued that "work brings children together . . . [T]he strong help the weak." The opportunity for six- and seven-year-olds to help the three- and four-year-olds she deemed especially valuable, as it would develop "altruistic feelings" in the older children while lending a "family character to the small commune." The image of the kindergarten as a new but natural family recurred in a department publication that took children's chores at home as a model for labor in preschool institutions. Just as children living at home were expected to look after younger siblings, stand in lines, or tidy up the house, "in the *ochag* children take part in all the housekeeping. . . . [T]hey know that if no one worked, there would be no lunch, no breakfast, no firewood."[59] Avoiding the family metaphor, Elizarova likewise emphasized the ability of labor to impress upon children of the tenderest age that "the commune cannot tolerate parasites."[60] Lazurkina concluded, "[I]n these small children's communes there is created, thanks to labor principles, the feeling of comradely solidarity and the habit of seeing in labor the general good."[61] By nurturing the impulse to work collectively, the kindergarten raised children who, never having felt the sting of arbitrary authority, experienced disciplined, collective labor as creative and natural.

The autumn ritual of accustoming wide-eyed three-year-olds to the rhythms and routines of the kindergarten evoked the most liberationist images of the Revolution. The preschool handbook, which presented free upbringing as the model program, cautioned that children probably would not be able to handle the responsibility of designing and regulating their own activities immediately. On their first day, children were likely to be overwhelmed, acting rather like "cowed beasts." But the teacher had to resist the temptation to take control of the situation, and instead had to calm the children and create an "atmosphere of mutual cooperation." Beyond the initial moment of chaos, the children would see a new world open before them. Soon, according to the handbook, "children begin to feel that they are members of this loving society and discipline themselves in the interest of general work."[62] "Free labor" accustomed children to living and working in a "commune."[63] In the kindergarten, the revolutionary liberation and transformation of society was played out in miniature. Free upbringing affirmed the inevitability of the spontaneous emergence of a "natural" community, in the kindergarten and perhaps beyond.

Setting the Limits of Freedom

While the language of liberation set the terms of debate, the impulse to enlighten was clearly visible in the constant reminders to impress upon preschoolers, even in the freest kindergarten, the importance of clean clothes and hands. It also showed up in the attempts of a group of teachers centered around Tikheeva in Petrograd to persuade their colleagues in Moscow that it was possible, and necessary, to teach kindergartners to read and count. Most fundamentally, any school project that took account not only of the child's present interests but also of the future needs of the Soviet state entailed some measure of enlightenment, control, or indoctrination.

The proponents of free upbringing who dominated discussions of pedagogy throughout the Civil War period dismissed all attempts to teach kindergartners to read or count as painful and potentially harmful infringements on the free life of the child. Viewed as dulling creativity, the introduction of literacy was conspicuously absent from the program outlined in the department's handbook. Doctors warned against burdening young children with abstract knowledge inappropriate to their level of physical and intellectual development.[64] If the emergence of natural collectives required releasing children from adult authority, then didacticism seemed to have no place in the kindergarten.

So pervasive was the commitment to resolutely child-centered pedagogy that even advocates of teaching reading and basic arithmetic in the preschool made their case in the language of *svobodnoe vospitanie*. The introduction to a 1919 article on preschool literacy suggested that the author opposed it. She argued that "the book at such an early age [before twelve] only paralyzes any independence, accustoms [children] to a superficial relationship with their surroundings and to an easy acquisition of sham knowledge." What she advocated was "living literacy" that allowed children to "set forth their thoughts . . . to count and note everything that is necessary in the practical course of work." She recommended that children remain in the kindergarten, where they could be introduced to literacy through the Montessori method and "of course, hand work and everything else" until age nine.[65] From this perspective, literacy became a vital tool facilitating the child's free activity.

Tikheeva, whose method resembled that of Montessori, likewise stressed that the acquisition of literacy was compatible with a child-centered curriculum. She eschewed books on the grounds that "the book reflects a kind of concrete world in its motionlessness and determinateness and excludes the possibility, motion, and activity of the preliterate child," a rather cumbersome formulation that suggests the pedagogical value of spontaneity in the classroom. Instead, Tikheeva employed a system of cards with printed words that corresponded to some object, toy, or picture that along with the cards figured in a variety of games. With the aid of beans, matches, buttons, chestnuts, sticks, or—best of all—small toys, numbers were similarly introduced through a series of specialized games. Advocating a fairly structured, teacher-directed program, Tikheeva insisted on its resemblance to "free" curricula.

Taking a somewhat different tack, an advocate of the Montessori method assured the largely unsympathetic delegates at a 1919 conference that students spent only a short time per day on didactic material. However, "these thirty to forty minutes have colossal significance for the development of character, will, persistence in achieving goals, self-fulfillment, and self-improvement." The emphasis on how reading and counting enhanced the process of self-formation co-opted the rhetoric of free upbringing. The delegate further noted that the Montessori kindergarten still allowed students time to build with blocks and draw freely, but simply did not give play and fantasy first priority, as "children have, if anything, too much fantasy already." Here a certain level of impatience with what free upbringing could mean in practice rises to the surface. The gathered teachers remained unconvinced, and the conference rejected the Montessori system as stifling creativity and suspiciously orderly. One delegate warned, "[B]eware of quiet."[66]

Such paeans to youthful exuberance notwithstanding, advocates of free upbringing sometimes gave in to the urge to teach, rather than observe, their charges. At the most fundamental level, the child's choice of activities and objects could never be entirely free, as teachers structured a carefully selected, possibly ideologically significant, range of options. The desire to foster, if not teach, a scientific outlook led teachers to supply kindergartens with aquariums and terrariums. That direct observations of plants and animals replaced dry textbooks did not eliminate the didactic component of the project. Similarly, teachers favored excursions to a park, forest, field, meadow, or pond over a formal course of nature study, but the goal of teaching children something about the world around them remained. While students were supposed to take an active part in planning the outings, it seems unlikely that the impetus came from the kindergartners themselves.[67]

Other choices made by teachers could also inculcate, however surreptitiously, specifically "socialist" values. The preschool handbook defined the selection of toys for the kindergarten as a scientific undertaking. Commissions of experts made up of teachers, doctors, and artists developed appropriate toys and sketches of model furniture. Yet the handbook did not detail the scientific rationale for deeming "ideal" large wooden building blocks in bright primary colors. Small blocks no doubt frustrate still clumsy hands, but the main appeal of the larger toys may have been the prospect of children discovering the need to work together in order to build with them. The department also suggested colorful, "primitively decorated" wood figures—a "crowd" of people and a "forest" of trees.[68] Children very likely found such toys both attractive and conducive to a wide variety of games. However, the department's description suggests additional concerns. The toys' "primitive" appearance, like the wooden village doll recalled by Vodovozova, may have been conceived as means of connecting children to the life of the *narod*. Calls for a "crowd" and a "forest" were perhaps grounded in the vision of a large group of children playing together, their attention focused not on individual people or trees, but on collectives. Teachers' "scientific" control of the environment could make the child's free choice a tool of enlightenment.

Science, Gender, and the Revolution

Teachers deflected political attacks on free upbringing with claims of the programs' scientific validity. Classroom practices that did more to perpetuate old values than to raise children in new ways could nonetheless be represented as "progressive" if they were grounded in universal laws of child development. By the same token, didacticism could be smuggled into the free kindergarten if it could be portrayed as responding to the true nature of the child. Nowhere was the tendency to submerge politics in scientific debate clearer than in the kindergarten's handling of gender and the Revolution.

Given the key role kindergartens played in Bolshevik efforts to emancipate women and Krupskaia's pre-Revolutionary criticism of the family's role in restricting girls' horizons, it would not have been surprising if the Soviet kindergarten challenged traditional gender roles. Its failure to do so was rooted in "scientific" evidence. Progressive educators had never seriously challenged the conventional notion that gender differences are inborn. American psychologist Stanley Hall maintained that a woman could realize her full potential only in marriage and motherhood. For Hall, the distinction between female and male development was so great that he advised against entrusting boys to women teachers. William James agreed that the limited and intuitive female mind could not reach the same level of "intelligent capacity" as the male mind. Even where progressive psychologists granted that individual variation (perhaps grounded in environment) played a role in development, they concluded that the male group was more "variable" and therefore contained "many more brilliant minds than are found among women." Dewey could manage only the negative conclusion that the data did not bear out the belief that higher education injures women.[69]

Russian psychologists, both before and after the Revolution, likewise concluded that women were biologically and psychologically made for motherhood. Updating his pre-Revolutionary study of play with dolls in the mid-1920s, psychologist Konstantin Nikolaevich Kornilov reiterated his earlier conclusion that "there is no doubt that girls' play with dolls is closely tied to their natural maternal instinct." He found it as impossible to imagine a girl without a doll as a boy without a rifle, pistol, or whip. "Scientific" observation led him to the highly ideological conclusion that a girl who never played with dolls was an "abnormality, like a married woman who never has children."[70]

Kornilov no doubt stated the case in the most extreme terms, but most researchers seemed to assume that observed gender differences were grounded in biology. In his study of early childhood sexuality, Efim Aronovich Arkin granted that some differences could be ascribed to "different methods of upbringing" that encouraged girls to help with the housework or play with dolls while giving boys toy soldiers. But, he argued, most such "peculiarities . . . carry the stamp of natural sex differences" that could be observed in the young of other species as well.[71]

Reports from schools suggest an unreflective acceptance of such results. In general, teachers noted differences in the play of boys and girls very matter-of-factly as a natural and predictable divergence scarcely worthy of mention. At one kindergarten, observers reported without comment that girls cleaned up after tea while the boys played.[72] At another, teachers described girls as busying themselves with singing while the boys organized war games.[73] One teacher observed that girls were more adept at housework than the boys, and therefore were given complete responsibility for it.[74] Such comments seemed to reflect an effort to be thorough rather than any abiding interest in studying the different upbringing of boys and girls. The very obvious gender distinctions did not generate debate. Krupskaia's pre-Revolutionary call to draw boys into work in the kitchen went unheeded. Since teachers made no effort to interfere with what they perceived as "natural" differences, kindergartens ended up perpetuating traditional roles in the name of progressive science.

"Science" produced very different results when applied to the task of teaching children about the Revolution. Here careful observations of children purportedly demonstrated that they preferred revolutionary to religious holidays and that political education could be made accessible to preschoolers. Teachers at a summer training course in 1920 reported that attempts to celebrate Christmas in the kindergarten failed miserably. An elaborate holiday show to which parents and siblings were invited suffered from an insufficient number of costumes and the inability of the distraught children to remember their lines. The teachers at a kindergarten in the country accompanied children to the forest to choose a Christmas tree to decorate, but the children reportedly lacked any understanding of the tree's significance and did not take to the project. In both cases, it was the children's lack of interest and investment in Christmas, rather than the specific activities, that teachers blamed for the failure of the projects.

By contrast, May Day celebrations reportedly succeeded in engaging children's interest. At the kindergarten where the holiday pageant proved such a disaster, an allegedly more spontaneous May Day celebration went extremely well. The children decorated the terraces with flags, then sang children's songs, had breakfast in the garden—the children themselves carrying the chairs outside—after which the students sat in a circle to listen to fairy tales and to share impressions of May Day processions they had seen. The report omits any mention of the teachers' role in organizing the celebration, creating the impression that the celebrations had been the result of the children's own revolutionary proclivities.[75]

Science further sanctioned efforts to introduce kindergartners to the significance of the May Day festivities, as long as such explanations respected the interests and imaginations of children. In an effort to keep May Day fun while bringing in its political dimension, Lilina prepared a small twenty-one page volume that turned the rise of the revolutionary proletariat into a fairy tale. "Once upon a time," the story began, "there were no rich people, no poor people, no masters, and no slaves in the world. Then all people were equal." It went on to describe how all people—even children—became divided into masters and slaves and how they might be equal again.[76] Children's "natural" love of fairy tales legitimized Lilina's clearly didactic story.

Of course it is difficult to determine how often teachers read (or told) this story. A 1920 survey of Moscow's children's homes indicated that in only five of the eighteen preschool homes did teachers engage pupils in conversations on the "unity of workers of all nations." However, fourteen responded that they had explained the "basic principles of Soviet power, in a form accessible to children." Six reported leading discussions on religious and antireligious topics, with two of these noting that such discussions took place "rarely" or only "when children ask." One home responded that such discussions did not occur because they were not "age-appropriate." The questionnaire itself did not necessarily assume that any of these conversations were appropriate for preschool children; preschool homes simply received the same form as homes serving school-age children.[77]

As long as children could be portrayed as evincing an interest in current affairs, lack of understanding might not constitute a reason for denying kindergartners the beginnings of a political education. Without any irony, one teacher noted that during the revolutionary year of 1917 her kindergartners' urge to participate in the dramatic events around them led them to the task of plastering the *raion* with posters they did not understand.[78] In this way political education became "hands-on," and therefore compatible with a program grounded in the immediate interests of the child, but also empty of any identifiable political content.

New Teachers

As the representatives of adult authority in institutions designed, at least in theory, to undermine the presumptively oppressive power of the old over the young, teachers in free kindergartens played a crucial and problematic role in cultural transformation. They performed as observers, facilitators, instructors, and role models. The kindergarten required new, ideally young, teachers capable of guiding the child while allowing full freedom for the development of the child's uncorrupted social instincts.

The central irony of a program of freedom for children was that it required more of instructors than traditional teacher-directed methods. The awareness of this fact may have done more than anything else to turn primary and secondary teachers against the new dispensation. First and foremost, teachers had to be scientists. They selected appropriate materials for children, quietly took notes on every detail of life in the kindergarten, and refined their initial choices on the basis of the observed preferences and capabilities of each specific group of kindergartners.[79] With its requirement that teachers respond to their pupils' shifting moods and interests, *svobodnoe vospitanie* ruled out the possibility of a universal or fixed kindergarten curriculum.[80]

Reports from teachers in the field attested to the difficulty of the constant improvisation demanded by free upbringing. Many kindergartens committed in theory to following the children's lead allocated only a few hours per day to "free activities and games," the rest of the time following a set schedule of organized games and activities, walks, story-telling, and nap time.[81] Even the Preschool Department's methods section, which "highly valued" free upbringing, granted that it could "take on different forms."[82] A delegate to a 1920 conference reported that two-thirds of the kindergartens in Vitebskaia province followed a "mixed method," tempering *svobodnoe vospitanie* with elements of Montessori and Froebelist programs. Such mixing and matching was perhaps not surprising where half of the preschool workers lacked formal training. Creating a kindergarten that appeared to run itself required a great deal of skill on the part of the teacher.[83]

Even in its purest form, free upbringing expected teachers to use the knowledge gained through unobtrusive observation to facilitate the children's self-directed activities. Rather than asserting themselves as authority figures, teachers were instructed to suppress every impulse suggested to them by experience rooted in the rotten past and simply to hold a mirror to the child's true nature. Shleger explained that "the teacher must go to the aid of students, of course painstakingly and carefully thinking about every step, ceaselessly observing children's lives to keep a close eye on the life of each individually and all together."[84] Lilina envisioned the teacher as something like a guardian angel: "He observes the revelation of children's independence and helps in especially difficult moments." Even at crucial moments, the teacher never interfered in the child's work, but only offered wise advice.[85] The teacher's touch was represented as almost certainly authoritarian and therefore corrupting.

Somewhat incongruously, teachers also functioned as role models for the children. Lazurkina affirmed that preschool teachers "as the source of many impressions" had tremendous impact on their charges.[86] Instructions for setting up playgrounds that listed as minimum requirements an even, empty lot and "experienced teachers who love their work" reflected the certainty that teachers played a decisive role in children's lives. Other educators suggested that, more than experience, the "personality of the teacher" determined the success or failure of the kindergarten.[87] An eager and enthusiastic teacher who "carries *dezhurstvo* together with the children" might by her example foster "willing and harmonious" participation in work.[88] Teachers became a positive influence on children by participating in kindergarten activities "with the rights of a comrade" rather than with the authority of an adult.[89]

Whether as a result of age, education, or the very experience of working with children, teachers had to be free of the prejudices of the past. The notion that teachers exerted a positive influence on children only to the extent that they shared their outlooks and activities suggested that kindergarten teachers themselves ought to be drawn from the rising generation. Lilina recommended the recruitment of young people who had forgotten the past and "believed unconditionally" in the future. The precise nature of that belief concerned Lilina less than the capacity to join in the life of the children. She envisioned a teacher able to sing, dance, draw, model, tell stories and fairy tales, make toys, and raise flowers, while remaining always cheerful and ready to participate in any enterprise.[90]

Lazurkina gave less emphasis to youth and childlike sensibilities, stressing instead that, while teachers did not have to be communists, they did need to be "imbued with the interests of socialist construction." She also suggested that drawing women workers into preschool work could speed the process of forgetting the past. The Zhenotdel agreed, and took an active role in recruiting preschool teachers.[91] Teachers that lacked youths' capacity for living in new ways would have to "re-educate themselves so as not to bring discord into the child's life." Conceived as a "small commune," the kindergarten not only required that adults learn to live collectively, but also facilitated their reeducation.[92] The kindergarten became a place where the past visibly gave way to the future.

The identification of teachers with their charges produced teacher-training courses in Moscow modeled after free kindergartens. With very few teachers and great ambitions for opening a national network of kindergartens, the department established two- and three-month programs designed to give students an understanding of the "child's spirit and interests" by immersing them in a sort of kindergarten for adults.[93] "Conversations" and hands-on work replaced lectures. The budget for the classes provided money for paper, clay, paints, brushes, scissors, and rulers.[94] Materials were presented just as they would be in a free kindergarten, gradually but without any guidelines for their use. Like their future pupils, student teachers had "to experience the difficult and joyous moments in working" with materials.[95] The courses worked on the assumption that in order to be qualified to work with children, teachers had to experience the free world of the younger generation firsthand.

Shleger, who organized the Moscow program, hoped to keep didacticism to a minimum. Instead of presenting a syllabus on the first day of class, instructors invited students to discuss what they hoped to get out of the course. Here the story parallels that of children's first days in the kindergarten. Unsure how to handle the responsibility of setting their own agenda, the student-teachers asked for a set syllabus. But according to the official report of the courses, with "persistent" coaxing the students warmed to the discussion, and nearly all offered suggestions. Conveniently enough, the student-teachers' desires and needs squared almost exactly with the tentative plan arranged by the department and the instructors (still called "lecturers" in the report). By the end of the course, all the students embraced the "active" method, correcting anyone who referred to classes as "lectures" rather than "conversations."[96]

The Moscow experiments in hands-on teacher training found little support in Petrograd. Reflecting a broader split between the Moscow and Petrograd intelligentsia, educators in the erstwhile capital viewed the Moscow program as sacrificing intellectual rigor to a specious revolutionary authenticity.[97] Cultural enlightenment played a more prominent role both in Petrograd's kindergartens, where Tikheeva's more structured approach was often in evidence, and in the city's teacher-training program. In the "scientific" atmosphere of Petrograd's four-year teacher's college, "finding oneself" was "not part of the curriculum." Where the shorter, more intimate and informal Moscow courses produced new teachers by furnishing adults with the experience of a "free" childhood, the Petrograd program utilized more traditional methods to train "educated pedagogues." Students followed a program of general education coupled with specialized courses in preschool pedagogy. Lectures were not rejected as a vestige of the past, but remained the primary method of instruction, with "practical activities and books" given second place.[98]

In the provinces, circumstances produced rather unsystematic training. A relatively small number of provincial teachers received stipends to attend short-term courses in the capital.[99] Training in the provinces was supposed to occur at weekly meetings between the teachers of the guberniia's "primitive" kindergartens and the faculty at its one experimental-model institution. Far from providing a thorough course on preschool pedagogy or an opportunity to find oneself, the meetings focused on teachers' immediate and practical concerns.[100]

Despite sharp divergences in methods and assumptions, a tone of tolerance characterized discussions of teacher training. Shatskii, Shleger, and other Moscow teachers criticized the Petrograd approach as too theoretical, teaching psychology and ignoring preschool practice, and the intercity debate at conferences and in the press could get rather heated.[101] However, even teachers in

Moscow admitted that the active method had a tendency to produce general disorganization.[102] Many teachers agreed with the conclusion of a delegate at a 1920 conference that the two programs complemented one another and that "each [city] works in the direction that it must work." Satisfying different needs and different styles of learning, lectures and the experience of "finding oneself" both contributed to the preparation of the "new cadre of workers."[103]

The training of the "new cadre" remained largely in the hands of the older generation of pre-Revolutionary kindergarten teachers, which it resembled in one very visible respect—it was predominately female. While a majority of school teachers (65.2 percent in 1923–1924) were women, preschool teachers were almost exclusively female (92.7 percent in the Russian Republic as a whole, 100 percent in some areas).[104] Not only the department's head but also the majority of presiding officers at its conferences were female. Women also constituted a majority of the delegates. At the 1920 Third All-Russian Conference of Preschool Teachers, the female majority denied the small male contingent's request to smoke.[105] Teacher-training courses welcomed men and women who wanted to work in kindergartens, but where statistics were kept one finds not a single male student and only a smattering of male teachers. Shleger noted with some regret that the student body at the 1919 courses in Moscow was exclusively female.[106] The department's publications often used the feminine forms *rukovoditel'nitsa* and *vospitatel'nitsa* generically. However "new" the cadre might be in terms of age, socialist convictions, or childlike experiences of creative freedom, it did not do much to sever the traditional link between women and responsibility for children of preschool age.

New Children

Free upbringing emphasized the *process* of revolutionary becoming, not its end result. At least in the preschool, the process never really ended. Each fall a new group of children entered the kindergarten and began the initially chaotic, always unpredictable work of building a small community. Along the way, advocates of free upbringing insisted, the child's present happiness, and not the effort to mold it to fit into some ideal future, drove the program.

Official tolerance of *svobodnoe vospitanie* rested on the assumption that the program of free upbringing and the goals of the Soviet state would naturally converge, that socialism necessarily produced and required "free" people. At the First All-Russian Congress of Preschool Education, Lazurkina confidently asserted, with no hint of potential incompatibility, that "we must raise not only a person but also a citizen of the Soviet Republic, who is capable of living in the future commune."[107] Her fellow educators often doubted that the two goals could coexist, even though the justification for their programs relied on the purportedly near perfect overlap of the present needs of the child and the future needs of the Soviet state.

The image of the child as creator that stood at the center of free upbringing seemed to rule out efforts to transform children into socialists or anything else. Free upbringing pictured the child not "as a kind of empty vessel," according to Venttsel', "but as a being gradually formed by means of creative activity." Representing the "child's soul" not as a "*tabula rasa*" but as "already from the moment of birth marked with a whole series of obscure signs,"[108] *svobodnoe vospitanie* viewed any effort to lead children toward a particular future as damaging to their "normal and natural" development.

Such "scientific" conclusions had political implications. Shleger distinguished her "purely pedagogical" approach from that of policymakers at Narkompros, whom she characterized as wanting "to give the rising generation political education [*obrazovanie*] and to prepare the citizen of the contemporary state order," an effort she deemed potentially at odds with the child's true interests.[109] Embedded in her argument, despite its claim to be "purely pedagogical," is the vision of revolution as liberation and a rejection of any sort of revolutionary discipline as unnatural and dangerous. The "purely pedagogical" premise that the child was not a blank slate turned the state's interest in political education into an authoritarian perversion of revolution. Shleger preferred raising people to raising citizens: "You say that we must prepare the child for life, and I say that we must create life for the child." Ending with the assertion that only "lofty" (*vysokii*) people made lofty citizens, Shleger received a loud round of applause from the delegates. When pressed to define the "*prekrasnyi chelovek*" that she envisioned, Shleger returned to the image of the child already marked with obscure signs and explained that "we cannot create a person. I cannot make a pear out of an apple. . . . I only know that in every child lies a mass of strengths, possibilities, capabilities, and instincts."[110] Venttsel' voiced the same unwillingness to tolerate any political authority over the child, even as he, like Shleger and other proponents of free upbringing, granted the legitimacy of efforts to enforce modern habits. "The free school must be really free," he argued, "independent of any politics, bourgeois or proletarian."[111] The vision of the child creating his or her own future motivated the conclusion that socialist upbringing could be just as oppressive and distorting as bourgeois education could be.

Embracing the image of the child as an empty vessel, proponents of discipline and enlightenment also framed political claims in the language of pedagogy. Both advocates of the introduction of literacy and of what Shleger termed "political education" insisted on the legitimacy and necessity of preparing children for the future. Emphasizing that "a change in conditions provides the opportunity for a sharp change in the character of individual personalities," proponents of a more structured program concluded that once revolution transformed the child's environment it became reasonable to talk about educating children in new directions.[112]

If contact with the outside world, rather than the child's innate capabilities, shaped his or her development, then children might have something to learn from their elders after all. Making children into socialists became the legitimate first task of the Revolution. A proponent of the Montessori system justified the use of didactic material on the grounds that the child's "poverty of mind, ignorance of the surrounding world," required that the teacher "guide it in a defined direction, toward a knowledge of the real world and toward labor."[113] Similarly, a delegate to the First All-Russian Congress of Preschool Education who spoke against the general endorsement of free upbringing contended that "*svobodnoe vospitanie* tells us: grant the child four walls, and all the rest children will create for themselves." It ignored the fundamental question of how to prepare children for the "struggle for right and justice for all." She urged that children be taught to think scientifically, "without mysticism or religion."[114] Understanding the child as a blank slate allowed teachers to represent adult intervention as a necessary means of rescuing the child from ignorance and of training them to build the future.

By contrast, free upbringing's suspicion of any program oriented toward the future potentially limited its usefulness as a tool for constructing Soviet socialism. Pavel Blonskii, an educator more interested in schools than preschools, labeled *svobodnoe vospitanie* "reactionary utopianism" because it ignored both genetics and environment and assumed that the "ideal and unchanging" nature of the child required only "freedom from" adult interference to ensure its full and normal development. Blonskii feared what Venttsel' affirmed—that "freedom from" potentially included "freedom from socialist upbringing."[115] As long as it was assumed that granting children freedom would be enough to produce a generation of socialists, the free kindergarten remained "revolutionary." But in the mid-1920s, as faith in the liberationist model of revolution faded and the spontaneous emergence of socialist society seemed increasingly unlikely, the Soviet state turned its attention to making children into socialists.

What free upbringing bequeathed to the programs that repudiated it was a faith in the revolutionary power of science and a purportedly scientific vision of revolutionary youth. *Svobodnoe vospitanie* was able to leave an imprint on later approaches to children largely because it, like more rigid programs, was a revolutionary hybrid of unlikely, if not contradictory, elements. At their most utopian, advocates of free upbringing insisted on the "scientific" conclusion that children were born with creative and social instincts that parents and teachers could distort but never recast. Freeing children from adult authority allowed them spontaneously to build a community of equals, a big happy socialist family. At the same time, commitment to the project of raising cultural levels led advocates of free upbringing to picture efforts to teach children the value of cleanliness, efficiency, and productivity as compatible with, even a tool of, liberation. Indeed, the equation of washed and rational children with revolutionary transformation was a leitmotif of radical pedagogy before and after the Revolution. If *svobodnoe vospitanie* had greater faith than more overtly "political" programs in the ability of the rising generation to develop revolutionary consciousness on its own, it nonetheless granted that teachers played a crucial role in organizing the small kindergarten commune. Even in its most liberationist incarnation, the revolutionary impulse was never singular. Changing circumstances and priorities produced complex and shifting amalgams of policies designed to liberate, enlighten, modernize, and discipline the oppressed masses — figured not only as workers and women but also as children.

part three

Rethinking Revolution
and Childhood, 1921–1932

5

The Withering Away of
the Kindergarten

Emerging victorious from the Civil War in 1921, the Bolsheviks faced an economic and social crisis of staggering proportions. As they sought to engineer recovery, the Bolsheviks jettisoned many of their earlier assumptions and policies, but they did not necessarily abandon or betray dreams of revolutionary transformation. The litany of problems is well known: the half-empty cities lacked food; industrial output stood well below prewar levels. Civil War food requisitions coupled with two years of drought brought famine to the Volga and other regions. Peasant resistance to the policies of War Communism culminated in massive uprisings in Tambov province in late 1920. Still more alarming was the March 1921 rebellion of the sailors at Kronstadt. The Soviet government responded with crack units of the Red Army and with a tactical retreat on the economic front that ended seizures of grain and allowed the revival of free trade. The New Economic Policy (NEP) marked a step away from the earlier methods of communism—from central planning and the nationalization of industry—and its impact on the economy was immediate and beneficial.

The NEP's impact on state services for children was equally immediate, but disastrous. It not only brought back private trade, but also mandated cost accounting and limitations on government spending. Efforts to reverse the economic devastation wrought by the war often meant diverting funds from education and other programs for the rising generation.[1] Preschools, never high on Narkompros's list of budgetary priorities, fared even worse than the hard-hit primary and secondary schools. Most of the institutions built at such an ambitious pace during the Civil War ended up closing their doors. Where institutions did manage to stay open, they often turned to parents to supply whatever the state did not. Far from replacing the family, the kindergarten came to depend on its aid. Circumstances made the dream of socialized child-rearing wholly unworkable.

Nonetheless, economic crisis did not so much quash the revolutionary impulse as redirect it. Increasingly skeptical that the new world could be counted on to emerge spontaneously and almost immediately from the ashes of the old, revolutionaries embraced enlightenment, indoctrination, and discipline as "practical" means of effecting sweeping change. As William Rosenberg has argued, the NEP did not entail renouncing the belief that "the legacies of the past had to be overcome: through attrition, absorption, . . . repression" or education.[2] The imperative mood is crucial; even as hopes of immediately replacing the family faded, revolutionaries could not walk away from the enterprise of overturning the old world. The lack of central funds meant that without parental support institutions simply would not exist. At the same time, policymakers at the Preschool Department continued to distrust family upbringing and to assert that even with a limited reach, educational programs would and should remake the lives of children and parents. Chapter 6 examines what the process of rethinking revolution meant for classroom practice and shifting visions of childhood. Here the emphasis is on the impact of the NEP on child care institutions and on the resulting complication of the already ambiguous relationship between the kindergarten and the family.

A Giant Step Backward

During the Civil War, despite administrative disorganization and shortages of materials and trained personnel, the number of preschool institutions in Russia had grown dramatically. Just one year after its establishment, the Preschool Department had organized 2,436 institutions. By December 1921, the new state had 7,784 preschool institutions of all types (kindergartens, day cares, playgrounds, children's homes) serving 350,280 children out of a total preschool-age population of perhaps three and a half million. In just one year, NEP budget-cutting reduced the number of institutions to 5,088 and the number of pupils to 226,260. Published statistics do not always agree on absolute figures and are sometimes vague about the sorts of institutions they include, but the trend is unmistakable (Table 4). The Preschool Department began the 1920–1921 school year with almost 4,800 kindergartens and *ochagi* and ended it with only 1,800. In the nation as a whole, the number of all types of institutions dropped 70 percent between November 1921 and November 1922.[3] The Preschool Department felt the effects of the decline for the rest of the decade.

The reason for the drop is not hard to find. NEP-mandated austerity meant that Moscow cut almost all central funding for schools and preschools. In 1917, the Preschool Department's total budget was 600,000 rubles. During the Civil War, state funding had expanded rapidly, and the department's budget for the first half of 1919 was 99,303,370 rubles, over 85 percent of which was allocated to day cares and kindergartens. The department received an additional

Table 4   Kindergartens and *Ochagi* in the RSFSR, 1920–1931

Year	Kindergartens and *Ochagi*	Number of Children Served	Preschool Age Population (ages 3–7)	Percent Served		
				Total	Rural	Urban
1920/1	14,046	235,725				
1921/22						
Oct. 1921	4,785	247,701				
Apr. 1922	1,800	88,595				
1922/23	766	36,134				
1923/24	647	32,946				
1924/25	766	38,962				
1926/27	1,244	54,258	9,839,800	0.6	0.1	3.3
1927/28	1,387	71,669				
1928/29	1,584	85,280				
1929/30	2,079	114,263				
1930/31	3,769	222,216	[13,802,236]	1.61	0.32	7.83

Sources: For 1920/21, *1917–Oktiabr' 1920* (Moscow: Gosudarstvennoe izdatel'stvo, 1920), 18. For 1921/22–1922/23, TsGA RSFSR, f. 1575, op. 7, d. 14, l. 116. For 1923/24, *Statisticheskii ezhegodnik* (Moscow: Izdatel'stvo "Doloi negramotnost'," 1925), 40. For 1924/25, *Statisticheskii ezhegodnik* (Moscow, 1926), X. For 1926/27, *Narodnoe prosveshchenie v osnovnykyh pokazateliakh* (Moscow-Leningrad: Gosizdat, 1928), 48. The 1926 census puts the number of children between ages three and seven at 14,944,341, *Vsesoiuznaia perepis' naseleniia 1926 goda*, vol. 17 (Moscow: Izdanie Ts. S. U. Soiuza SSR, 1929), 50. For 1927/28-1929/30, *Narodnoe prosveshchenie v RSFSR v tsifrakh* (Moscow-Leningrad: Gosudarstvennoe uchebno-pedagogicheskoe izdatel'stvo, 1932), 38. For 1930-31, *Narodnoe prosveshchenie v RSFSR v osnovnykh pokazateliakh za 15 let sovetskoi vlasti (Kratkii statishcheskii sbornik)* (Moscow-Leningrad: Gosudarstvennoe uchebno-pedagogicheskoe izdatel'stvo, 1932), 8. Population calculated from reported percentages.

3,811,400 rubles for teacher-training programs.[4] Two years later, the preschools had been all but cut out of the state budget. As of 1922, the salaries of workers in kindergartens, day care centers, and colonies as well as the funds to set up preschool institutions became the responsibility of the localities.[5] For the 1923–1924 school year, state appropriations for primary, secondary, and preschool education (i.e., for Sotsvos, the division of Narkompros responsible for these tasks) amounted to 193 million rubles, which funded 0.03 percent of institutions in European Russia and just over 2 percent in Siberia. Limited central funds went overwhelmingly to professional education, funding almost 35 percent of higher education.[6] The state contributed less than 95 million rubles to Sotsvos institutions for the 1924–1925 school year, less than the Preschool Department's 1919 budget. For the 1925–1926 school year, political education for adults constituted a higher budgetary priority for Narkompros than primary, secondary, and preschool education combined.[7] The statistics do not mention what proportion of state funding reached preschools, but the department's decision to fund only two model-experimental institutions per *guberniia* suggests that its share of state funds was quite small.[8]

Schools and preschools relied primarily on appropriations from the *uezd* (county, 83 percent of funding) and the *volost* (township; 9.5 percent). At the same time, the *uezdy* became responsible for public health institutions and for local administration and police.[9] In the Russian republic, the localities continued to bear at least two-thirds of the cost of Sotsvos institutions through 1932.[10]

That local authorities would prove unable or unwilling to bear the new burdens was well known. Central authorities "uncomfortable" with the idea of dictating the percentage of local budgets that had to be earmarked for education set no minimum figure despite the appeals of teachers. They generously established a 35 percent maximum.[11] At the same time, hard-pressed local administrations began the unsanctioned and "unconstitutional" practice of merging the departments of education, public health, and social welfare at the *uezd* and even at the *guberniia* level in order to save money. Warnings not to cut education below some vaguely specified minimums went unheeded.[12] In an international comparison published by Narkompros, the Soviet Union ranked last in the percentage of the education budget spent on primary schools (for 1925–1926), behind both British India and Egypt.[13] As local funding for schools and preschools increased from 1927 to 1931 (from almost 270 to 646 million rubles), the percentage allocated to primary schools, the institutions that served the largest numbers of pupils, fell from 55 to 49 percent.[14] Most of the remainder presumably funded secondary schools. An even lower priority than primary schools, preschools received very little.[15]

Even in Moscow, the leader in preschool education, the NEP severely reduced the number of institutions. Before the NEP the city boasted 296 kindergartens, the *guberniia* outside the city, 135. By October 1922, those figures had fallen to 126 and 62, respectively. By January 1923, the Moscow city figure stood at 123, ten of which received funding from the city soviet. Between four and six relied on food aid from the American Relief Administration (ARA). Only four *uezdy* had preschool instructors, and all peasant kindergartens had been closed.[16]

In the provinces, and especially in the famine areas where they were most urgently needed, preschools all but disappeared. Statistics from the provinces suggest grim circumstances. In Archangel *guberniia* the number of institutions fell from a pre-NEP high of forty to just three in October 1922. Novgorod went from sixty-eight to thirteen institutions, Vologda from ninety-four to twenty-one. As of January 1923, Kaluga had lost all but nine of its ninety-five institutions, and Ivanovo-Voznesensk had less than half of its ninety-six.[17] Where kindergartens had to cope with the effects of not only budget cuts but also the famine, very few preschool-age children received care, let alone education, in state institutions.[18] In June 1922, Kindergarten No. 7 in Tambov appealed to the ARA for support, explaining, with a degree of understatement, that the kindergarten had lost its government NEP funding the previous November and that "no hope can be placed upon private initiative and local resources, for the conditions of life in the city of Tambov are extremely difficult." Food prices had reached unprecedented levels, "and the Gub. Department of Education has not even the means to pay its employees in time."[19]

The downward spiral continued into 1924, and although a revival began shortly thereafter, the number of preschools did not return to 1921 levels. The number of institutions in Moscow *guberniia* went from 91 for the 1924–1925 school year to 224 in 1926–1927. In the same period, the number of institutions in Leningrad *guberniia* went from 61 to 113. Ivanovo-Voznesensk had only 13 preschool institutions in 1924 and 21 by 1927, still well short of the 1921 total of 96.[20]

Whether the institutions that opened in the mid-1920s were of higher quality than their more numerous pre-NEP counterparts is impossible to tell from the statistics. Given the budgetary constraints and the constant appeals in the press and at conferences to raise standards, this seems unlikely. For the 1927–1928 school year, Saratov *guberniia* reported 372 institutions, 301 of which were playgrounds. Permanent kindergartens and *ochagi* served only 0.8 percent of the province's preschool-age children. In general, the number of playgrounds grew much more rapidly than the number of permanent institutions that required better-trained personnel and more substantial material resources.[21] In terms of quantity if not quality, the entire NEP period marked a giant step backward for the Preschool Department.

Holding Firm on the Ideological Front

As five years of work disappeared almost overnight, the Preschool Department resolved that it would allow the current policy to affect the "organization, but not the ideology" of preschools.[22] From the beginning, kindergarten teachers had struggled against limiting their task to the provision of food and clothing, and even in the face of widespread misery, they insisted on the preschool's broad educational mission. Budget cuts and famine compelled teachers to scale back educational work in order to deal with a new wave of hungry and abandoned children. Yet preschool policymakers at Narkompros, including the non-Bolshevik experts who had shaped policy during the Civil War period, continued to reject the notion that kindergartens were nothing more than feeding points.

The department's commitment to educational work seemed to require a willful disregard for reality. The shortages of pencils, paper, books, and toys, not to mention dishes, shoes, and linens, that had long plagued children's institutions became critical. The teachers at the Krupskaia Children's Home complained in 1925 that even with funds from Moscow, the home "suffers from the lack of supplies and materials for activities," a description that does not sound like exaggeration.[23] Kindergartners in Saratov in 1927 were reportedly so overjoyed with the rare appearance of colored pencils for drawing that when they finished their work, they helped the teacher pick the pencils up off the floor and counted to make sure all were returned.[24]

The emphasis on education appeared particularly out of place in the famine region. In 1922, doctors examined 47,000 school children in Kiev and Kharkov and diagnosed over 75 percent of them as tubercular. A school dispensary in Petrograd reported to ARA doctors that "if marked anaemia and malnutrition are included, 100 percent of the 27,000 children examined in 1922 presented symptoms requiring treatment."[25]

Viewing the new crisis as a transitory, if painful, phenomenon, the Preschool Department refused to allow reports of shortages and malnutrition to govern kindergarten policy. Horrendous shortages led Lazurkina to concede only that a temporary reduction in "scientific-theoretical" work was probable. The establishment of "feeding points" continued to be defined as a solution of last resort; she urged preschool workers to build institutions to relieve the famine without "forgetting pedagogical tasks." Likewise, the Third All-Russian Congress of Preschool Education that met in 1924 recognized that playgrounds temporarily might have to take the place of more costly indoor kindergartens, but rejected playgrounds where children "just play." From the policymakers' point of view, inauspicious conditions did not excuse or necessitate the abandonment of educational "principles."[26]

The department spent much time and money on curricular issues throughout the NEP.[27] Apparently ignoring the tremendous constraints, Lunacharskii reported optimistically that "methodological work" was being pursued intensively. The department's publications continued to focus on pedagogical questions, for example, on the importance of building materials in the classroom. Teachers were advised that the kindergarten required building blocks in a wide variety of "harmonious" shapes and sizes and "conditio sine qua non, a sufficient quantity of material that is not too small in size." Realities outside the classroom did occasionally intrude. If necessity dictated, the required materials might be reduced to four large blocks and two boards that would allow the children to build two trams, two airplanes, two locomotives, or two automobiles. Even the most bare-bones kindergartens had to give children the opportunity to construct icons of the modern age.[28] That a teacher might be more worried about feeding her charges than about helping them to build an airplane did not emerge as a real possibility.

The most telling manifestation of the department's commitment to its educational ideals was its decision to fund a handful of experimental-model kindergartens rather than to assist "primitive" kindergartens struggling to survive on the paltry sums allocated by the localities. In 1922, the Second All-Russian Congress of Preschool Education resolved that limited central funds ought to go to experimental-model institutions with local governments, factory committees, and professional organizations supporting the rest. Ideally, each *guberniia* would have two centrally funded model institutions—for a national total of ninety-four—which would serve as an inspiration and guide to primitive kindergartens.[29]

As it turned out, even the model schools had trouble fulfilling their educational mission. Figures for the 1923–1924 school year seem to indicate that the goal of two centrally funded institutions per province was met. But the statistics are so regular—each *guberniia* listed has the same ratio of students to teachers as well as teachers to institutions—that the numbers are probably better read as a plan for the future than as a reflection of reality. A more detailed 1925 account of model institutions listed only nineteen.[30] Many model institutions, such as the Krupskaia Children's Home and Kindergarten No. 11 in Saratov, complained about shortages of basic teaching supplies. Still, the department favored educational quality—however compromised—over a mass of purely care-taking institutions.[31] Famine relief was not the primary "practical consideration" to which the Preschool Department responded.

"Organizational" Compromises

What seemed unavoidable in the context of NEP budget cuts was the indefinite postponement of free, universal, socialized child care. Reluctantly, the department began to charge tuition and to give its hesitant blessing to privately organized kindergartens. The compromises were labeled "organizational," essentially pragmatic responses to the department's dwindling funding and institutions. They did not, according to policymakers, connote the abandonment of the kindergarten's role in cultural transformation. Such claims required the redefinition of the preschool's revolutionary mission. Overflowing with orphans from the famine regions, children's homes lost their status as beachheads of the socialist future. Instead of envisioning a parentless utopia, policymakers at the Preschool Department increasingly emphasized that spending even a few hours per day in the right sort of kindergarten would revolutionize children. Revolution no longer required fully socialized child-rearing.

In the face of famine, economic crisis, and budget cuts, children's homes could not possibly realize the dream of raising all children under conditions that met up-to-date scientific criteria. The dislocations of the early 1920s coincided with a massive influx of children (ages three to seventeen) into children's homes. Between 1920 and 1922, the number of children receiving state care increased 77 percent (to 473,949 children), while the network of children's homes and "reception centers" for orphaned children (*priemniki*) grew less than 50 percent. After 1922, the number of children served by state institutions dropped slowly, while institutions organized to deal with the worst of the crisis quickly disappeared. If the "average" home in 1920 housed forty-nine children, by 1927, it had to accommodate eighty.[32] For the 1926–1927 school year, over 64.8 percent of the children in children's homes were orphans, and an additional 20.4 percent had only one parent, usually the mother. Less than 3 percent of children for whom information was available had both parents. Although they constituted about half of the total cohort between ages three and seventeen, children between ten and seventeen—perhaps less vulnerable but more publicly disruptive than their younger siblings—filled 75 percent of places in children's homes.[33] Raising all children from earliest childhood in state institutions clearly was not the state's first priority.

Despite the inauspicious circumstances, the Preschool Department sacrificed its commitment to free public upbringing only grudgingly. The promise of universal child care was apparently too central to policymakers' understanding of the department's revolutionary mission to be easily surrendered. While secondary and primary schools began to charge tuition in 1922 in order to make up for Narkompros budget cuts, preschools did not.[34] A 1923 teachers' conference denounced privatization and tuition as solutions to reduced funding and insisted that a fixed percent of local budgets be set aside for preschool education.[35] Even after tuition became a reality, some within the department continued to voice the fear that by charging tuition kindergartens lost their revolutionary status. Teachers objected that the policy left proletarian children "outside the doors of institutions," and condemned sliding tuition scales as undermining pedagogical work.[36] Not everyone was persuaded by the department's rhetoric that "organizational" matters, like tuition, could be separated from educational practice.

Ultimately, the social dislocation that had seemed such a golden opportunity during the Civil War became in the cold light of the NEP an unbearable burden on overtaxed, underfunded institutions and teachers. By the summer of 1924, the Commissariat of Enlightenment ordered preschools to charge tuition on the basis of the parents' ability to pay as a means of keeping institutions open. At the Third All-Russian Congress of Preschool Education the same year, a number of delegates defended the policy as a necessary evil. Under the present circumstances, was it fair, one delegate asked, that the child of a worker earning

100–120 rubles per month as well as the child of an unemployed worker or one earning only 20–30 rubles all attended kindergarten free of charge? People who worked eighteen hours per day in addition to their party or Soviet duties clearly needed child care, but not necessarily free child care. She concluded that free four-hour kindergartens that served no meals met no one's needs. A delegate from Petrograd agreed, noting that charging tuition did not reduce the number of children enrolled.[37]

Privately organized kindergartens were also justified as necessary organizational evils. The department's commission on preschool policy had rejected private kindergartens as "serving a defined layer of the population, destroying fundamental pedagogical principles, and detaching institutions from central control."[38] Delegates to the third congress focused on the fear that private kindergartens would undermine the program of public upbringing.

Those favoring such institutions emphasized that they represented nothing more than an organizational compromise, unrelated to the kindergarten's larger goal of transformation via education. One delegate, calling herself a "liberal" with regard to the question of private kindergartens, saw nothing wrong with allowing private groups to set up institutions; "we must only—and this is of primary importance—guarantee our control, so that something we do not need, something that is dangerous to us does not go on there." By "us" she apparently meant not so much public kindergarten teachers as the communist state. She located the kindergarten's link to revolution not in its ability to provide universal child care, but in its curriculum. As an example of the sort of institution that was not needed, the delegate recounted a visit to a private kindergarten where she asked the children if they wanted to be communists; only one of the fifteen pupils replied in the affirmative. A delegate from Moscow reported that in the last two years, factory organizations had founded sixteen kindergartens in the city. She saw no danger in these institutions as long as the "initiative is not of an NEP-man character." If private kindergartens could raise children devoted to the Soviet state, the department was willing to tolerate them.[39] Increasingly, the kindergarten curriculum supplanted the socialization of child care as the preschool's chief contribution to revolutionary transformation.

A New Reliance on Parents

Relying on the material and financial support of parents put preschools in a rather awkward position. While the ultimate goal for many Bolsheviks remained the creation of institutional "families," the expected date for achieving this goal receded deep into the future. Given the "new pedagogical conditions" created by the NEP, the department displayed a new willingness to consider the full-day *ochag* as the basic type of preschool, and some educators went so far as to label the department's "war on the family" a "serious mistake." At the very least, the need for parental aid made denunciations of the family as an "enemy camp" particularly tactless—and self-destructive.[40] Nonetheless, assessments of the family's ability to raise children were, if anything, more pessimistic than they had been in the Civil War years. Even the department's non-Bolshevik experts, who were ready to grant the family a vital role in child-rearing, had serious reservations.[41] Teachers continued to believe that the preschool had to become the most powerful influence in the child's life.

Preschool teachers had always assumed that their programs would do best if working mothers viewed them as useful. With NEP budget cuts, the depth of the mutual dependence of parents and day cares became clear. The keynote address at the Third Congress of Preschool Education in 1924 emphasized that institutions served both children and their mothers, who would not be able to work without child care and who would not be able to support their children without working.[42] The department concluded that studies of the family circumstances of preschool children demonstrated a general need for "long day cares."[43]

In making this recommendation, preschool policymakers responded to a predominately and increasingly urban clientele. For the 1923–1924 school year, 86 percent of kindergartners for whom information was available lived in cities and towns. Preschool children's homes were also a largely urban phenomenon. By contrast, less than 18 percent of primary-school pupils lived in urban areas. Figures for the 1926–1927 school year were almost identical.[44] Since summer playgrounds were more common in rural areas than kindergartens, figures that include *all* preschool institutions indicate a bit more balance. However, as the number of all institutions rebounded in the cities in the mid-1920s, the gap between urban and rural enrollments widened (Table 5).

Largely urban, kindergartens did not necessarily serve only or primarily the children of workers. Based on information from less than half of all children enrolled in preschool institutions, Narkompros statistics on the social origin of preschoolers for the 1923–1924 school year are not definitive, but they are suggestive. Rural preschoolers from whom information was collected were predominately the children of workers (66.4 percent) or peasants (26.2 percent). In the cities, just under half of pupils were children of workers (41.4 percent) or peasants (7 percent). An additional 27.6 percent of urban pupils were children of white-collar employees "of Soviet and other institutions." The survey also identified relatively small numbers of urban kindergartners as children of artisans (4.6 percent), of merchants and industrialists (2.4 percent), of members of the "free professions" (2.3 percent), and of Red Army men (1.9 percent). The remaining 7.8 percent fell into the "other" category.[45] Statistics for the 1926–1927 school year suggest a proletarianization of the kindergarten. However, the result may

Table 5   Rural-Urban Distribution of All Types of Preschool Institutions, 1920–1926

Year	Institutions		Children Enrolled	
	Urban	Rural	Urban	Rural
In absolute numbers				
1920/21	2,378	2,345	131,925	113,602
1921/22	1,960	1,600	106,956	77,951
1922/23	1,159	367	60,589	18,034
1923/24	996	233	48,202	10,935
1924/25	940	195	49,823	10,353
1925/26	1,139	230	62,071	10,553
Percent				
1920/21	50.3	49.7	55.7	46.3
1921/22	55.1	44.9	57.8	42.2
1922/23	76.0	24.0	77.1	22.9
1923/24	81.0	19.0	81.5	18.5
1924/25	82.8	17.2	82.8	17.2
1925/26	83.2	16.8	85.5	14.5

Source: "Statistika uchrezhdenii doshkol'nogo vospitaniia," *Pedagogicheskaia entisklope-dia*, Vol. 2, ed. A. G. Kalashnikov (Moscow: Rabotnik proveshcheniia, 1929), 113–114.

also be an artifact of the narrowing of possible categories to "children of work-ers" (53.1 percent of an unspecified number of pupils), "children of peasants" (41.1 percent), and "other" (5.8 percent). White-collar employees' children may have been folded into the "children of workers" rubric. Whatever the real-ity of these categories, by the mid-1920s, kindergartens enrolled substantially higher percentages of "workers'" children than any other Sotsvos institution.[46]

Although female unemployment rose steeply in the early 1920s,[47] kinder-gartens continued to serve a large number of working mothers. The mothers of at least one-third of the students attending Pskov's Kindergarten No. 3 in 1921 worked outside the home.[48] Moscow institutions reported that between one-third and one-half of their pupils' mothers worked.[49] Some Moscow kinder-gartens reportedly charged as much as 16 rubles per month, roughly half of the average woman's income. To induce working mothers to bear this financial bur-den, kindergartens had to pay serious attention to their needs.[50]

Not surprisingly, even as institutions were forced to close, the department pushed those that remained open to operate for the entire workday and even into the evening to free women to engage in "public political work."[51] Paradoxically, teachers considered full-day care more necessary for preschool children than for nursing infants. It was easier for a working mother to keep her infant "under lock and key" all day long and run home to feed it every few hours than to leave a three-year-old locked up from nine to five. After work, bringing an infant to a meeting, while not quite "sanitary," was less disruptive than bringing a three- or four-year-old who could not be quieted with her mother's breast or a *soska* (pacifier).

Such sensitivity to the needs of working mothers became increasingly important as teachers turned to them to help keep kindergartens functioning.[52] That parents proved willing to pay tuition and to provide both money and materials suggests that preschools were of real value to working families. At a kindergarten where educational supplies consisted of thirty black pencils, two pounds of lined and unlined paper, and one doll, parents met in October and again in December to organize a monthly collection to pay for the materials children desired. Parents provided funds for construction paper, paints, brushes, clay, and six pairs of scissors.[53] At another kindergarten, parents met to agree to a one-time fee to buy materials and arranged a schedule for helping out in the classroom.[54] At a Saratov "model" kindergarten funded primarily and inadequately by the *guberniia* department of education, parents contributed the 320 rubles necessary to hire an additional teacher for the 1924–1925 school year. Nonetheless, the kindergarten ran a deficit of about 60 rubles and lacked sufficient dishes, cots, kitchen equipment, and teaching materials.[55] Parents seemed to see more value in preschools than did officials at Narkompros or local departments of education, who preferred to spend money on training technical specialists, who might make an immediate contribution to the economy, rather than on providing education and day care for young children.

Parents' support for kindergartens no doubt grew in large part out of their need for day care for their children, but they also seem to have valued the preschool's educational component. Some, perhaps many, parents may have shared the Soviet state's interest in raising a generation of socialists. Elena Bonner, who attended kindergartens from the time she was three (in 1926), describes her mother's decision to enroll her as purely ideological, a consequence of Ruth Bonner's "antibourgeois" maximalism.[56] A child at Sventitskaia's kindergarten told her teachers that her communist parents never told fairy tales — neither did Bonner's parents.[57]

That most parents shared such revolutionary commitments seems unlikely. Since the beginning, the Preschool Department had operated on the assumption that food, clothing, and day care, not ideology, induced parents to enroll their children. Parents' willingness to do without the ration, as many parents did in order to keep kindergartens open, was therefore of tremendous symbolic as well as practical significance. But foregoing food aid did not necessarily constitute an endorsement of the kindergarten's increasingly politicized curriculum. Parents chose to provide funds for Christmas parties, not May Day celebrations.[58]

What parents seemed to appreciate most was the kindergarten's ability to teach their children to be orderly and disciplined and to prepare them for school. At meetings where parents confronted the problem of keeping preschools open, educational matters received a great deal of attention. As part of the campaign to attract funds from the center, the reports of such meetings may reveal more about local understandings of what policymakers in Moscow wanted to hear than about parents' motives for sending their children to preschool institutions. Still, parents' enthusiasm for the kindergarten's educational program seems genuine, if perhaps overstated. In the accounts of two parents' meetings in late 1921 at Pskov's Kindergartens No. 6 and No. 3, the overall tone was one of effusive gratitude for the fine educational work being done in the kindergarten and of real eagerness to keep the institutions open.

The meeting at Kindergarten No. 6 began with an overview of its imminent dissolution. The head of the kindergarten reported that because the provincial government could not make up the funds withheld by the center, it planned to close four institutions in the city, including Kindergarten No. 6. In its place, the *guberniia* planned to open a dining room to serve the neediest segments of the population.[59]

Immediately after this announcement, a number of mothers rose to testify to the kindergarten's positive influence on their children and to voice their commitment to keeping the kindergarten an *educational* institution. The first to speak noted that the kindergarten had sparked her youngest daughter's interest in drawing, and that the child constantly brought games, songs, and fairy tales home from the kindergarten. Policymakers who hoped that kindergartens would transform the lives of children still living at home should have been pleased. The grateful mother concluded that she herself "undoubtedly could not provide for the children what the kindergarten did." The second speaker went further to proclaim that the kindergarten teachers had worked nothing short of a "miracle" in bringing her son out of his shell. After a year of attending kindergarten, he was more quick-witted and had learned to count.

Another mother related that a little over a year at the kindergarten had transformed her daughter into a model child. Once an unbearably capricious girl, she now busied herself with work brought home from the kindergarten or by helping around the house. She swept the floors until not a crumb remained and never went to bed without putting her toys in their place.[60] As reported, the parents' accounts echoed to a remarkable degree the Preschool Department's own goals of nurturing creativity and good work habits. However, parents seemed less concerned with raising future socialists than with having more cooperative and creative children.

The minutes of the meeting at Kindergarten No. 3 also emphasized the powerful and positive influence of the preschool. According to the report, it was the "opinion of the parents" that "in these difficult times, parents do not have time to spare to raise their children; upbringing is turned over completely to the kindergarten." The kindergarten was given credit for developing the ability to speak in children who entered barely able to talk; after one or two years in the kindergarten these same children were able to retell fairy tales. Parents also testified that the kindergarten made children more attentive and observant and developed their "love of cleanliness and order, love for work." Teachers, with their pedagogical experience and training, were characterized as understanding their charges better "than the majority of parents."[61]

The parents resolved to do whatever was necessary to keep the kindergartens functioning. At Kindergarten No. 6, parents planned to send a delegate to the All-Russian Congress of Preschool Education to make their appeal heard in Moscow. They declared their willingness to supply the kindergarten with firewood. They announced that they would take on the responsibility of providing food for the children at the kindergarten because "they value the kindergarten as an educational [institution], not a feeding point." The teachers at Kindergarten No. 3 also asked parents to renounce government rations in order to show "that what is important to them is not the ration, but the raising of children."[62] While kindergarten teachers took parents' needs for full-day child care seriously, parents apparently shared the teachers' sense of the importance of preschool *education*.

Whether the parents at the meetings in Pskov were somehow "typical" is impossible to say. At least one of the fathers present was himself a first grade teacher. He might reasonably be expected to have greater than average respect for the wisdom of preschool teachers, and in fact observed that children who attended kindergarten came to school better prepared than those raised at home. Kindergarten No. 3 included a rather unsystematic sketch of the "social and material circumstances" of the thirty-eight children enrolled. One father who refused the rations provided by the kindergarten worked for the Council of National Economy (Sovnarkhoz); his wife did not work. A few other fathers also had direct connections with the state, as Red Army men or teachers. One father was identified as a shoemaker, another as working at a mill. But in most cases, no occupation was recorded. There was no indication of what sort of work any of the mothers did, only the occasional notation "mother at home" or "mother works." There were nine of each. In a few instances, the list provides more specific, but still very abbreviated, glimpses of family life: "husband in jail," "mother and grandmother at home," "awful poverty." Three of the parents present at the meeting were unable to sign their names to the resolutions.[63] The kindergarten appeared to draw children from a wide variety of backgrounds, but whether the "very poor" parents valued the kindergarten primarily as an educational institution remains obscure.

While parents seemed to have confidence in the expertise of teachers, the teachers' attitudes toward parents were more ambivalent. Teachers sometimes expressed more enthusiasm than did parents for building a child-rearing partnership between the family and the kindergarten. One educator suggested modeling parent-teacher meetings on American PTA meetings that recognized the role of parents in raising their children and allowed for the cooperation of mothers and kindergarten teachers.[64] Yet many parents seemed content to leave their children's education in the hands of the professionals. At one kindergarten, meetings to organize aid were well attended, but a meeting focused on pedagogical matters drew only thirteen parents. A final meeting that was to feature reports from teachers had to be canceled when only four parents showed up.[65] The lack of interest may indicate that parents had few complaints about how the experts were doing their job. It is also possible that however satisfied parents were with the kindergarten, they understood that teachers had little respect for the job they were doing at home. Along with a strong dose of didacticism, a measure of condescension could permeate teachers' exchanges with parents.[66] Relying on the family's trust and support, teachers—and perhaps some parents—believed that they did a far better job of raising children than did "the majority of parents."

The NEP marked a decisive shift in the Preschool Department's priorities. In its first years, the department established no fixed educational "ideology," and it modeled its curricula on progressive systems in the West and on the free kindergartens of pre-Revolutionary Russia. The kindergarten's role in revolutionary transformation was to be more institutional than pedagogical; children's homes would supplant individual family upbringing. As the NEP made universal public child-rearing less and less practicable, the department responded by investing the kindergarten curriculum with increasingly "ideological" significance. At the same time, teachers worked to understand and meet the needs and desires of parents, who provided essential material and financial support. Abandoning the initial vision of parentless child-rearing by relying on parental aid was written off as an "organizational" necessity that freed kindergartens to pursue their revolutionary pedagogical program. Practically speaking, educational theories cost less than efforts to replace parents, although it might have been more "practical" still to have spent the department's meager funds on a large number of care-taking institutions rather than on a small number of experimental kindergartens. By the end of the NEP, the policymakers at the Preschool Department had decided that the "ideology" that could not be compromised, although it could be contested, was the kindergarten's educational program.

6

Rescripting Childhood

The NEP has been characterized as both pragmatic and as fostering an efflorescence of cultural experimentation. Indeed, the 1920s witnessed gradual economic recovery as well as some of the Revolution's most exotic cultural experiments. NEP's move away from the policies of War Communism spawned, alongside the neocapitalist NEP-men, conductorless orchestras, utopian science fiction, and fanciful city planning. Yet despite their "relative laxity and pluralism,"[1] the NEP years also marked a shift toward a conception of cultural transformation that was neither particularly pragmatic nor especially tolerant of cultural diversity. The utopian impulse remained, but discipline and indoctrination (if not yet coercion) began to emerge as the privileged, "practical" means of effecting revolutionary change.

Nowhere was the emerging emphasis on what Robert Tucker has called the "tutelary state"[2] more visible or vivid than in discussions of how to reconcile the state's material incapacity to provide universal socialized child care and the deeply felt necessity of raising a generation capable of building socialism. Viewing the "watershed"[3] years that followed Lenin's death in 1924 through the lens of social and educational policy foregrounds not political intrigues or the polemics of the industrialization debate but the work of re-envisioning the Revolution. Wendy Goldman describes the legal wrangling on the new family code of 1926 as pitting "protectionists," who "distrusted spontaneity" and hoped the new code would act as a "compulsory device," against "progressives," who maintained, as one jurist put it, that the law was not meant "to instruct citizens in good behavior."[4] A similar dynamic appears in even sharper relief in educational debates, where the issue was not overcoming the legacies of the past but raising the heirs of revolution.

Civil War programs for children had been constructed on the (contested) premise that freeing children from the arbitrary, sometimes dangerous, authority of adults would naturally produce a generation of socialists. The new reliance on, if not respect for, parents mandated by budget cuts and by the task of restoring order and productivity could render the notion of children's liberation both unworkable and ideologically suspect. The specialized debates among legal experts, public health workers, and educators hinged on whether families and children could be trusted to revolutionize themselves—a question with important implications not only for real families but for the metaphorical social family as well.

In 1924 the State Academic Council (Gosudarstvennyi Uchenyi Sovet, or GUS) for the first time devised a uniform preschool and school curriculum designed to train children to construct and participate in the socialist future. Among preschool teachers, debate on the new program revolved around how to balance didacticism with the desire to create a small world in which children would feel free and happy. The GUS curriculum retained many traditional kindergarten activities, and its proponents insisted that it respected, without holding as inviolable, the immediate needs and interests of children. But it required the abandonment of the image of the self-disciplined, instinctively creative small comrade so central to earlier descriptions of children. At the core of the new scheme stood a vision of the child as a blank page on which teachers could write the future. Far from possessing "social instincts," the child had to be taught how to live collectively.[5]

The new conception of childhood required a general rethinking of the "science" of pedagogy. Although still willing to borrow from Western and pre-Revolutionary models, the department came to deny the existence of universal laws of child development. Psychologists "discovered" that proletarian children required a uniquely proletarian upbringing. What teachers had to pay attention to, they advised, was not the child's individual inclinations and capabilities but the process by which children *learned* (and here the teacher could play an active role) to work as a model community.

Reconceiving children as boundlessly impressionable played a crucial role in the reimagination of revolutionary transformation as compatible with, perhaps dependent upon, discipline and social control. Still, the new approach to children hardly signaled the unalloyed victory of authoritarianism or bureaucratic rigidity. The pedagogical literature offers a revealing view of the compromises and paradoxes involved in rethinking revolution at a moment when immediate transformations seemed unlikely. Alongside the emphasis on adult supervision and guidance stood the still powerful image of the revolutionary young generation.

From Free Upbringing to "Socialist" Upbringing

In the early 1920s, the language of free upbringing still dominated discussions of preschool education.[6] Advocates represented its insistence on liberating children

from the constraints of teachers and especially of parents along with its emphasis on independence and creativity as revolutionary. But free upbringing had
never lacked critics, and by the mid-1920s the same emphasis on "liberation"
that had originally made *svobodnoe vospitanie* attractive to socialists became
its undoing.

On the pedagogical level, it received criticism for its refusal to introduce
reading and for its overreliance on the ability of preschoolers to discipline themselves. Marxists objected to *svobodnoe vospitanie*'s failure to address the needs
of the future communist society and to its contempt for efforts to make children
into socialists. Attempts to stem the critical tide by moderating kindergarten
practice—celebrating revolutionary holidays or introducing literacy—could do
little to answer attacks grounded in a new vision of the nature of childhood and
of the role of children in the Soviet future.

By the third preschool congress in 1924, the department no longer couched
its aims in the rhetoric of free upbringing. The transfer of authority over
preschools to the newly created Administration of Social Upbringing and Poly-
technical Education (Glavsotsvos) in February 1921 perhaps anticipated the
new emphasis on discipline and didactic activities. The discussion at the congress revolved around the reorganization of the curricula of all schools undertaken by the State Academic Council (GUS), which before 1921 had authority
primarily over higher education.[7]

In many ways a product of the progressive, child-centered tradition in education that shaped the kindergarten, the new program received a warmer reception among preschool teachers than schoolteachers. The "complex" or project method utilized by the new approach drew on the work of American
progressive educator William Kilpatrick. Schoolteachers tended to reject such
innovations as an attack on the most fundamental elements of traditional pedagogy—discrete subjects and grades. By contrast, preschool teachers found
much that was familiar and looked for ways to adapt current practices to the
new program. Whether or not they were enthusiastic about the new dispensation, preschool teachers repackaged (or said they repackaged) familiar kindergarten activities as tools for raising socialists. Only in the kindergartens did the
new curriculum spark efforts to fit established practices into the "socialist"
program.[8]

What distinguished the new curriculum from Civil War programs was its essentially conservative view of revolution. The program valued not rebelliousness, liberation, or self-expression but stability, enlightenment, and state-build-
ing. The interests of the proletariat, argued the delegate who introduced the
GUS curriculum to the congress, were not served by *svobodnoe vospitanie*'s
"cult of personality."[9] Statements of the aims of preschool institutions became
encrusted in ideology, and declarations of the need to raise "hearty builders, the

creators of communist society," became commonplace.[10] The "socialist" curriculum took as its point of departure the future needs of the Soviet state.

The implementation of the centrally planned curriculum did not entail closing down kindergartens based on free upbringing or silencing advocates of *svobodnoe vospitanie*. But the stock phrases and images of free upbringing no longer shaped discussions of preschool education. Tikheeva found the limits of the new program's tolerance for progressive models when she suggested at the third congress that the new program had roots in the work of Froebel and Pestalozzi. Her effort to look for precedents was rejected on the grounds that Pestalozzi, Froebel, Montessori, and the rest had said absolutely nothing that applied to proletarian children.[11] A more generous delegate who had spent a year working in the United States conceded that although the Russians had much of a "technical-organizational" nature to learn from the Americans, lessons from U.S. schools had to be "recreate[d] in our Marxist spirit and in the spirit of the construction of a new form of social life."[12]

While the new program made many concessions to established practices, older professionals feared the implications of the emerging lack of tolerance for pedagogical eclecticism. Sventitskaia reminded her colleagues that the greater the number of systems practiced, the firmer the guarantee of progress in pedagogy.[13] Tikheeva, whose methods were ostensibly vindicated by the rejection of free upbringing, joined Sventitskaia in arguing that no pedagogical system could be written in stone; good teachers thrived only when allowed the "joy of being flexible." "There is not and can be no greater danger for the living work of education," she concluded, "than that one or another system be understood as the Creed, as the path that must be slavishly followed."[14] What teachers objected to was the injunction that all children follow the same "path" to a predetermined and unchanging destination. Although it paid obeisance to the importance of the child's present happiness, the "socialist" curriculum's main concern was its future. Such an emphasis seemed to open the door to purely tutelary, if not authoritarian, upbringing.

As a means of raising children in, to borrow Kollonati's phrase, "our spirit," the "socialist" curriculum provided teachers with a new blueprint for organizing the lives of children. The script provided by GUS altered the terms of discussion of preschool practice, retaining familiar activities, but endowing them with new meanings. The preschool remained a place of drawing, modeling, and building with blocks and sand, but such activities were incorporated into a fairly rigid framework that emphasized "socialist" values. The third preschool congress resolved that the basis of preschool work had to be a "connection with the present time [*sovremennost'*] and surrounding life [and] the development in the child of a materialist world-view and collective habits." Delegates received a detailed sketch of how the GUS "theme" for the autumn trimester—autumn—

might produce the desired results.[15] Activities fit into the three broad categories of "nature," "labor," and "society." In this way, the new curriculum introduced unprecedented structure into the life of the kindergarten and infused with explicitly "socialist" content activities that had never needed more justification than their appeal to preschoolers.

Narkompros's script for the "socialist" kindergarten called for children to have fun while being transformed into Soviet citizens. It recognized the need to engage children in age-appropriate activities, although some of the tasks it recommended seemed designed less for actual preschoolers than for the iconic children who embodied the future of the Revolution. Under the heading "nature," the curriculum prescribed work in the preschool garden, excursions in the *raion* and outside the city, the organization of a nature corner, and ongoing observations of the temperature and water level of the Moscow River—all familiar kindergarten occupations, although a bit more structured and teacher-directed than in the past. More novel was the suggestion that building snow statues of the leaders of the October Revolution constituted a "nature" activity, a label that apparently covered a combination of play, political education, and a scientific understanding of snow.

"Labor" included such utilitarian tasks as making necessary repairs in the kindergarten, helping to prepare vegetables, and shoveling snow, along with more creative pursuits such as having children keep journals of their impressions of winter or making decorations for the celebration of the October Revolution. Under "society" came directives to acquaint children with the problem of *besprizornost'*, to introduce them to the biographies of the leaders of the socialist movement, to have them meet with troops of young Pioneers, and to take them to visit a local factory. The program assumed children would enjoy such activities.

Where children showed little interest in the correct sorts of occupations, the new program required active teacher intervention. Instructions to teachers in the provinces mandated that they take a more active role in shaping the lives of their pupils. While free upbringing was not banned, teachers were warned that their kindergartens had to have a "systematic character" and a clearly articulated plan of work.[16] The teacher had to become an "active creator . . . guaranteeing the correct growth of the child."[17] The "socialist" curriculum put clear limits on the degree to which the current interests and desires of children shaped the program. It counted on teachers to find a way to interest kindergartners in what adults knew to be best for them.

A Day in the Kindergarten

Because both teachers and policymakers insisted that the new program required not the abandonment but the restructuring of current practices, the degree to which the new script affected the experiences of teachers and children is difficult to gauge. If the meanings ascribed to various activities changed, but the activities themselves remained more or less the same, would children or even teachers have noticed the difference? Did the translation of old practices into the language of the new curriculum occur only on paper, or did the translation itself somehow remake the day to day life of the kindergarten? Did a new tone and style in teachers' descriptions of their classrooms reflect or help to create a different mood and feeling in the classroom? Relying primarily on teachers' notebooks and reports, it is impossible to offer definitive answers.

Nonetheless, a narrative account of a day in the life of the kindergarten may be the best way to compare Civil War and NEP kindergartens and to visualize what the new conception of childhood may have meant for children. But if the narrative of the free kindergarten was tentative, that of the NEP kindergarten is perhaps even more so. While the constant refrain that pupils followed their individual inclinations could have been boilerplate, the 1924 GUS curriculum actually provided teachers with a clear and obvious model for their reportage. Still, it is possible to suggest the look and feel of efforts to implement the program, especially since many teachers (although of course not all) seem to have made a good faith effort to recast practice in the image of the new program. The question of how much things "really" changed must remain an open one.

For the children who reside at the kindergarten, the day begins at about seven, and the first activities are washing up, getting dressed, and making beds.[18] The work is overseen, at least in theory, by the children on the *san–komissiia*—the sanitary committee. By eight, the children adjourn to the activity room, where the members of the "living corner" committee feed the animals and water the plants. Another group of children might help to prepare the morning coffee, while the rest occupy themselves with free activities. The children on duty (*dezhurnye*) help to serve breakfast and to clean up afterwards. Breakfast consists of tea or coffee with milk or occasionally cocoa and bread with butter or, rarely, cheese.

After breakfast, the children work in the garden for a bit and then participate in organized activities "according to the plan" (*po planu*). The late morning hours might be set aside for games devised by the children themselves, a stroll, or, in nice weather, sun-bathing. Whatever the activity, children wash before lunch. Once again, the *dezhurnye* assist in the serving and cleaning up of the meal. Lunch is followed by an hour or in some cases a two-hour nap, ideally outside in the fresh air.

The late afternoon is taken up with walks or excursions, organized and free games, creative work, and conversations led by the teacher. The children might meet with a troop of Pioneers, observe the seasonal changes in the city, or visit a workshop or the vegetable market. The children have a snack of tea and bread with butter at about four. Preparations for dinner, including another round of hand-washing, begin between five thirty and six thirty. After dinner, the children get ready for bed; they wash up, brush their teeth, and undress themselves. They are in bed by eight.

At first glance, the contours of the kindergarten day appear to have changed only minimally. Not surprisingly, the activities designed to inculcate habits of cleanliness and orderliness—hand-washing, dressing oneself, and *dezhurstvo*—retain their featured roles. Time, albeit less than before, is set aside for "free" activities and games. Nonetheless, the overall mood seems to have shifted. The classroom is represented as a calmer, quieter place, as teachers take an active role in planning activities and opportunities for children to do as they please diminish. In the accounts from "socialist" kindergartens, there are no children gossiping in the corridor or devising loud and unruly games. A new emphasis on task-oriented committees replaces attention to grouping children by age and interest. The preschoolers' leisurely afternoon stroll is in many cases represented as a more purposeful excursion. Whether or not the children felt constrained by efforts to direct their attention to, say, the river's water level is impossible to tell. Teachers picture themselves as more often directing the conversation of their charges. And perhaps most significantly of all, the content of conversations as well as games and activities are suggested not by the children themselves or even by the teacher on the basis of "scientific" observation, but by the "plan."

The New Program from Above and Below

The new program's potential appeal was both pedagogical and political. The more structured approach of the new curriculum seems to have struck a chord with preschool teachers frustrated by the contradictory and nearly impossible role assigned to them by free upbringing. The GUS plan encouraged teachers to assert more control in the classroom. Making kindergartens "socialist" also offered a new revolutionary mission to kindergartens that had lost their status as institutional substitutes for the family. Preschool teachers gained authority not only within the kindergarten, where they assumed active leadership, but also beyond the classroom as they helped to lay the foundations for the "habits and emotions which guarantee the construction of the new communist life."[19]

Many kindergartens had moved toward a more teacher-directed approach well before the implementation of the GUS program, apparently on their own initiative. Teachers at an experimental-model *ochag* in Iaroslavl reported that they had embarked on their work with the "naive belief" that the children would discipline themselves and that the teachers would spend their time filling notebooks with careful observations. However, it soon became clear that discipline was necessary to the "development of freedom" in the child.[20] The "socialist" curriculum rested on precisely this understanding of the child's nature and needs.

The teachers at the Polonskii Kindergarten in Moscow reported coming to a similar realization. They found that their commitment to allowing children to follow their own interests succeeded only in creating a noisy, disorganized atmosphere. Moreover, the oldest children displayed serious gaps in their personal habits and lacked concentration and organization. Increased discipline and teacher involvement produced a "calm atmosphere in which groups did not bother one another—and in this way real freedom was achieved."[21] The new curriculum did much the same thing, presenting increased order and structure as the true route to revolutionary transformation.

The new task of "socialist" upbringing may also have made the impossibility of "socialized" upbringing easier to bear. In the mid-1920s, there continued to be a higher proportion of Bolsheviks in the preschools than in the primary and secondary schools, and this may help account for the willingness of many preschool teachers to embrace the new program. But party affiliation was not necessarily the most crucial factor. Teachers who had long imagined themselves as combating the superstition and poor hygiene of the home could find in the new emphasis on active teaching a call to intensify efforts to thwart the negative influence of parents. Such a program could have appealed not only to the 7.3 percent who were active in the Party or Komsomol, but also to any teacher committed to raising cultural levels.[22] One educator noted that "experience shows us that where there is a lack of other conditions that aid the development of collectivism in the child's personality, free development—the total non-intervention of the pedagogue"—succeeded only in giving children over to the damaging influences of the family and the streets.[23] She represented active teaching as both scientifically ("experience shows") and socially necessary, since children at home were portrayed as facing the same dangers as children on the street.

The reports of official visitors to Moscow children's homes and kindergartens in 1924 suggest that not all teachers embraced the new program. At the Tolstoi Kindergarten, authorities found that "contemporary life" was not incorporated into the children's art projects, although the kindergarten did build connections to the outside world through parent meetings and home visits. At the kindergarten on Largozhilov Street, *sovremennost'* was not very much in evidence, but the events of Lenin's death had attracted the pupils' attention. Not even that could be said of the Red Flower Kindergarten, where inspectors found no connections to contemporary life, no children's meetings, and little willing participation in work. Instead, the children listened to "mystical and fantastic" fairy tales.[24] Whether failure to implement the new curriculum was the result of willfulness or ignorance is difficult to gauge. What is clear is that teachers were being held to standards imposed from without.

Teachers' own reports from the field could mimic the GUS program almost word for word, a correspondence seemingly too good to be true. Rather than register any objection to the new program, teachers rescripted their accounts of life in the kindergarten. In Saratov, the spring curriculum revolved around the "Volga and changes in it in connection with the arrival of the spring-summer season"—a literal translation into local geography of the model program's observations of the Moscow River. In terms of nature study, "excursions and strolls along the Volga gave children the opportunity to follow the rise and fall of the water and variations in the water temperature." "Labor" consisted of collecting wood and fish at the river and holding a meeting, which teachers admitted did not go very well, in order to organize a committee to oversee the "living corner." The "social moment" of the program consisted of a meeting along the banks of the river with a troop of school-age young Pioneers with whom the preschoolers went swimming.[25] The only failure was the meeting, vital to the new program, but perhaps not particularly age-appropriate. However, the teachers did not use the difficulty of organizing children's committees as an argument against the new program or even suggest that in the future they would deviate from this portion of the script. The report can be understood both as a shrewd attempt to tell the center what it wanted to hear and as an indication of teachers' tolerance of, if not enthusiasm for, the "socialist" program.

A less transparent effort to recast familiar practices as revolutionary can be seen in the nearly one hundred pieces of student artwork sent to Narkompros from the Central Library Children's Home in Moscow.[26] The exemplars of pupils' work suggests a high degree of teacher involvement and a concerted effort to make it appear, at least, that the faculty brought *sovremennost'* into the kindergarten. The clearest evidence that the outside world penetrated the kindergarten was perhaps unintentional: The projects were all small in scale, on paper of about the quality of a brown paper sack. In making paper cut-outs, the children often used the pages of discarded books. Relatively few pictures made use of crayons, watercolors, colored pencils, or chalk. The drab cut-outs in brown, yellow, and red underlined more clearly than any catalog of shortages the poverty of the kindergartens. Regardless of what else changed, scarcity remained a constant in the experiences of Soviet children.

Despite the self-described "free" nature of the kindergarten, most of the drawings reflected a limited number of themes clearly connected to contemporary life, if not modern technology. Several pictures illustrated excursions to a factory and to the post office. Another series of drawings showed a train and a signalman. A handful of pictures was based on the rather prosaic folk tale "Repka." Of course children may have produced more fanciful images, but those that teachers chose to send to Narkompros drew their subjects from life and labor.

The existence of a number of extremely similar representations of a given theme suggests either teacher intervention or a tremendous amount of group work. The overall impression is that the kindergarten was interested not in developing each child's individual voice but in instilling appropriate values and understandings. All seven pictures of the train, for example, showed the train itself, the signalman, and, in all but one case, red and green flags. The one exception had red and orange flags; perhaps the child was too impatient to wait for the green pencil. Whether the teacher or the children themselves suggested the topic is unclear, but the similarity of the end products sent to the department evidences a desire to demonstrate that the kindergarten raised children in the correct spirit.

Even Sventitskaia, who never adopted the new curriculum's definition of the child as entirely malleable material, attempted to describe her kindergarten in the language of the GUS program. Her efforts to accommodate the official line demonstrated both the pervasiveness of the new formulations and, unwittingly, the gulf that separated her practices from the revolutionary curriculum. Under the heading "the appearance of *sovremennost'* in games, conversations, stories, and questions," Sventitskaia presented pupils aware of circumstances beyond the kindergarten but often lacking in the "correct" understandings of the world around them. One six-year-old declared his intention to become a *militsioner* like his uncle, who "lives well; every day he has white bread and apples." Another bragged that his father had become rich; "he is a commissar, and he has flour, salt, and sugar." A group of six- and seven-year-olds with a cart full of various objects informed their teacher that they intended to sell everything at the market. Asked what they would do then, they replied, "We are going abroad. It is impossible to live here."

Teachers at Sventitskaia's kindergarten apparently limited themselves to recording, not correcting, such attitudes. In some cases, parents seemed to do a better job of inculcating revolutionary ideals than the kindergarten did. One child related that she had no favorite fairy tales because her father and mother were communists and did not tell any.[27] From the point of view of the new curriculum, the life of Sventitskaia's kindergarten could not be considered ideal. Yet even here, the new categories structured the discussion. Teachers, if not pupils, viewed the kindergarten experience differently.

Proletarian Science

Free upbringing had dictated that teachers move from scientific study of children to the construction of an environment that met their observed needs and interests. The new program ostensibly reversed the sequence of events; the center devised a "socialist" curriculum, and teachers observed how it worked in practice. Still, the framers of the new curriculum—Shatskii, Krupskaia, Blonskii, and Viktor Shulgin—insisted that it too grew out of the study of preschool children, or, more specifically, proletarian preschoolers. The science of pedology, a study of children that combined social psychology and pedagogy, was built on the assumption that under revolutionary conditions children could be fundamentally remade.[28]

The emphasis of research shifted from uncovering the obscure signs that marked the child from birth to delineating its response to the social environment. The new science emphasized the formative importance of children's interactions with each other and of the conditions of their lives at home. Studies of the child's neighborhood, street, apartment, and family gained new prestige. However, reports tended to omit detailed descriptions of the methods used in interviews with parents or home visits. Data on the child's home life were apparently collected much as they always had been.[29] What changed was the relative weight assigned to such research.

Observations within the classroom were supposed to become more structured. The idea was not simply to describe children's activities but to come to an understanding of how pupils interacted.[30] The system devised by psychologist S. S. Molozhavyi directed teachers to the right sort of observations through the use of a series of rigid categories. In line with the GUS program of nature, labor, and society, the Molozhavyi method required teachers to tease out the "social," "industrial," and "everyday" reactions of the pupils to their work. The categories were designed, according to Molozhavyi, to focus the teacher's attention on the influence of "surrounding circumstances" on the child's development.[31] The results looked more uniform and scientific than earlier research. Records of teachers' observations took on a more quantitative appearance as graphs and tables replaced or supplemented anecdotal journals. A mere five-minute-long activity might generate detailed descriptions of the work performed as well as a folio-size graph charting teachers' observations.

Child study of this type became an important feature of many experimental-model kindergartens. At least Kindergartens No. 11 and No. 2 in Saratov seem to have taken their scientific mission quite seriously. Teachers filled numerous notebooks with cramped handwriting, detailing the processes of "children's labor" in particular. The kindergartens also collected data from parents and conducted research into children's relationship with nature. Both kindergartens in Saratov adopted the "Molozhavyi method" or some variant of it.[32] That teachers ultimately scaled down their research because it interfered with pedagogical work suggests the painstaking detail of their observations and reports.[33]

The compact, densely annotated teachers' notebooks from Saratov teem with life even as they illustrate the process by which teachers squeezed experience into tight, and seemingly poorly understood, categories. The notes capture children playing, talking, and working. They are full of small, sometimes moving, pictures of childhood in a period of great upheaval. We learn that "Verochka V. is well acquainted with the fact that her mother threw her father out, with the judicial process that her parents went through, and with how hard things are for her grandmother, ..ho is raising her without the parents' help." Her story is included as a means or demonstrating the children's "orientation toward the new way of life [novyi byt]," a key goal of the GUS program.[34] Only those episodes teachers deemed relevant to the socialist curriculum were detailed, and all of the observations were self-consciously, if often rather confusingly, structured. Here the lives of children and the visions of teachers are inextricably intertwined.

Each entry began with a short note regarding what the children had been doing before the observed activity began, who suggested the activity, and the overall physical environment in which the activity was conducted. Teachers recorded without comment their observations that, for example, before sitting down to work with clay, the boys had been busy building ships out of furniture and the girls had been playing house. An activity might be suggested by the teacher (when she saw that the children had lost interest in their pursuits) or by the children themselves. That the children had colored pencils for drawing might also be viewed as worth mentioning in this opening section.[35]

In the remainder of the report, teachers described the activity itself in terms of manifestations of the children's labor and social habits, their understandings of everyday life, and their relative levels of physical and mental development. Because the very structure of the report established the existence of social, labor, and everyday "moments" in children's activities, the "observations" often do more to illuminate educators' assumptions than the experiences of children. Teachers did not have to prove that the categories made sense, and the title of each column did not necessarily constitute an accurate reflection of its content. No research challenged the notion that labor, nature, and society provided the correct basis of the kindergarten curriculum. The research program was built on the assumption that the new curriculum might have to be refined, but that it was the only truly "socialist" and "scientific" approach to children.

By filling out reports in often minute detail, the teacher made labor along with the interplay of the individual and the collective central aspects of kindergarten "reality." The sections of the reports on the "children's social [sotsial'nye] reactions" noted "collective moments" in the process of drawing: With one exception, the children willingly showed one another their work, and they discussed the content of their pictures. "Individual" moments included instances of children hiding the prized colored pencils in their fists as well as cases of polite sharing. Illustrations of each "moment" were quite specific. The teacher noted that Tamara informed a fellow pupil proffering advice that she did not want to make the hills yellow, but white; Vova, Tania, and Lelia were particularly good about relinquishing their pencils.[36] Why conversation constituted a "collective" moment while hoarding or sharing pencils was defined as an "individual" moment is not explained. The details of life in the kindergarten did not so much illustrate as concretize and legitimize abstract qualities.

Similarly, children's labor was conjured out of a rather mixed bag of details. The section on labor could contain a wide variety of unrelated observations. Teachers seemed to have no clear idea about exactly what constituted "productive reactions." Under this heading, one teacher noted that the drawings contained many "technical moments (a ship, a boat, a train)." The same report explained that the pencils were quite fragile, and, although the children were careful, at the end of the activity, of eleven pencils (for sixteen children) only the infrequently used yellow, brown, and black remained intact; the gray one had arrived broken. The teacher further observed under the same rubric that most of the children drew right-handed, that two drew with both hands, and that one recent arrival, three-and-a-half-year-old Vitia, held the pencil almost in his fist. None of the children were able to sharpen their own pencils, and they asked the teacher for assistance.[37]

Less descriptive approaches to filling out the "productive labor" category were also possible. The important thing was the act of somehow connecting the children's activities to the category of "labor." One account of "productive-labor habits" noted simply that the students displayed interest in "labor processes" and in the results of their work. A report with ambitions of quantitative accuracy listed the tools used by the students and graphed the "productive-labor tendency" of the observed exercise as rising over the course of seven minutes from "2" to "2 1/2." I have been unable to determine exactly what the scale of 0 to 5 was intended to measure or to locate the source of this approach.[38] That all reports contained some "scientific" examination of "productive labor" seemed to matter more than the actual content of the category.

"Everyday reactions" (bytovye reaktsii) proved an equally nebulous subject. Under this rubric one report included both the observation that the children had refused to straighten up the furniture before sitting down to draw and that children's drawings contained many scenes of life at home and on the street. Another report simply noted that no one except the teacher and the students were present during the activity and went on to describe how the children took turns on duty in the dining room, a fact with no relevance to the activity at hand.[39]

The sections more loosely connected to the ideology of the new curriculum, those detailing the "complexity and organization" and "liveliness and stability" of the children's activities, contain less varied, often formulaic observations. Teachers might note that pupils completed their task, or simply that it developed the senses of hearing and sight.[40] A more descriptive report outlined the themes of the children's drawings and the relative realism of their images ("Zina drew a girl with a red face") and noted that the children had been so absorbed in their drawing that they managed to ignore a toy revolver for an entire half hour.[41]

Conspicuously absent from teachers' accounts of the lives of children in the kindergarten are the categories associated with free upbringing, and, more broadly, a clear sense of childhood as distinguished by anything save its malleability. The notions of "social instincts" and "innate capacities" have been banished from the kindergarten. Activities that occur in the interstices between episodes of "productive labor" are sometimes noted, but they are granted no formative influence on the child and therefore have no analytical significance for the teachers. The accounts provide no pictures of "chaotic moments" and display no wariness about quiet in the kindergarten. There is little sense of childish fantasy in the reports and few instances in which teachers transcribed the interests or desires of the children themselves. Instead, the investigators concentrated on physical description as a means of giving body to the abstract qualities they assumed must be present in the child's world. The emphasis on labor and the new way of life makes the children seem like miniature adults, moving toward "correct" understandings and habits. There was no room in the researchers' rigid columns for childish mischief.

Science and Classroom Practice

Curricular changes that allegedly grew out of scientific research usually had less to do with new data than new analytical assumptions. Calls to reassess the appropriateness of telling fairy tales or giving girls dolls invariably made reference to the latest research. But in most cases, current findings did not point to the sorts of changes advocated by proponents of the revolutionary curriculum. "Science" continued to indicate that preschoolers enjoyed fairy tales and that girls liked dolls. However, the assumptions of "Marxist" child study made it possible to draw new conclusions from old observations. Just as the Saratov research shoehorned observations of children's behavior into predetermined categories, "research" on fairy tales and gender roles managed the data to fit the desired conclusion.

The new curriculum's concern that the life of the kindergarten reflect the "new way of life" made telling fairy tales increasingly suspect. Early concerns about *skazki* had revolved around whether listening to stories constituted an inordinately passive and structured activity. But fairy tales had been tolerated because researchers had concluded that children loved them. At the third preschool congress in 1924, opposition to filling children's heads with magic and fantasy became louder. Research still pointed to the conclusion that children loved *skazki*, but new assumptions diminished the importance of this finding. As R. Prushitskaia, the delegate who introduced the GUS program, noted, "Children also love the circus, but it is no substitute for natural interests."[42] In the mid-1930s, when the "socialist" strictures against childhood fantasy were finally abandoned, Kornei Chukovskii, a well-known literary critic and author of children's stories, recounted the turn against fairy tales with biting sarcasm, portraying as "gravediggers or professional mourners" the "overpersuasive specialists," who in their overzealous quest to raise rational people were blind to the simple truth that the technological progress they hoped to facilitate required "the most uninhibited fantasy and imagination."[43]

As a "scientific" substitute for fairy tales, teachers proposed realistic stories. Prushitskaia suggested that since "fantasy has its roots in real events," new *skazki* ought to revolve around the "wonders of technology, the achievement of the radio." She did not mention the source of her assertion regarding the nature of children's imaginations. As an example of how modern life could become the basis of a new children's literature, she pointed to an American collection focusing on the "sounds, rhythm, and dynamics of New York." A "scientific" study of the fairy tale suggested how stories might focus not only on modern technology but also on specifically Soviet themes. One delegate, adopting the formalist distinction between form and content, argued that, if it obeyed the formal rules of fairy-tale construction, a story about a visit to the Lenin Mausoleum could be a *skazka*. A story based on "contemporary facts" qualified as a fairy tale as long as it "dressed real acts in fantasy" and included "the unexpected, exaggerations, and generalizations."[44] In either case, fantasy had to be tempered with material or political "realities."

A survey of Leningrad kindergartens found that 55.4 percent of stories told in them were "realistic," a frequency that suggests that modern *skazki* may have appealed to children. However, researchers did not note children's reactions to such stories.[45] Attacking the banishment of fantasy, Chukovskii argued that the usual dry fair failed to engage pupils. He cited as evidence the overwhelming enthusiasm with which a group of nine-year-olds responded to *Baron von Munchausen*. But whether or not children liked the new stories was essentially beside the point. If one accepted the assumption that the best fantasies — or the only legitimate ones — were those that grew out of real life, then *skazki* about radio or the Lenin Mausoleum made scientific sense.

Proletarian science also called into question the conventional wisdom that all gender differences noted in the classroom could be ascribed to natural "instincts." Here again the argument did not rely so much on new observations as on a "Marxist" reading of old data. The notion that girls' love of dolls or boys' fascination with guns grew out of biological differences had fit smoothly into the theoretical framework of *svobodnoe vospitanie*, with its emphasis on children's innate talents and inclinations.[46] By contrast, the hope that the Revolution would fundamentally remake social relationships had led Krupskaia to emphasize the cultural construction of gender roles long before October 1917.

"Marxist" child study privileged the child's "social circumstances" and rejected the notion of fixed and natural gender roles. At the third congress of preschool education, Prushitskaia noted with regret that even in the best institutions, teachers tended to accept a sexual division of labor that "had its roots in the remote past." But, she insisted, it was not instinct that led the girls to cook for the boys at Pioneer camps; "there is no doubt that the conditions of upbringing create the difference in interests between boys and girls." In the realm of gender roles as in labor, the new curriculum assigned teachers the task of directing children along the "correct path" as early as possible.[47] Prushitskaia did not need new "data" to back up her claim that gender roles were culturally determined. The conclusion flowed smoothly from the "Marxist" assumption that the existence of gender differences was a social, not a biological, phenomenon.

In part because teachers continued to understand gender differences as natural and in part because the new curriculum accorded sexual equality secondary importance, the "Marxist" approach to gender seems to have had little impact in the classroom. When observers in Narkompros's experimental kindergartens noted differences between boys and girls, they continued to represent them as predictable and trivial. That boys used furniture to build boats or factories while the girls used it to play house or hospital warranted no more than a casual comment.[48] Responding to questions about what they wanted to be when they grew up, a group of seven-year-old boys expressed interest in joining the Red Army, inventing machines, and becoming factory engineers. By contrast, the girls dreamed of becoming teachers and artists. But the differences mattered little because "all wanted to be Pioneers when they went to school and communists when they got older." Similarly, it was not necessary to attempt to alter the girls' preference for playing "mother and daughter" and the boys' for "at the barricades" and "the war of the Whites and the Reds" as long as all "willingly participate in the same kinds of labor."[49]

The new curriculum uncoupled the task of raising new Soviet people from the notion of emancipating women from traditional stereotypes. As long as boys and girls alike could become communists, other inequalities seemed to matter little. Reports from teachers seemed to assume that while it was possible to train both boys and girls to be communists, "natural" gender differences could not—or need not—be effaced. Most policymakers, most of whom were women, valued the goal of raising the future of Soviet Russia over the task of inculcating a "consciousness of equality" between the sexes.[50] One teacher reported that when her students got into a debate over whether boys or girls were better, a boy had tried to settle the argument with the statement that "Lenin was a boy." At that point, the teacher joined the discussion and reminded the children that "in order to be good, it is not enough to be a boy like Lenin"; one had to love and work for the people as he did.[51]

Work and Play

The process of adjusting to the new script is clearly visible in efforts to reconcile existing practice with the "socialist" insistence that the life of the preschool child revolve around work rather than play. Every system that had vied for recognition in the early years of the Preschool Department's existence had been based on the "scientific" conclusion that play facilitated both the intellectual and physical development of preschool children. The GUS triad of "labor, nature, and society" signaled a shift in emphasis. Unwilling to abandon the emphasis on play, senior members of the preschool teaching community found new justifications for old practices. Eager to retain the support of teachers, advocates of the GUS program downplayed the practical significance of the accent on labor. Children, it seems, were exposed to a wide range of schemes to make work fun. The preschool may have become a less playful, but no less joyful place.

For teachers committed to progressive methods, any effort to coerce or even cajole children into doing work that did not interest them was anathema. Tikheeva spoke for many teachers trained before the Revolution when she maintained that play—defined as any activity that did not "carry the character of a responsibility" or direct itself to some practical end—was the "fundamental element" of preschool education. According to Tikheeva, utilitarian tasks had no place in the kindergarten. She condemned the new curriculum's suggestion that kindergartners make field trips to factories as completely inappropriate to the age and as the "crudest pedagogical mistake."[52] Sventitskaia concurred, warning that a visit to a candy factory had succeeded only in frustrating the children, who could not afford the goodies they saw being produced.[53]

However, labor was acceptable where it was freely chosen and truly interesting to the children themselves, where it was, in other words, largely indistinguishable from play. On this basis, even free kindergartens had long included labor in the form of dezhurstvo and self-service. Sventitskaia approved of labor as long as it had a "natural character," and her kindergarten included many types of chores. Children hung up their own coats, put away their toys, and helped the younger pupils get dressed. Scientific observation led her to define truly interesting work quite narrowly. Preschoolers liked to make toys and other necessary items, to build snow hills in the winter, and to collect berries and mushrooms in the summer. Beyond such activities, Sventitskaia concluded, work became an intolerable burden.[54]

Such attitudes were too deeply ingrained to be ignored by advocates of the new program, who worked to expand the repertoire of appealing labor activities by effacing the gap between work and play. The new program conserved familiar child-centered activities by fitting them with appropriately forward-looking justifications and represented its most teacher-directed activities as appealing to preschoolers. The newly organized toy museum in Moscow invited children not to play with the collection but to build their own toys.[55] Children "worked" with building blocks, developing not so much creativity as respect for labor and the habit of working collectively. Art projects and games lost their status as play and became tools for connecting children to the world around them.[56]

The new program represented the required field trips as responding to the children's interest in technology and nature, and therefore fully compatible with child-centered pedagogy. Strolls in the forest became more "systematic" as teachers taught their charges the names of various flowers, but were counted no less enjoyable for the dose of didacticism.[57] Prushitskaia suggested that preschoolers would easily relate to small enterprises like a candy factory, a factory manufacturing school materials, or a blacksmith's shop. She also recommended trips to the post office.

A teacher at the congress reported that her pupils did indeed love to see machines in action and, more importantly, that they brought valuable impressions home from their field trips. She related that an excursion to a local factory prompted the children to incorporate the factory whistle and increased discipline into their games. Attributing an astonishing level of understanding to the preschoolers, she went so far as to suggest that the visit had given rise to a spontaneous and spirited debate over the issue of equal pay. With perhaps more attention to following the script than to descriptive accuracy, the teacher recounted how children *on their own* juxtaposed the knowledge that their mothers earned less than their fathers with the fact that they had observed no real difference in men's and women's work at the factory.[58]

Sventitskaia's account of unhappy kindergartners at the candy factory rings truer; it seems to better reflect the psychological and intellectual development of preschoolers. Yet if one accepts the terms of the "socialist" script for life in the kindergarten, the impromptu advocacy of equal pay for equal work becomes necessary and even believable. The new program co-opted progressive rhetoric by defining efforts to raise socialists as inherently age-appropriate. Labor and the wide world became the topics most interesting to children.

In the GUS program, play became simply one species of work, no more valuable or engaging than any other. Delegates speaking in favor of the new program at the third congress emphasized that, contrary to what the slogan "labor, nature, society" might suggest, play remained central to the life of the kindergarten.

The absence of the term "play" simply reflected the fact that "it is impossible to make a sharp distinction between play and labor." Introducing the GUS program, Prushitskaia argued that characterizing work as a "means to the achievement of a defined aim" and play as an "end in itself" made little practical sense. She asked her audience to consider whether children who decided to sew clothes for their dolls were working or playing. She dismissed the work–play dichotomy as a capitalist atavism.[59]

The same blurring of the line between work and play that had allowed proponents of free upbringing to reconcile labor with the principle of free choice now made it possible for supporters of the "socialist" curriculum to contend that a kindergarten organized around labor remained responsive to the needs of preschool children. No doubt, as Prushitskaia noted, there exists no bright line between work and play. But by equating work and play, the new curriculum went further and suggested that children were as eager to perform their chores as to participate in more conventionally playful activities. Kindergarten No. 2 in Saratov reported that pupils participated in two kinds of labor: "self-service" [*samoobsluzhivanie*] and creative work. The former included hand-washing, straightening up the classroom, assisting younger children, watering plants in the "living corner," and helping the teacher decorate the room. Creative work involved building with blocks, playing with sand, modeling with clay, and drawing. Clearly work could shade into play, as in decorating the room, but nowhere was it suggested that children might find some types of work more appealing than others.[60]

In any event, the new program did not rule out work that children did not consider play. Instead, it took as its central task training children to enjoy labor. After her question about sewing doll clothes, Prushitskaia went on to describe how teachers could get children to feel "that work is not imposed from without by adults." She suggested a gradual approach, whereby three-year-olds began with the simple tasks of buttoning each other up or making beds. Four- and five-year-olds might be required to set the table or water the plants. Then the oldest pupils (ages six to seven) would be ready for the transition to "socially useful labor": assisting with the housework, caring for the animals in the "living corner," and helping peasants in the summer. Another delegate recommended a more ideologically charged approach that subordinated the child's desires to the inculcation of "socialist" values and habits. She recounted that a boy who always tried to get someone else to make his bed changed his ways after his teacher reminded him that "in the past, only the bourgeoisie forced others to work for them."[61]

The new importance of labor in the kindergarten was reflected in accounts of classroom practice that wasted little time on descriptions of play. One report reduced its record of children's play to the observation that the pupils were fascinated with construction materials. A chronicle of the program of the Working Moscow Children's Home ignored creative work entirely. Instead, it stressed that all children participated in housekeeping and noted that the key to the materials cupboard was held by the child on duty.[62] Activities at the Karl Liebknecht Children's Home included housework, self-service, hand-work, and visits to a power station and a mill to observe adult labor.[63]

Where teachers described play, they cast it as a manifestation of the kindergarten's efforts to bring contemporary life and labor into the classroom. A report from model-experimental Kindergarten No. 2 in Saratov noted that games reflected the "social orientation of the group." The children themselves reportedly organized games of "barricades," "the First of May," "at the Lenin Mausoleum," and "how the workers used to live." Civil War games apparently did not last very long as no one wanted to be a White.[64] Less worldly peasant children played "wedding," "requiem," and "making home brew," but, noted their teacher proudly, by the end of the summer the whole village "was singing our songs."[65] In the "socialist" kindergarten, play was valued as a means of connecting children with contemporary life and labor. In this way, the progressive injunction to put the child's interests first was ostensibly observed while the most child-centered of activities—free play—became a powerful tool in the work of raising socialists.

Political Education

At the heart of the new program stood the conviction that socialists were not born, but made. Here "socialist" upbringing's rejection of the liberationist vision of revolutionary transformation becomes unmistakable, if not yet categorical. The new understanding of children as endlessly plastic made direct political training both possible and necessary. Although cast in the language of child-centered education, the directive to teach even the youngest children about the Revolution and its leaders represented the most potentially constraining aspect of the new program and its most striking departure from progressive the models it claimed to—and often did—respect.

Such indoctrination became particularly urgent in the wake of Lenin's death in January 1924. His death, or more specifically fears of what his death might mean for the future of the Soviet state, spurred, according to Nina Tumarkin, a "massive campaign . . . to launch a cult of his memory" in order to "ensure political stability, inspiring in the populace loyalty in the regime that would continue to rule Russia in Lenin's name."[66] Since no segment of the population was as crucial to the long-term future of the Soviet state, or as impressionable, as its children, the Preschool Department worked to ensure that future socialists had

Figure 2   "We are young Leninists" 1924

at least a rudimentary knowledge of the life and work of the founder of the communist state. A March circular directed to all *guberniia* and *uezd* departments of education contended that in order to raise "fighters for communist ideals," all schools had to introduce children to the "personality of comrade Lenin." In the kindergarten, such work could take the form of a "Lenin corner" or a "Lenin morning" organized in conjunction with nearby institutions.[67] Teachers responded with requests for stories about Lenin for preschoolers who knew him only as a "good uncle" and not as a leader.[68]

Children's reported reactions to the shock of "Uncle Lenin's" death provided Narkompros with a convenient measure of the degree to which "contemporary life" penetrated kindergartens and with a means of justifying in the language of progressive education the newly articulated call to bring political events into the classroom. Prushitskaia, who introduced the GUS program at the third congress, noted that children in Leningrad had taken part in a whole series of activities revolving around Lenin's death. Apparently with their teacher's guidance, they made albums of the events of the days of mourning and built a mausoleum and a monument to Lenin out of blocks. She concluded that such activities demonstrated that "children's interests go far beyond the limits of their family life and their institution" to embrace the whole of contemporary life.[69]

Teachers no doubt hoped that glowing reports of their pupils' political consciousness would be read as proof that they were doing a good job of implementing the new curriculum. And if preschool policymakers chose to take such reports at face value, they gained evidence that political events touched and engaged children in just the way that their directives had predicted. Teachers at the Klara Zetkin Children's Home in Moscow proudly asserted that their charges knew to hate the bourgeoisie and love the workers, without elaborating on what sorts of meanings these concepts had for kindergartners. What was important was that pupils eagerly awaited a visit from "grandmother Klara," loved Lenin, and respected Trotsky. Upon learning that Lenin was very sick and would probably die, one four-year-old girl reportedly asked, "What will become of us now? If Lenin dies, who will show us how to drive out the German bourgeoisie?" When the news of Lenin's death arrived, the children reportedly asked to play sad music and to visit him lying in state. Because of the cold weather, teachers took only the oldest children, who did not, they assured the center, allow the frailty of the man they saw to destroy their image of him as "some kind of uncommon hero, a myth." Upon returning home, the literate children spent the remainder of the day writing "Lenin, Il'ich, Il'ich, Lenin," and the others talked only about Lenin. The teachers pictured the children as appropriately inconsolable.

Besides stories and activities revolving around Lenin, the Revolution entered the kindergarten mainly through the celebration of socialist holidays. Joyful celebrations, particularly of May Day, were supposed to create occasions for making political education fun. It was hoped that Revolutionary holidays would not only replace religious festivals but also make a deep and meaningful impression on the rising generation. Since everything in the kindergarten had to be "imbued with the spirit of solidarity and collectivism," the "Christmas-tree tradition" that nostalgic teachers dragged into the "contemporary child's world" had to be abandoned. Interesting children in the Revolution's holidays was viewed as the first step in the process of turning them into "future fighters for communism."[70] The new curriculum aimed to make November 7 and May 1, rather than Christmas and Easter, the most anticipated dates on the preschool calendar.

Prior to the implementation of the GUS curriculum, a Christmas tree (*elka*) holiday was often the highlight of the kindergarten year. Parents' preferences and contributions played a key role in maintaining this tradition. At the Krasnovo-Malokhovskii kindergarten, children celebrated a number of holidays, but the "fullest and most successful" was the January 28 Christmas tree party. With the help of parents, the kindergarten provided each child with cookies, *pirozhki*, candy, and a new doll. By contrast, the First of May was commemorated with a "modest celebration"—a large lunch and sweets. Another group at the same kindergarten celebrated the October Revolution with games, dramatizations, songs, and a tastier-than-usual lunch. But the section of the teachers' report on "children's holidays" devoted most of its attention to the late December Christmas party, which "thanks to close ties to the parents and the material means supplied by them" was better than in previous years. A third group's celebration of the October Revolution ended up being quite modest due to its teacher's illness. Rain cut short their May Day celebration. The biggest, best celebrations of the year came at Christmas and at a "spring holiday" in late May. At a model-experimental *ochag* in Iaroslavl, kindergartners celebrated Christmas, Easter, and the "day of the International," apparently on equal terms.[71] Socialist holidays did not dominate the ritual life of the kindergarten.

Where kindergartens had declined to celebrate Christmas, the decision often had less to do with politics than pedagogy. Organizing a party implied some, perhaps too much, interference in the lives of the children and was the source of a great deal of Christmas-time angst for teachers at the Third International Children's Home. Before 1924, teachers designed and abandoned a whole series of celebrations. One year, the children began making decorations for the tree in October. Sventitskaia worried that the task took on the character of a "responsibility," in a negative, constraining sense, and limited the scope of free activity. The following year, the children decorated the tree on Christmas Eve. The holiday proved unduly chaotic. Sitting the children around the tree to sing Christmas carols was also discarded in an effort to allow for greater "freedom" and "direct expression."

Only a nearly aimless holiday seemed to satisfy the requirements of free upbringing. After changing the holiday every year and engaging in much debate, the teachers finally arrived at a workable solution. The new "winter holiday" retained the Christmas tree "as a symbol of trees that did not lose their leaves and of winter" and because the children were accustomed to it. The traditional chorus was abandoned. The children simply entered the room where the tree was set up and were left to sing and play games as they wished. This provided, Sventitskaia noted, an interesting moment for observation. In this way, teachers dedicated to free upbringing reduced Christmas to an occasion for children to run and jump around the room because such activity allowed them to feel "at ease and cheerful."[72]

Emptying the Christmas holiday of any religious content made it less politically inappropriate but also less useful as a pedagogical model for the "socialist" kindergarten. By 1924, the introduction of the GUS curriculum prompted Sventitskaia to recognize that a "socialist" kindergarten had to combat the religious ideals children picked up at home. On the basis of her scientific observations, she concluded that "children have no innate religious feeling." In this sphere, if nowhere else, she viewed the child as a truly blank slate. While Sventitskaia may have considered the "winter holiday" stripped of religious symbols sufficiently revolutionary, the logic behind the "free" holiday seemed to rule out the organization of socialist celebrations.

Far from advocating a formless celebration, the GUS program represented socialist holidays as both didactic and fun, very much like the religious festivals they were designed to replace. May Day, more than the commemoration of the October Revolution, was touted as the quintessential children's holiday. One article on planning First of May activities informed teachers that "children must love this holiday above all others and await it with impatience." Rather than culminating in a dry, uninvolving spectacle or in the passive watching of a parade, the day was supposed to be spent playing a well-orchestrated game that gave concrete form to the slogan "Workers of the world, unite." At the same time, teachers had to explain the significance of May Day, to "raise in the children consciousness of the international solidarity of the working class." Teachers were instructed to tell stories about the "life and childhood of the leaders of the working class." Organizers assumed that such lessons would not interfere with the "creative and vivid joy" of the holiday, but teachers had no choice but to include them.[73]

The ideal May Day celebration at once transformed kindergartners and allowed them to transform themselves into "small proletarians at the bench." As early as March, the teacher had to begin introducing six- and seven-year-olds to "accounts of how the workers are the masters of life; that they must take first place everywhere in the world; that when they realize that, there will be no more hunger and everyone will work well and gladly." Once children became familiar with the different forms of labor, through art projects and playing with dolls, each group chose a specific job for itself. The kindergarten was filled with chimney sweeps, blacksmiths, sailors, miners, and bakers (but not peasants) each busily setting up shop in the weeks before the holiday. By May 1, the kindergarten might contain a large oven, a mine shaft, and a forge. On the day of the holiday, teachers hung new portraits of "proletarian leaders," and pupils dressed in costume to work at their shops, "feeling themselves to be . . . small workers—the future masters of life." Somewhat incongruously, a "vital" visit by young Pioneers would show the kindergartners "their future leaders, whose bidding they must follow." The transformation was planned by teachers but was not, on that account, superficial or coerced. Children were supposed to experience themselves as workers.[74]

Whether such elaborate holidays actually came off is difficult to say. Reports from kindergartens usually offer only the barest sketches of their celebrations. Often teachers deployed the formulas of progressive education as the explanation of modest celebrations. In an account of "social-political upbringing" at the Third International Children's Town, the institution's director did not mention any preschool celebration of May Day. He related only that the children reacted strongly to Lenin's death and that on International Women Workers' Day, the boys "volunteered" to do all of the girls' chores. The problem was that "of course, with preschoolers it is impossible to carry out political work in the narrow sense of the word." Children could take part in revolutionary holidays, but they were not "organically connected" to them. The same concerns seem to have been behind the decision at a Saratov kindergarten to celebrate the October Revolution with songs and a show rather than by following directives to put together a wall newspaper and a "red corner" with the children's artwork on themes related to the Revolution.[75] In some cases, teachers trained by the older generation of experts may have been simply unprepared to undertake political education; lectures on socialist history became prominent features of teacher "retraining" courses in 1924.[76] The "socialist" curriculum may not have accomplished much more in the realm of holidays than meeting its minimum goal of rooting out Christmas trees.

The Children's Collective

The conception of children as shaped by outside pressure rather than innate interests implied a new vision of revolutionary transformation. A child who needed to be taught to live and work collectively could not be expected to transform his or her world without substantial guidance. Still pictured as revolutionary, the younger generation was increasingly seen as dependent on its revolutionary elders. The emergence of a model children's community (*obshchina*) had been a goal of free upbringing, but whereas the process of building a community in the free classroom was represented as organic, instinctual, and a bit messy, the procedure prescribed by the GUS curriculum was orderly, rational, even bureaucratic. The concept of "*obshchina*," with its connotations of the ancient Russian peasant commune and Populism, was a long way from the Latin-rooted, technical-sounding "*detkollektiv*" (an abbreviation of *detskii kollektiv*, children's collective). The self-consciously "socialist" GUS program replaced the image of the spontaneous emergence of self-directed communes that functioned as a "big happy family" with the *detkollektiv*'s committee work overseen by adults.

The new curriculum's insistence on student self-government at all levels may have been strictly for show. Certainly it meant little in the schools, where teachers committed to traditional methods usually viewed student representatives as, at best, an extension of their own disciplinary power.[77] In the kindergarten, self-government was largely unworkable, since it was unlikely that even the oldest preschoolers would be able to allocate tasks or enforce discipline. The rhetoric of self-government becomes more significant when it is read not as a insincere window dressing but as a means of accustoming children to highly structured work. This aspect of calls for student meetings and commissions is especially clear in the field of preschool education, where teachers harbored few illusions about the ability of kindergartners to run their own institutions, but advocated "self-government" anyway.

The general consensus among preschool teachers was that the impetus for organizing the collective had to come from teachers, but that once children were given specific responsibilities, they usually understood them and took them seriously. Typically, kindergarten teachers added to organized *dezhurstvo* in the dining room longer-term commissions of two to six children responsible for "housekeeping," "sanitation," and caring for the plants and animals in the "living corner." Commission members might go marketing with an adult; check to see that hands, faces, and ears were clean; or water the plants.[78] None of this necessarily came naturally or easily to the children. However, Prushitskaia, the delegate who introduced the GUS program at the congress, noted that once children received their assignments, "refusal to participate in commissions is rarely observed."[79] That pupils picked up the language of the kindergarten bureaucracy was held up as proof that they had become "conscious of the expediency of these groups": "Kostia has dirty feet, but the sanitary commission is not watching! Where is the commission?"[80] Such "successes" suggest that the purpose of so-called self-government was to impress upon children the importance of discipline and order.

The entire program relied on the image of the child as pliable. Presenting the GUS program at the congress, Prushitskaia conceded that for the "little ones . . . the rudiments of self-government have no direct meaning, but," she argued, "the whole atmosphere of an institution established on the principle of children's participation in its construction, has great educational significance for them." Anticipating the objections of advocates of free upbringing, she added that even the youngest children take an interest in general meetings that touched on issues "close to them," like their participation in a holiday. However, the fundamental justification for including kindergartners in a process that they barely understood and had little interest in was that "for us, the child is no longer just a child but also a future person." Prushitskaia maintained that the refrain "return childhood to childhood" had to be discarded when one realized that "there is a threshold of entry into more mature childhood, into youth, and into life."[81] A rather precocious kindergartner in Saratov reportedly expressed similar sentiments, warning a comrade who wanted to play with a ball instead of working that "if we don't learn to work now, we won't know how to work when we grow up."[82] The *detkollektiv* did not indulge the child's immediate interests; it shaped children to fit the future.

The normative narrative of the child's adjustment to the kindergarten changed dramatically, as the new curriculum directed teachers to keep the initial chaos to a minimum. The first step in the process of building the kindergarten community might include giving the children "materials for general and collective use, primarily large building materials (blocks and other wooden forms), sand, clay, etc." or organizing simple games. Where children missed their mothers too much to join their comrades, they might be drawn into the collective by helping the teacher to put toys away or water plants.[83] The teacher was not supposed to wait for children to organize such activities on their own.

Teachers emphasized that new arrivals did not work as well as children who had been enrolled for a while. Even members of the "old collective" reportedly noticed the difference. One of the veterans complained to the teacher that the new pupils "still don't know how to work in the kindergarten." Another was reported as confiding, "You know, auntie, it's difficult for them to work." Teachers confirmed that by the end of the semester, all the children had learned the importance of straightening the activity room, washing their hands, noticing when other children were dirty, working on their own initiative, and completing their tasks. The teacher together with the "old collective" taught newcomers how to work and live collectively in the kindergarten.[84] The reports imply that without leadership, children would not build their own free communes.

Teachers who did not share the new curriculum's vision of the child as a "future person" found the sort of structured community it required an imposition on the child's freedom. Sventitskaia, whose kindergarten became part of the Third International Children's Town, refused to compromise the fundamental belief that the child is not "a blank sheet of paper on which it is possible to write whatever you like, but a being processing a mass of inheritances and instincts." She convened kindergarten meetings only on the rare occasions when the children fully understood their "cause and aim." The youngest children held no meetings at all. A typical meeting confronted a "wave of terror" perpetrated by two children hiding hats and mittens. Sventitskaia believed that such meetings gradually developed in the children the sense that they themselves controlled the kindergarten—rather than the appreciation of structure and order valued by the new curriculum.[85]

The Child as Revolutionary

For all its emphasis on discipline and indoctrination, the new curriculum never entirely abandoned the vision of the revolutionary rising generation. On the one hand, the plan curtailed children's freedom in the classroom and expanded the teacher's authority. On the other, children continued to be understood as the "real revolutionaries," counted on to rebel against old-fashioned teachers and, even more importantly, their "backward" parents. The material circumstances and political priorities reflected in the NEP clearly ruled out efforts to replace the family, but the children's collective could steel children against the family's "antisocial" influence and give them the tools to see beyond it. The new program amplified the revolutionary role of the generational conflict stirred up by the kindergarten.

Even as they encouraged teachers to take a more active role in guiding the young generation, the drafters of the new curriculum worried that adults could not always be trusted to raise children in the proper spirit. The curriculum assigned to young Pioneers the crucial tasks of connecting the children's collective to the wider world and of protecting their younger peers from "bourgeois" teachers who tried to foist their views on their pupils.[86] Regular visits with Pioneers were pictured "as a factor in deepening the organization of the children's collective and in revolutionizing the environment of the children's institution." Working with "older and more enterprising comrades" was supposed to strengthen the kindergartners' habits of work and hygiene. The Pioneers might help out with the organization of special events and holidays, but "experience shows" that "systematic work" required at least one, perhaps two, meetings per week during which the Pioneers could help to plan the work of the kindergarten or the kindergartners could join the Pioneers as they organized rural children.[87] Untarnished by any memory of the old way of life, the school-age Pioneers were cast as the best role models for kindergartners.

As the logical extension of Lilina's insistence on the need for young preschool teachers, the plan of bringing Pioneers into the kindergarten points to the ways in which the new curriculum continued to incorporate, in a minor key, the assumptions of free upbringing. While the GUS program had more confidence in the possibility of training children to be socialists, it shared *svobodnoe vospitanie*'s sense that the best teachers would be those who were themselves liberated from the weight of the past. Apparently pessimistic about the possibility of adults extricating themselves from the residue of their lives before October, the revolutionary curriculum located the most reliable teachers among children themselves. Faith in the transformative power of education existed alongside the deepening suspicion that announcements of the old world's demise had been premature.

While the new curriculum suggested that teachers might occasionally have to defer to the purer revolutionary impulses of the rising generation, it assumed and hoped for an even more confrontational relationship between the young revolutionaries and their parents. Children spent fewer hours in state institutions than policymakers might have wished, but as the kindergarten curriculum became increasingly focused on the task of raising "socialists," the lessons learned at home and in the preschool diverged more dramatically than before. As one delegate to the third congress pointed out, "in the family, they celebrate Christian holidays, and in the kindergarten the holidays of the October Revolution." At home, children acquired their parents' superstitions; in the kindergarten, they gained a scientific understanding of nature. Having learned the basics of cultural and political literacy at the kindergarten—the importance of cleanliness and of May Day—the child was supposed to "bring the new way of life to the family."[88] Here is a vision of revolutionary change that distrusts untutored instincts while retaining a faith in the revolutionary agency of the rising generation and a commitment to undermining, if not exactly smashing, patriarchal authority.

7

"Thank You, Comrade Stalin, for Our Happy Childhood"

The Stalinist Revolution of the late 1920s did not so much abandon the humanist and liberationist aspects of October as it purposefully redefined or—to use a verb favored by the Stalinists themselves—perverted them. The Stalinist program purported to be completing the task of throwing off the weight of the past and constructing the communist future. The euphoric atmosphere and the military rhetoric surrounding the "cultural campaigns" of 1928–1931 recalled, often self-consciously, the frenzied excitement of the first optimistic years of the Revolution. But whereas the revolutionary enthusiasm of the Civil War period had bred all manner of utopian schemes, the cultural revolutionaries of the late 1920s sought to impose a uniformly "proletarian" culture. However disruptive it might have been in practice, the new vision generally favored the formulaic over the experimental, the state-directed over the spontaneous. The notions of building a new way of life and of raising new people that had evoked the Revolution's Promethean possibilities became, in the context of the militarized millenarianism of the First Five-Year Plan, tools for smothering dissent and enforcing social order.[1]

Such revolutionary inversions produced a complex composite of attitudes and actions in the sphere of family policy—visions and programs contradictory enough for historians to have characterized them as both pro-family and anti-family.[2] On the one hand, the reconciliation with the family that had been justified as a short-term expedient during the NEP took on the character of a permanent feature of Soviet life. From merely tolerating family upbringing, the state moved by the mid-1930s to an unabashed sentimentalization of motherhood. At the same time, the vision of the "backward" family as a social and potential political threat and of the rising generation as truly revolutionary persisted. The Stalinist approach to parents and children managed to combine a commitment to "emancipating" women by providing state child care for working mothers, an insistence on the social importance and personal satisfactions of family upbringing, a reliance on parental authority as a bulwark against social dislocation, and an idealization of the revolutionary impulses of children.

The "preschool campaign," an effort to aid and transform both women and children, offers a particularly revealing view of the contradictions in Stalinist family policy. Touted as a vital means of freeing working women from child care responsibilities, the expanding, but still poorly funded, network of kindergartens had the additional, paradoxical aim of promoting more intensive and enlightened family upbringing. Alongside often minimal day care, the kindergarten was supposed to offer programs designed to train working mothers to do a better job with their children at home. Stalinist "emancipation" meant a double, even triple, shift for women, who were enjoined to work outside the home, undertake public political work, and devote themselves to the task of raising future communists.

While representing the double shift as liberating could strain even the socialist realist imagination, revitalizing the bonds between parent and child constituted a conventional approach to improving the lives of children. But in embracing family upbringing, the state did not relinquish its control over the rising generation. On the contrary, political education became an increasingly prominent feature of the education of even the youngest children. The clearest symbol of the Stalinist Revolution's success became the beaming faces of Soviet youngsters. The policy of making childhood (appear) happy had at least as much to do with the state's need for disciplined and devoted communists as with the best interests of children. The iconic children of the Stalinist state were at once hardworking and carefree, forward-looking and boundlessly happy in the present. The joys of childhood were grafted to the aims of a regime bent on rapid industrialization.

The Preschool Campaign

The drive to build preschool institutions as rapidly as possible, dubbed the "preschool campaign" (*doshkol'nyi pokhod*), grew out of the conviction that economic modernization required efforts to provide day care for the children of working mothers and to raise cultural levels within the family. While raising "new people" from earliest childhood remained a goal for policymakers at Narkompros, the task constituted a distinctly less urgent priority. As it turned out, even day care failed to receive adequate funding. By 1932, the number of preschool institutions of all types finally exceeded pre-NEP levels. However, "primitive" kindergartens, many offering only part-day care, predominated. The state education budget continued to favor institutions devoted to training technical experts, while parents continued to help cover the costs of child care services for preschoolers.

During the First Five-Year plan, planners viewed state child care as a means of minimizing the "social costs" as opposed to the "human costs" of women's labor

Figure 3 "Organizing nurseries, children's playgrounds, factory kitchens, dining rooms, and mechanical laundries—we will give 1,600,000 new women workers toward the fulfillment of the Five Year Plan" 1931

at home.[3] Lenin's 1919 characterization of household labor as "barbarously unproductive, petty, nerve-racking, stultifying, and crushing drudgery" suggested concern (and perhaps condescension) for the woman condemned to such tasks. By contrast, S. G. Strumilin, one of the men behind the First Five-Year Plan, emphasized that the industrializing Soviet state had to find a way of harnessing the labor of the estimated thirty million people, mainly women, devoting all their time to "unproductive" cooking, cleaning, and child rearing.[4] During the Stalinist revolution from above, Lenin's dictum that communism would be possible only when public dining rooms, laundries, nurseries, and kindergartens freed women from housework sounded less like a call for liberation than a strategy for drawing women into the work of socialist construction.[5]

Advocates of preschool education adapted to the new priorities by underlining the direct connection between kindergartens and modernization. Narkompros's brief for preschool education hinged on the argument that working parents both needed and demanded it. A 1930 article on the Pioneer movement that ran under Krupskaia's byline observed that as parents, and especially mothers, became involved in work outside the home, the development of a system of public preschool education, along with after-school care for older children, became indispensable.[6] One year later, at a conference of preschool workers, Krupskaia's speech quoted Stalin to the effect that "workers, who work so heroically, who participate in shock work, in socialist emulation, also present specific demands on the cultural front," including the demand for "the broad development of preschool education."[7] Educational literature often downplayed the benefits for children and stressed that the preschool had "tremendous significance in the work of the party and of Soviet power in involving women in the industrial and public life of our country."[8] Pamphlets geared toward involving women in the preschool campaign pictured inadequate child care as a threat to the economy. "Can a mother work calmly when her child is without supervision?" asked a periodical published by the Moscow Department of Education. Linking a mother's worst fears to planners' anxieties about productivity, it continued, "How can she keep her mind on work, when her child might be run over by a tram or drown in the river?"[9]

Additionally, proponents pictured the kindergarten's educational program, especially its efforts to raise cultural levels, as a prerequisite of industrialization. Addressing the Fourth All-Russian Congress of Preschool Education in 1929, Lunacharskii expressed the conviction that with enough resources preschool education could remake humanity within a generation. While the grand task of raising "new people" animated discussions of the preschool curriculum, the more concrete, if no less utopian, task of facilitating industrialization emerged as the chief justification for preschools. The congress's resolutions affirmed both the kindergarten's role in bringing women into the workforce and the connection between industrialization and the preschool's work of "cultural construction."[10]

Neither the dream of transforming humanity nor the promise of modernizing the economy aroused as much passion from the 1929 gathering of preschool workers as did the more prosaic problem alluded to by Lunacharskii—sufficient funding. The poverty of preschools, especially in comparison to the Commissariat of Health's nurseries for infants and toddlers (newborns to age three), constituted the fundamental theme of the congress. The discussion of preschool funding elicited horror stories of local departments of education that cut all funds for preschools, repeated calls for Narkompros to require that a fixed percentage of local budgets go to kindergartens, and reflected some measure of resentment toward the "aristocrats" at Narkomzdrav's Department for the Protection of Motherhood and Infancy (Okhrana materinstva i mladenchestva, or OMM), who enjoyed more substantial and more predictable funding than their peers in the preschools. E. E. Tsyrlina, who addressed the congress on the budget issue, noted that in the *guberniia* of Ivanovo-Voznesensk alone, OMM nurseries received half a million rubles from welfare funds drawn from salary deductions (*fond na zarplatu*) and the Fund for the Improvement of Workers' Lives (*Fond po ulusheniiu byta rabochikh,* or FUBR), while kindergartens received a total of about 30,000 rubles from both sources. The situation was especially galling since, according to Tsyrlina, workers reported that they needed preschool institutions more than the nurseries (*iasli*).[11] The state's commitment to funding child care seemed to end inexplicably when the child turned three.

The problem for the Preschool Department was its location in the Commissariat of Enlightenment, where the need for child care and the goal of raising a generation of socialists carried less weight than the task of training industrial specialists. The First Five-Year Plan earmarked more money for education than had NEP budgets, but all schools remained dependent on local funding (Table 6). Moreover, preschool education continued to constitute one of Narkompros's lowest budgetary priorities. The division of Narkompros responsible for preschool, primary, and secondary education (*Sotsial'noe vospitanie,* or Sotsvos) received a smaller percentage of the total planned education budget in 1932 (55.33 percent) than it had at the beginning of the Five-Year Plan, when it accounted for 57 percent of total spending on education. Preschools and children's homes lagged furthest behind, falling from just over 9 percent of the total education budget to just over 5 percent. Privileging educational expenditures that seemed to promise immediate benefits to the economy, the planned 1932 budget allotted more funds to eradicating illiteracy (41.2 million, or 2.5 percent of the total) than to kindergartens (19.8 million, or 1.1 percent of the total).[12]

Under these circumstances, teachers had to rely on the enthusiasm and contributions of parents to build and maintain kindergartens. Expenditures on food constituted at least one-quarter of the average kindergarten's budget, and policymakers proposed more systematic efforts to transfer this cost to the parents able to bear it.[13] Sometimes having to turn away as many children as they admitted, preschool workers viewed parental contributions for food as the most effective means of expanding the reach of their institutions. Teachers informed the congress that parents eager to obtain state child care were willing to pay for their children's meals. Even the "lowest paid group of workers, female textile workers" reportedly told preschool teachers, "Take our children, and we'll pay for feeding on our own."[14]

To meet the need for child care, parents and social organizations (*obshchestvennaia organizatsiia*) such as trade unions and housing cooperatives organized their own day care centers, often with little or no government funding. One success story recounted at the congress was the Central Housing Union's (*Tsentrozhilsoiuz*) kindergartens to which local departments of education contributed only the amount of a single teacher's salary. The union and the parents covered

Table 6   Central and Local Funding for Education in the RSFSR, 1924–1932 (in Millions of Rubles)

	Rubles		Percent		Actual	Planned
	State	Local	State	Local	Total	Total
1924–1925	94.7	157.9	37.5%	62.5%	252.6	N/A
1925–1926	135.6	213.4	38.9	61.1	349.0	N/A
1926–1927	139.3	305.1	31.3	68.7	444.4	N/A
1927–1928	146.2	371.0	28.3	71.7	517.2	577.8
1928–1929	146.9	472.9	23.7	76.3	619.8	N/A
1929–1930	220.0	651.5	25.2	74.8	871.5	N/A
1931	242.4	1,076.8	18.4	81.6	1,319.2	N/A
1932	371.0	1,384.9	21.1	78.9	1,755.9	1,803.2

Sources: Narkompros, *Narodnoe prosveshchenie v RSFSR v tsifrakh za 15 let sovetskoi vlasti (ckratkii statisticheskii sbornik)* (Moscow: Gosudarstvennoe uchebno-pedagogicheskoe izdatel'stvo, 1932), 37. Issledovatel'skii insitut nauchnoi pedagogiki Moskva 2 Gosudarstvennyi Universitet. *Narodnoe prosveshchenie v piatletnem plane sotsialisticheskogo stroitel'stvo* (Moscow-Leningrad: Rabotnik prosveshcheniia, 1930), 186.

the cost of the building, food, materials, and any additional teachers. Roughly half of the 228 kindergartens funded in this way were "primitive."[15] Many parents in need of child care "spontaneously" organized their own "private groups" (*chastnye gruppy*) or "wild" (*dikii*) playgrounds that often lacked trained personnel. Tsyrlina, the delegate presenting the report on the budget, guessed that the number of private groups equaled the number of public kindergartens, but conceded that no accurate accounting had been made. Teachers pointed to such arrangements as a clear sign of the value of kindergartens, even as they worried about their inability to control the "ideological" direction of such "institutions."[16]

The number of preschool institutions increased substantially between 1927 and 1932, but most children remained outside the state child care system. According to Narkompros statistics published in 1932, the number of kindergartens in the RSFSR rose over 80 percent between the fall of 1929 and the spring of 1931. Still, both the number of children served and number of institutions remained behind those for the fall of 1921 (see Table 4). Less than 8 percent of urban children, and less than 2 percent of *all* children, attended some type of kindergarten. In the United States, where kindergartens served only five-year-olds, 777,899 children were enrolled in public preschools. A far smaller percentage of American children were enrolled in nursery schools. In Soviet Russia, where the target population was ages three to seven, there were 222,216 kindergartners.[17]

Other sorts of "institutions," primarily supervised playgrounds, accommodated more children. By one count, the number of children served by "all types of institutions," apparently including nurseries as well as all types of preschools, went from just over 1.1 million in 1930 to about 3.7 million in 1931—a one-year increase of "220–225 percent." Narkompros statistics published in 1932 suggest more modest growth. The figures for the 1930–1931 school year put the total number of children enrolled in kindergartens, *ochagi*, "preschool groups," and playgrounds at about 1.2 million, with almost 80 percent served by the most primitive and temporary of these institutions, the playgrounds.[18] By 1932, perhaps 8 or 9 percent of all children attended some kind of preschool, a rather substantial increase, if still a long way from universal public child care.[19]

As during the Civil War period, impressive increases in absolute numbers tended to obscure the fact that most preschools were of the so-called "primitive" variety. The seemingly innocuous phrase "all types of institutions" is at least as important as the numbers. In the preschool campaign, as in campaigns in other fields and the First Five-Year Plan generally, "objective" difficulties, such as the shortage of adequately trained teachers, were not allowed to slow the breakneck pace.[20] But of course such "objective" factors did impact the sorts of care and education children received. The ideal kindergarten cared for children for the entire work day (up to nine or ten hours), but inadequate funds made such "normal" institutions a rarity, especially outside of Moscow and Leningrad.[21] Providing full-day kindergartens proved particularly difficult where women worked two and three shifts. A delegate to the 1929 congress from Ivanovo-Vosnesensk noted that even eight- and nine-hour kindergartens failed to meet the needs of textile workers.[22]

Without the resources to open full-day *ochagi*, preschool workers and parents improvised. "Primitive" institutions could take the form of summer playgrounds or rooms for children in dormitories and clubs that provided supervision for part of the day or a few hours. In factories, "work with children" occurred in the corridors, kitchen, or the "red corner" of the workers' barracks. In the summer in Moscow, teachers organized preschoolers "on the boulevards, in the squares, in courtyards." Occasionally the places where children gathered were fenced. More often they were not. Such "primitive" programs, the delegate from Moscow assured the congress, had a "very big effect."[23]

The educational content of such "institutions" was likely to be low. In 1929, three quarters of all preschool workers lacked specialized training. Preschool teachers suggested that much of the difficulty in attracting qualified people could be traced to preschool teachers' low salaries and difficult working conditions.[24] In Moscow and Leningrad, several kindergartens built by cooperatives had to be shut down when local departments of educations failed to provide teachers. A Zhenotdel delegate complained that preschool workers often came "straight from the Labor Exchange" without any qualifications. Without enough trained teachers,

Figure 4   "All children to the summer playground" 1930

many institutions relied on Zhenotdel, Komsomol, or factory activists. One such untrained preschool worker from Briansk, who described herself as "semi-literate," argued that teachers and activists could learn from one another. "Wildflowers" among more qualified "carnations," the untrained workers, she suggested, helped the teachers to be more socially minded, even as they deferred to teachers on pedagogical matters.[25]

Confronted with parents' demands for child care and severe shortages of funds and trained personnel, most preschool workers viewed "primitive" institutions as necessary but temporary. Whatever their shortcomings as educational institutions, "primitive" preschools were tolerated largely because, as a worker-activist from Briansk pointed out, it was "impossible to raise 12 people according to the highest standards (*po vsem pravilam iskusstva*), while leaving 112 without supervision." Some delegates to the 1929 congress worried that the desire to provide minimal child care threatened to undermine the project of preschool *education* and spoke in favor of better, rather than more, institutions. However, the congress's resolutions reflected the more optimistic view that primitive kindergartens could be held to minimal pedagogical standards and that they constituted a necessary first step in involving parents in preschool education and organizing permanent, higher-quality institutions.[26] Establishing "primitive" care-taking institutions did not necessarily entail abandoning the preschool's educational mission.

Restoring Social Order

Although collectivization and industrialization had spurred renewed state interest in the preschool as a means of freeing women to work outside the home, the preschool campaign never aimed to replace families. Practically speaking, full-day kindergartens were less expensive than children's homes. Emphasizing the effects of scarcity, Sofia Smidovich, a member of the Party's Control Commission, pointed out that "we are still far too poor to give the children the social training they should have; therefore, the family must be preserved."[27] But this sort of practicality did not constitute the defining characteristic of the preschool campaign. Behind the decision to favor family over state upbringing stood not only budgetary considerations but also fears about what the destruction of the traditional family would mean for social order.

The First Five-Year Plan fundamentally disrupted the lives of millions of people in a way that the even the Revolution and Civil War had not. Between 1928 and 1935, industrialization drew 17.7 million peasants into urban areas. This "rural-ization" of the cities overloaded the already strained housing situation and added an alarmingly "uncultured" element to the working-class population. At work, the newly arrived peasants lacked discipline and were condemned for their drunk-enness, absenteeism, and tendency to break expensive and unfamiliar tools.[28] At home, overcrowding coupled with the migrants' low cultural standards produced not only high infant mortality rates but also the "debauched" family situations observed by visiting teachers and nurses. Further undermining the family by so-cializing child care seemed likely only to add to the social chaos.

The Stalinist Revolution did briefly revive calls for raising children in isolation from parents, but in the context of city planning, not education. For those Bolshe-viks who continued to advocate state upbringing, the chief concern was no longer the liberation of children but instead the productivity of parents. In a widely read urban utopia, L. M. Sabsovich, a Gosplan economist, proposed "children's cities" built at a distance from adult housing as a means of rationalizing everyday life and of releasing women from "unproductive" domestic chores. Viewing child-rearing as a distraction from the important work of socialist construction and ac-cusing parents of doing a poor job of raising children in any event, Sabsovich proposed that the state take full responsibility for the rising generation.[29]

Policymakers at Narkompros rejected such schemes not because they held a significantly higher opinion of family upbringing or because they viewed state care as impractical, but because eliminating the family appeared to be an unduly disruptive means of freeing women to work outside the home and of remaking childhood. The First Five-Year Plan called for massive increases in the number of children enrolled in kindergartens and *ochagi*, indeed in every sort of educational institution, while prescribing a reduction in the number of places in preschool children's homes.[30] An article by Krupskaia that appeared in *Pravda* in 1929 deemed "children's cities" inimical to the best interests of both children and socialist society. Employing liberationist rhetoric to argue against the "liberation" of children from the family, Krupskaia took issue with Sabsovich's characterization of children as "property" that could be transferred from parents to the state. She further objected to Sabsovich's contention that "parental feeling" was necessarily harmful to children. Making an argument that in a few years would permit the exultation of maternal instincts and justify the recriminalization of abortion, Krupskaia's article contended that new material conditions had altered the content and meaning of family life. She favored children's "floors" or "sectors" in workers' dormitories, where professional educators, assisted by parent volunteers, would remake upbringing without removing children from the family.[31] Such arrangements combined respect for parental, especially maternal, feelings and disdain for what Krupskaia termed the "evils" of current family upbringing practices.

For educators, parental failings increasingly became evidence of the need to strengthen, rather than replace, the family. Pictures of disintegrating families functioned as a stand-in for social disorder generally and as a warning of the dire consequences of eliminating the family as a unit of social control. In the first few heady years after the Revolution, Zlata Lilina had been an ardent advocate of "liberating" children from their parents. In 1921, her case against family upbringing had taken the form of a picture of the horrors of pre-Revolutionary families. In 1929, she related equally dreadful scenes from the lives of post-Revolutionary families. But rather than calling for rational public upbringing, she implored, "Parents, learn how to raise your children!"[32]

The familiar litany of charges against parents gave concrete form to abstract fears about social dislocation and the lack of "socialist" values among the older generation. Even as they heap up detail, the accounts of family life seem formulaic. Lilina's description of the physical and moral filth encountered at the workers' barracks at a factory outside of Moscow is typical of the genre. Foul smells and foul language emanated from the communal kitchens. At one end of the corridor, one could find a group of loafers playing the accordion; at the other end, a drunk hurling choice epithets at his wife and shaking his fist. "And in this environment, the children knock around among the adults and play." The children lacked all supervision. A group of seven- and eight-year-olds might be sprawled out on the concrete kitchen floor losing stolen money in card games and swearing "no worse than their parents."[33]

Lilina emphasized that such situations were not exceptional, and the accounts of educators and visiting nurses agree with her in most particulars. In all cases, what is striking is the degree to which observers continued, over a decade after the Revolution, to characterize family life in terms of drunkenness, immorality, and filth—in short, in terms of the family's failure to assimilate modern and "socialist" values. Lilina reported that at the Livers factory in Moscow, one could find alcoholic parents giving their little ones wine, saying that "it will make them stronger." A five-year-old in Leningrad demonstrated an abnormal interest in being alone with girls. A little research into the "life of the family revealed that the boy slept with his mother and had the opportunity to observe his parents' sex life." Rather than setting a public-minded example for their children, even working mothers, who were expected to know better, did not participate in volunteer work or visit clubs. Teachers also found more mundane problems, including "irrational" children's clothing and mothers who failed to change the bed linens in a timely manner. To the question, "How do our children live?" Lilina could only respond, "badly."[34]

Underlying such descriptions was the assumption that the failings uncovered by investigators could be traced to parental incompetence or ignorance rather than to the larger social context. In line with "Marxist" methods of child study, teachers developed elaborate questionnaires to determine what sort of example parents set for their children. They asked about parents' social class, party membership, and participation in "collective forms of public life." Educators looked for "expressions of culture" in the family: the newspapers, books, and magazines that various members of the household read; the number of illiterates; visits to church and the presence of icons; "elements of the new way of life." Scientific thoroughness required questions about whether or not "the children in the family observe sexual displays of one sort or another" and about the parents' relationship with one another.[35] Out of view entirely were the profound changes in the structure of Soviet society that could also account for the family's impairment.

Still imagined as a source of social ills, the family in the course of the industrialization drive also came to be viewed as an indispensable ally in the regime's effort to enforce social order. The shift in attitude is most visible with regard to the "freest" children—the *besprizorniki*. Hailed in the early years as the harbingers of the future communist society, the *besprizorniki* came to be understood as a threat to the stability, productivity, and discipline of the socialist state. The move away from romanticizing "emancipated" children had roots in the 1920s. The clearest break with previous policy came in the early 1930s, when the law made parents responsible for policing their children and allowed juvenile offenders to be tried as adults. Rather than acknowledging that the social and demographic dislocations associated with the First Five-Year Plan produced a new wave of homeless children, the regime insisted that *besprizornost'* and the juvenile crime that accompanied it could be traced to parental failings.[36] Social order would be restored not by making all children wards of the state, but by holding parents accountable for the actions of their offspring.

The "Resolution" of the Woman Question

The link between public upbringing and women's liberation that had been weakened during the NEP was severed in the 1930s. Even as the state committed itself to providing child care facilities, the dissolution of the Zhenotdel in 1930 signaled the diminishing commitment to "emancipat[ing] women in their daily lives."[37] The maternal instinct that Kollontai had assumed would find broader application in public work became the object of extravagant praise and the centerpiece of pronatalist social policy that culminated in the 1936 family code that prohibited abortion except in cases of medical necessity, made divorce more difficult to obtain, and instituted a program of providing stipends to mothers of seven or more children. Trotsky labeled the shift in outlook the Russian Thermidor, but it was more complicated than the betrayal of the October Revolution usually implied by the analogy. Promises of liberation were subordinated to other items on the original revolutionary agenda—the productivist ethos, the commitment to overcoming social and cultural backwardness.

While the First Five-Year Plan drew large numbers of women into the workforce and provided some of them with child care services that helped relieve domestic responsibilities, such "liberation" was never its aim. Instead, as Gail Lapidus has argued, women's entry into new roles was largely "instrumental," a component and by-product of the modernization drive. Massive female employment had not been part of the original five-year plan. Only when "manpower" shortages became acute in 1930 did women's employment begin to increase significantly. Thereafter, the number of women workers grew rapidly. Women accounted for 82 percent of all newly employed workers between 1932 and 1937. By 1937, the over nine million employed women in the Soviet Union constituted over 40 percent of the industrial labor force. The provision of services for working women, most significantly child care services, failed to keep pace not only because resources were scarce, but also because the chief concern of state planners was modernization, not liberation.[38]

The preschool campaign had the ironic consequence of reinforcing—indeed, extending—women's traditional responsibility for child care. Promises to lighten the working woman's domestic burden coexisted with efforts to train her to carry out traditional child care duties in scientific, "revolutionary," and generally more burdensome ways. Even as they complained about the lack of funds for opening kindergartens, preschool teachers planned to open a network of classes for mothers and of "consultations" modeled on those operated by the Commissariat of Health for pregnant women and newborns. Preschool workers imagined that a "consultation" staffed by a doctor and an educator would allow teachers not only to provide child-rearing advice, but also to make sure that it was carried out.[39] While teachers' suggestions may have improved the overall quality of children's lives, they added to the working mother's responsibilities.

In the name of modernizing child-rearing, and in the absence of adequate funding, working women were called on to help out in the kindergarten and, where state institutions did not exist, to establish their own makeshift kindergartens.[40] Advice pamphlets described the organization of "preschool cooperatives" among mothers who lived in the same neighborhood as the ideal response to the shortage of public facilities. Sharing child care responsibilities was supposed to give all the mothers involved more free time, while raising children in small groups functioned as a substitute for the "collective" atmosphere of the kindergarten.[41] Looking after several children was represented as at least as easy as caring for one. Educators assured women that all they needed to do was provide some simple furniture and boxes for the children to play with; "three or four children of the same age playing together require almost no adult intervention, and," they suggested helpfully, "the mother on duty observing the children could busy herself with some work, for example sewing or mending."[42] That working mothers might find it difficult if not impossible to squeeze their days on duty into their work schedule did not emerge as an issue. Certainly there was no suggestion that fathers might help the cooperative run more smoothly.

For those mothers unable or unwilling to cooperate with their neighbors, building a makeshift kindergarten at home did nothing to ease the burden of child care. Mothers were supposed to find time to take their children on excursions, either to study nature or to observe socialist holidays, and to organize revolutionary celebrations at home. Educators advised parents to "find an hour in the course of the workday for conversations with your children, in order to answer the questions which are troubling them—then your children will be your best friends." Accustoming children to useful work required that parents spare a minimum of two hours a day to teach their children to use scissors, knife, hammer, and nails. A sample schedule of daily activities for children who did not attend kindergarten kept a mother busy from seven in the morning until eight at night.[43] One wonders how even a woman who did not work could manage such a full program.

The dual image of women "as an active economic and political agent of society and as a mother and nurturer of new communists"[44] suggested that it was possible to assign mothers primary responsibility for child care while encouraging daughters to reject traditional female roles. Advice pamphlets stressed that preparing women to build "our future socialist society" had to begin "with earliest childhood." Parents were criticized for viewing their daughters as future wives and mothers and there-fore raising girls who had "weaker habits for public work" than did their broth-ers and who enrolled in college in smaller numbers. Yet the remedies perpetuated the image of women as wives and mothers. "Each family, *especially the mother*," parents were told, must make an effort to put girls on the same level as boys and allow them to participate in the same activities.[45] Parenting classes targeted moth-ers. The revolutionary dream of raising new people was domesticated, and in the process uncoupled from the promise of remaking family relationships and roles. The new utopia not only tolerated women's double shift but also required it.

Raising Cultural Levels

If family upbringing was to serve the needs of the industrializing state, it had to be both modernized and "Sovietized." Counting on parents to raise communists and to maintain social order, policymakers looked for ways to raise cultural levels within the family and to ensure its ideological reliability. It has been argued that what most clearly separated the Cultural Revolution of 1928–1931 from earlier Soviet efforts to revolutionize culture was the strident rhetoric of class war and the rejection of what one activist characterized as the "peaceful, classless raising of cultural standards—a conception that does not distinguish between bourgeois and proletarian elements of culture."[46] Yet especially with regard to children and families, the two categories of cultural revolution overlapped and reinforced one another. The struggle against "backwardness" could encompass both parent edu-cation in the largely apolitical spheres of health and hygiene and militant attacks on religion. The propaganda of the preschool campaign suggested that class war could be effectively waged only where basic standards of "culture," defined with-out reference to class, were met.

As the battle against cultural "backwardness" intensified in the early 1930s, much of the child care advice to parents continued to focus on standards of health and hygiene. To guide parents, Narkompros published a "whole series of popular brochures, in which all aspects of the child's life and needs are sorted out," in Russian as well as minority languages. The goal was to reach even the least "cul-tured" groups in the minority republics and in the village. The department pre-pared informational slides and movies, broadcast lectures on the radio, and set up exhibits at factories and schools that demonstrated appropriate toys and books as well as proper hygiene, clothing, and sleeping arrangements. Preschool teachers intervened to try to get women off work to attend meetings at the kindergarten.[47]

The minutely detailed nature of the recommendations suggests that the audi-ence was envisioned as lacking what educators took to be the most basic of un-derstandings. Cold food along with canned goods, sausage, and sunflower seeds were banned as dangerous. Parents learned that a healthy diet for children consisted of vegetables, fruit, butter, milk, meat, groats, and perhaps the occasional sweet. An entire number of *Doshkol'nyi pokhod* was devoted to the dangers of sharing beds, plates, and towels. Parents had to accustom their children to washing their hands before meals and to using their own individual towels and spoons as a means of checking the spread of harmful bacteria. The practice of children sleeping in their parents' bed was condemned on the grounds that it deprived preschoolers of their requisite ten to eleven hours of sleep. Educators also warned that rubbing against another body could lead to the "very early manifestation of unhealthy desires" that could destroy a child's body and nerves. Teachers suggested chests, trunks, benches, or a couple of chairs as alternatives to sleeping with parents or siblings.[48] Some kindergartens organized competitions for parents, who pledged, among other things, to provide a separate bed, towel, and toothbrush for each child; to see that children's hands were washed before meals; to serve meals at regular hours; and to put children to bed by ten o'clock.[49] Such advice echoed what the Preschool Department had been telling parents since its establishment.

The propaganda of the preschool campaign usually justified the prescribed regimen in terms of universal rather than class-specific science. Advice pamphlets labeled all forms of punishment medically unsound. Educators informed parents that physical punishment stunted children's growth and weakened their characters. Frightening children in order to get them to behave was also deemed a bad idea from a medical point of view. Without delineating the science involved, teachers warned that if a child finished everything on his or her plate out of terror, the food would do no good. Even telling frightening fairy tales or taking children to see acrobats at the circus could be hazardous to their health. Rational conversations with children were promoted as the healthy alternative to beatings and threats.[50]

Ideally, such modern and friendly parent-child relationships facilitated the inculcation of specifically Soviet culture. Preschool propaganda provided parents with guidelines for talking with their children that collapsed the distinction between sound pedagogy and sound politics. Parents received detailed advice on "how to answer a child's questions": Do not correct a mispronounced word until after the question is answered, and do not respond with a simple "yes" or "no." When parents did not know an answer, teachers recommended that they read and find out. Teachers advised that it was best to answer all questions as straightforwardly as possible, including difficult ones such as "Why are there boys and girls?" Questions about the existence of God were to be answered with a simple, "there is no God."[51]

In a narrative presented by *Doshkol'nyi pokhod* as an illustration of the normative relationship between kindergartens and parents, improvements in children's

Figure 5   "Down with the punishment of children. For a new life — new upbringing." 1930

health became the first steps on the road to the establishment of "proletarian" values. The titles of the story's short chapters make the progression clear, moving from "the kindergarten fights illness" through "give me a corner for games and activities" to "down with the priest's narcotic, long live the brotherhood of peoples!"[52]

In the story, the kindergarten is emphatically an educational institution. Liza, apparently a working single mother, decides to send her children to kindergarten, despite the fact that her mother could look after the children. She seems to understand intuitively that her landlady's warnings about children being beaten, learning to swear, and bringing illness home with them from the kindergarten have no basis in reality. That such stories actually circulated at a time when kindergartens were underfunded, understaffed, and perhaps rather unsanitary seems likely. Popular reactions to kindergartens might also have included concerns about their hostility to religion.[53] The story quickly belies fears about disease and bad habits, as Liza finds that the kindergarten can teach her much about basic hygiene. When she implements teachers' suggestions, the health benefits are immediate. She learns that if the children wash their hands after playing with the dog, they are less likely to get worms. To the skeptical landlady's questions about the large number of clean rags hanging on pegs, Liza responds with the explanation that individual towels prevent the spread of infections.

In the story, the ultimate triumph of the preschool program comes with the children's refusal to get involved in their grandmother's and the landlady's frantic preparations for Easter, preferring instead to make decorations for May Day. Always a model parent ready to follow her children's lead, Liza helps to prepare the children for May Day by sewing costumes. Vania goes as a Black child, Petia as a Chinese child, and Mania as a woman worker. When the landlady and her children mock the international delegation as "Negro-shoe polish" and "slant eyes," Liza and her children patiently explain the importance of the solidarity of all workers against the bourgeoisie. What better example of the family and the kindergarten "hand in hand building the new life, realizing the new upbringing"?[54] The ideal kindergarten did far more than improve children's health. If parents would only follow its advice as Liza did, it could remake the life of the entire family.

Since the preschool campaign represented the transformation of family life as beginning with the politically neutral task of raising standards of health and hygiene and of encouraging parents to be hardworking, sober, and chaste, teachers could count the introduction of "modern," if not specifically proletarian, child-rearing practices as a major achievement. How much of the kindergarten's advice parents really followed is of course difficult to gauge. That teachers proposed "consultations" designed to follow up on educators' prescriptions and even to take charge of family spending on children suggests some frustration with parents' inability or unwillingness to act on recommendations in the sphere of health and hygiene. Calls at the 1929 congress to undertake "antireligious upbringing" may reflect the difficulty of persuading parents to abandon Easter for May Day.[55] On the other hand, teachers reported many improvements in family upbringing. At Kindergarten No. 11 in Saratov, founded during the famine of 1922, teachers initially had a difficult time convincing parents that the preschool was more than a feeding station. The faculty got parents to the lectures on preschool pedagogy and health only by offering free stockings and underwear to those who showed up. But, teachers reported, with the arrival of slightly better times and the opportunity to witness the kindergarten in action, parents began to look to its teachers and doctors for advice in raising their children.[56] Other kindergartens reported that many of their pupils' parents had made improvements in household hygiene, providing separate beds and towels for each child. The number of parents administering corporal punishment declined. Many made an effort to supply children with materials recommended by teachers and stopped taking children to evening

Figure 6   "How children fight against alcoholism" 1930

movies.[57] In teachers' accounts, parents often welcomed changes that made their children healthier, although not necessarily more "Soviet."

Educators instructed parents not only to adjust the way they treated their children but also to change radically their own way of life for the sake of the younger generation. While the preschool campaign underlined the crucial role of the kindergarten, advice manuals often emphasized that parental examples constituted the most potent influence on children. Preschool propaganda tried to impress upon parents that "science demonstrates that the child is not born with prepared habits and knowledge. The child grows up to be good or bad depending upon whom he meets and who surrounds him." Since even children who attended kindergartens spent more time at home than in state institutions, change required parental support. Before they could raise their children well, adults had to "educate themselves." "Children," Lilina maintained, "copied adults in bad and good."[58]

The "good" was presumptively "communist," but ostensibly often quite middle class. Parents were warned to watch their language in front of the children and to shield youngsters from the intimate lives of adults who shared the apartment. Educators explained that if parents hoped to raise sober, productive children, they had to stop drinking and going to movies that featured murder and drunkenness. The ideal parent was both a publicly minded citizen and a fit moral example for children. Only if parents rationalized their own lives and disciplined themselves could the family function as a pillar of social order.

The Real Revolutionaries

During the years of the First Five-Year Plan, the rising generation was linked, both sociologically and symbolically, to the proletariat. In part, the association reflects the fact that in the early 1930s, the working class as a whole became visibly younger.[59] Moreover, young people seem to have been the most active and enthusiastic cultural revolutionaries. Sheila Fitzpatrick explains the Komsomol's antibureaucratic zeal, epitomized by the attack on the educational establishment, as the result of the "real grievances of the younger generation."[60] At the same time, less "real" factors worked to reinforce the image of revolutionary youth. At a time when class distinctions became both increasingly significant and increasingly blurred by massive urban migration and the promotion of workers into white collar jobs, youth provided a clear and potent index of commitment to the Revolution. According to Victoria Bonnell, the visual propaganda of the First Five-Year Plan made "youth and a general appearance of vigor, freshness, and enthusiasm" the "first and perhaps most important" feature of the heroic citizen.[61] Whether or not they were the work of actual young people, the most ambitious construction projects of the period were represented as fueled by "youthful" idealism. Stories about the building of the dam at Dneprostroi and the new city of Magnitogorsk were deemed particularly appropriate and appealing subjects of children's literature.[62] Witnessing a conflation of age and class, journalist Ella Winter suggested in 1933 that "the division between a generation of parents and children in Russia today may be the chasm between two social orders."[63]

The image of a revolutionary rising generation clearly evoked the Civil War's emphasis on generational conflict, but the youthful "revolutionaries" that populated Stalinist propaganda had little in common with the earlier image of emancipated young people liberating themselves from the weight of all authority. In the 1930s, the rebellion against teachers and parents was not the germ of a spontaneously generated "family" of equals, but instead an act of obedience to the Soviet state, a "big happy family" of a very different sort. The central paradox of the Stalinist effort to reinvent revolutionary ideology may be the simultaneous attack on and rehabilitation of the patriarchal family.

Children had long been represented as both the chief beneficiaries of the Revolution and as its purest exponents. What changed during the Stalinist Revolution was the degree to which the interests and "revolutionary" impulses of the young were equated with the policies of the Soviet state. Drawing heavily on the

"socialist" curricula of the 1920s that amalgamated progressive methods and ideologically charged content, educational policy in the early 1930s assumed that
children as a class would naturally find satisfaction in building socialism. At the
primary and secondary levels, traditional disciplines gave way to theme-oriented
"projects" that often included industrial or agricultural labor. The hands-on work
emphasized by progressive educators became a means of fulfilling the Five-Year
Plan. When Komsomols or young Pioneers asserted their authority vis-à-vis non-
communist teachers, they seemed to prove that the administration and curriculum
of the schools could be at once responsive to the demands of (some) pupils and re-
flective of the goals of the Soviet state.[64]

The identification of the state's and the child's best interests also informed policy toward the smallest members of the rising generation. The propagandists of
the preschool campaign envisioned children as "our future," by which they meant
to suggest both that the October Revolution and the great leap forward had been
undertaken on behalf of children and that children had to be trained to complete
the job begun by adults.[65] In other words, Soviet policy recognized no conflict between guaranteeing the present happiness of children and preparing them to build
the communist future. Educators represented a program of intensive labor and
immersion in the world of adults as the chief source of childhood delights.

At the preschool level, the "socialist" curriculum articulated in the mid-1920s
became the basis of an increasingly labor-intensive and ideological, but still
avowedly child-centered, program. The "socialist" kindergarten curriculum of
the mid-1920s had tempered free upbringing's emphasis on the child's "instinctive" interest in labor with an insistence on the role of adults in training children
to work collectively. The kindergartens of the preschool campaign were supposed
to go even further in the direction of guidance and indoctrination, not only teaching children proper work habits, but also raising their class consciousness and
"purposefulness" (napravlennost'). The holidays of the "Red calendar" structured a series of "organizational moments" that were designed to appeal to children while laying "the foundations for the future fighter for the realization of
socialism." The planned activities that comprised each "moment" were supposed
to revolve around "productive labor" (proizvodstvennyi trud). For example, the
"organized moment" on May Day required the teachers to acquaint themselves
and the youngsters with the holiday's slogans, to teach the children through conversations that workers made everything that surrounds them, and to organize
work in the garden after the thaw. The "moment" on "preparation for spring
work" included an excursion to observe nature, conversations about the signs of
spring, work in the garden, art projects related to the excursion, and the construction of notebooks to record observations. Such "organized moments" were described as "giving general purposefulness to the child's life and connecting to the
children's interests."[66]

Policymakers in Moscow hesitated to devise a rigid formula for translating "organizational moments" into practice. Instead, the experts at the Preschool Department provided various possible patterns of organized activities coupled with the admonition that all institutions must celebrate "political holidays" and raise children devoted to building socialism. The delegate presenting the lecture on curricula provided data on the number and types of "organized activities" at a small number of institutions, but insisted that she viewed the programs as a starting point for analysis rather than a model for teachers to follow. What is most striking in the presentation is its near total disregard for "free" activities and play. The delegates learned the average number of "organized activities" engaged in by children of various ages in a single day (generally between two and four), the percentage of "organized activities" related to "organized moments" (an average of about 70 percent), and the percentage of organized activities that fell into various categories. The mix of activities varied. At the "Red Poppy" kindergarten, over half the organized activities for the three- and four-year-olds involved "labor." By contrast, the youngest children at another institution devoted a third of their time to art activities, and only 15 percent to labor. Absent entirely from the accounting was any sense of how much time was or should be devoted to free activities. Unstructured play carried little pedagogical significance, except when it "reflects the content of the organized moment."[67]

While the more experienced educators in the audience applauded the department's commitment to avoiding "recipes" that interfered with the teacher's creativity, teachers in "primitive" institutions expressed frustration with the center's efforts to couple flexibility of implementation with nonnegotiable content. Presenting themselves as lacking both the time and the expertise to work out the specifics of the program on their own, they asked for "definite and clear directives from the center." Teachers whose qualifications may have consisted of a several month course wanted to know how long each "organized moment" ought to last, what sorts of activities should be included, and, most importantly, how the prescribed activities could be adapted to "primitive" conditions.[68] Insisting that teachers would be able to find the best ways to make political education accessible to their charges, policymakers supplied the title and basic content of the mandated "organized moments," but offered few unequivocal answers about practice.

Repeated reminders that Soviet educators had "entirely dissociated themselves from the influence of bourgeois pedagogues" signaled not a rejection of child-centered approaches so much as an effort to link progressive practice to increasingly ideological aims. In her closing remarks on the curriculum, Surovtseva distinguished American kindergartens where children acquired necessary "habits" from Soviet kindergartens where much the same "habits" were coupled with a "definite purposefulness."[69] By 1932, the "chief task of the kindergarten" was "to arm the child with the temper of Soviet communism, to kindle his love for and his devotion to our factories, machine tools, our fields, our Red Army men, etc.—in short, all that which characterizes us, *our* world, *our* society, *our* struggle." Such formulations left little doubt about who the "us" might be. Progressive education, and *svobodnoe vospitanie*, with its slogan "the harmonious development of the personality" in particular, was rejected for its tendency to produce "fops and dandies" rather than hardworking Soviet citizens. Children, it was assumed, understood the new exigencies at least as well as adults. Teachers claimed that the "reactionary character" of kindergarten programs that looked to Rousseau, Pestalozzi, or Froebel for guidance "is now obvious to every Soviet preschooler."[70] If it was an exaggeration to suggest that kindergartners were likely to appreciate the references to educational theorists, it was a basic premise of pedagogy of the Stalinist revolution that the even the youngest children of the Revolution had a natural interest in learning about and promoting the new way of life.

Soviet pedagogy wholeheartedly embraced the progressive dictum that the school program became relevant and interesting to children only when it was connected to the wider world. Visiting Soviet Russia in the late 1920s, John Dewey found much that was familiar in "the idea of a dovetailing of school activities into out-of-school social activities" that he viewed as the core of Soviet education. What distinguished the Soviet program from American progressivism was the degree to which it elided the distinction between the enthusiasms of children and the state's educational agenda. Dewey found that the chief difference between Soviet schools and those "from other national systems and from the progressive schools of other countries (with which they have much in common) is precisely the conscious control of every educational procedure by reference to a single and comprehensive social purpose."[71]

Soviet educators denied that ideological content limited the program's appeal to children. To the contrary, Soviet children allegedly clamored for toys, books, and plays steeped in ideology. Perhaps nothing better summed up the desired relation of the child to the state than the poster that hung in every Soviet school that proclaimed, "Thank you, Comrade Stalin, for our happy childhood."[72] In the Soviet kindergarten, politics permeated even the ABCs. Children learned that "A is for Atheist, whom the priests try to kill," and "D is the death, the legal lynching by a dried-up old New England judge of brave class-war prisoners—Sacco and Vanzetti." Echoing the official line, journalist Ella Winter reported that children found the political alphabet just as interesting as the more traditional ABCs illustrated with antelopes and monkeys. An educator who claimed that "everything follows the child's interest" proved the point with a collection of apparently self-evidently fascinating "books illustrating socialist construction." An article advocating "polytechnic" toys—such as a burlap conveyer belt—that appeared in *Komsomolskaia pravda* in June 1930 suggested that it was misguided adults rather than the rising generation itself that judged toys solely on the basis of their ability "to amuse our proletarian children."[73]

Figure 7   "We will be
Leninists" 1934

At the Children's Theater in Moscow, children's enthusiasm for real life was
translated into a repertoire of propaganda plays. The theater solicited the comments
of its young audiences and even involved children in the development and staging of
its plays. The theater, in short, went to great lengths to assess and respond to the interests of children. Yet, somewhat paradoxically, the productions, as described by a
sympathetic British observer, seem less than captivating. Most dealt rather unimagi-
natively "with the planning and building of the Socialist State."[74]

Where children were understood as deriving present satisfaction from the task
of preparing for the communist future, solicitousness about the child's happiness
could be divorced from any concern for his or her inner life. The lack of regard

for the child's inner life had already been a feature of the research program of the 1920s that emphasized physical descriptions of the world of the child. Outward conformity to Soviet norms and the appropriation of the Revolution's vocabulary became irrefutable evidence of the child's investment in and enthusiasm for the task of building the future. Recollecting his own pre-Revolutionary childhood, children's author Samuel Marshak explained that for children "words are inseparable from meaning, and meaning from image." Since the child apparently used only those words that he or she could connect to something both visible and meaningful, the child's language could be taken as a straightforward index of consciousness.[75]

Educators looked for clues to the rising generation's mentality in children's efforts to redeploy the Revolution's words for their own purposes. Although what emerged most clearly was the child's inability to grasp abstractions, experts drew the somewhat paradoxical conclusion that children understood and internalized, often more fully than adults, the meaning of the Revolution. The roots of this practice in earlier Soviet pedagogy is clear in the best-known Soviet study of children's language, Kornei Chukovskii's *From Two to Five* (*Ot dvukh do pyati*), which was originally published in 1928 as *Little Children* (*Malen'kie deti*). Initially rooted in the pedagogical debates of the 1920s, it nonetheless ran through over twenty editions before the author's death in 1969. Chukovskii related numerous dialogues in which children took words too literally. In a typical exchange, a child who is asked if he is a Muscovite (*Moskvich*) connects the word to the automobile of the same name and answers that he is a "Victory" (*Pobeda*), another car.[76] Journalist Ella Winter suggested that such confusion was common. She reported that children "apply the ideology and politics of the day with amusing literalness," although her examples are not particularly funny. One little girl worried that a cab driver whose mare had had a foal would be classified as a kulak and would "have to be liquidated."[77]

Such misunderstandings did not become proof that children failed to understand or take an interest in the Revolution. Instead, the child's speech taken at face value became evidence of the profound influence of technology and Soviet ideology on the rising generation's picture of the world. The child who connected "Moskvich" to an automobile rather than the city or who described a broken shoelace as a "motor out of order" could be understood as more "correct" and up-to-date than the adults who chuckled at such charming confusion. Chukovskii marveled that "[e]ven before this child knew how to pronounce the words correctly, he already knew how to apply technical terminology to his tiny shoe." He explained that whereas an earlier generation of children attributed human or animal characteristics to machines ("Mother, look at that red-cheeked bus!"), the "new generation" understood animals and people in technical terms ("Oh, Mama, what a beauty you are! Like a new motorcycle!") An extreme example came out of the mouth of a four-year-old, quoted, Chukovskii assured his readers, with "stenographic exactness": "I am as exhausted as a 120-volt electric bulb connected with a 22-volt circuit—without a transformer." The rising generation was apparently no less precocious in the sphere of politics. Chukovskii recorded without comment the words of a child who responded to the news that "When it is day here, it is night in America," with a vehement, "Serves them right, those capitalists!"[78] Was a six-year-old who managed, with a bit of prompting from his mother, to propose the "bourgeoisie" as the "enemies of socialism" and to define them as "damagers" who "eat and sleep and take the money that the workman earns"[79] merely repeating phrases learned by rote? The question did not exist for Chukovskii. Despite his sensitivity to the child's age-specific capacities, he does not wonder what meaning "capitalist" could have had for a preschooler.

Ultimately, the image of the child as an empty vessel coupled with the equation of the child's and the state's interests ruled out such questions. Drawing on her own remembrances of childhood, Krupskaia argued that words had the power not only to reveal the child but also to shape his or her perceptions and "whole development." She recalled that her father's explanation, poorly grasped at the time, of a peasant's anger as a manifestation of the "age-old hatred" of the peasant for the landlord made the moment meaningful and, even more important, memorable for the six-year-old Nadezhda. Much later, she identified the episode as the source of her interest in "the question of why peasants hate landlords."[80] Children would learn in time to understand the strange new words that peppered their teachers', and sometimes their own, speech. In the meantime, that children listened to, remembered, and attempted to duplicate the speech, if not yet the meanings, of adults became evidence of the profound appeal of the task of building the communist future.

Teaching children the language of socialism and training them to be "future fighters" for socialism often meant raising children to defy the anti-Soviet influence of the older generation. Along with the intensification of class war came the intensification of generational conflict. If parents failed to reeducate themselves, policymakers reasoned, then children had to be taught to turn against their politically and culturally backward families. The kindergarten's "international, antireligious, collective upbringing" aimed to overturn the lessons learned at home. Where teachers "agitated against Christmas trees" and children reported that they had Christmas trees at home, it seemed clear, as one delegate to the 1929 congress expressed it, that "we must resolutely battle against the old way of life."[81]

Here the preschool campaign can be seen at its least practical and most tutelary. Enlisting young Pioneers to undertake systematic work with preschoolers constituted one method of minimizing the impact of the old generation on the young, both at home and at school. At the same time, teachers were directed to inculcate the "purposefulness" and class consciousness that prepared children to

Figure 8   "May Day parade" 1930

fight what Lunacharskii termed the "reactionary" influence of the family. Such plans ignored both the difficulties of making "primitive" kindergartens effective educational institutions and of enlisting parental support for institutions devoted to undermining parental authority. Turning children into revolutionaries at home rested on a vision of children as the happy and malleable agents of the Soviet state.[82]

Perhaps nothing more clearly illustrates the way in which rebellion against an actual father could become a sign of devotion to the metaphorical father than the story of Pavlik Morozov. In 1932, Pavlik, a young Pioneer, denounced his father as an enemy of the people only to be murdered by his grandfather and an accomplice. Almost immediately, Pavlik's story was mythologized. He became the first "Hero-pioneer of the Soviet Union," immortalized in poems, opera, movies, and statuary.[83] In the 1950s, the "cult of Morozov" still flourished at Pioneer camps. Paul Thorez, the son of French Communist Party leader Maurice Thorez, recalled, with a large measure of adult disgust, that the Pioneers knew Pavlik's biography by heart, and learned from it that "if family ties keep you enslaved to the past, they must be severed for the sake of the future."[84] The young generation remained the revolutionary class par excellence, but only in the most conservative sense of devoting itself to the tasks laid out by the state. Children retained the revolutionary prerogative to liberate themselves from antisocialist parents, but in doing so they only underlined their filial piety with regard to the social family.

While educational policy during the Stalinist Revolution emphasized the (contained) revolutionary rebelliousness of the rising generation, other policies equated the authority of (reeducated) parents with social order. The family, as Katerina Clark has argued, functioned as a "root metaphor" for the Stalinist state, "enhancing its increasingly hierarchical structure by endowing it with a spurious organicity."[85] The family metaphor also provided a powerful means of attaching the Revolution's most emancipationist images to a state committed to patriarchal order, productivity, and discipline. Positing the identity of the child's (if not always the parents') deepest desires and the state's interests made it possible to turn obedience to the authority of the great father into a revolutionary act. While educational and legal policy implemented "the disciplining of youth" derided by Trotsky as an authoritarian betrayal of the October Revolution, the image of a liberated rising generation building the bright Soviet future remained a powerful icon of revolution.

conclusion

Revolution and the Rising Generation

As the embodiment of the inevitable victory of the new over the old, as the agents and benefactors of the Revolution, children, or the rising generation as both a social category and symbolic construct, played a central role in Bolshevik conceptions of cultural transformation. Perhaps no "binary model" shaped the Russian revolutionary tradition more deeply than the conflict between fathers and sons—the old versus the young, the obsolete versus the modern.[1] At least since the 1860s, generational conflict functioned in radical circles as a means of visualizing, naturalizing, and even realizing cultural change. Drawing on this legacy, the Bolsheviks, who as Marxists defined the proletariat as the moving force of the revolution, often identified the young with the victory of the working class. If the proletariat began the Revolution, then the children of October would finish it. Ultimately, the contest over the nature of childhood was a battle between conflicting visions of the process of creating socialism—and socialists.

By 1932, the revolutionary optimism that had led officials during the Civil War to predict that the family was on the verge of withering away and to view homeless children as the harbingers of the future communist society had been eclipsed by calls for order, productivity, and discipline. Such optimism had been on the wane since the 1920s. Faced with the reality that world revolution was not imminent and with the task of restoring an economy ravaged by revolution and civil war, the Bolsheviks had backed away from predictions that full communism would take root spontaneously and almost immediately.

But fading optimism did not coincide with a straightforwardly, or even predominately, "pragmatic" approach to children, family, or the question of revolutionizing culture generally. Revolutionary priorities and conceptions of cultural transformation certainly shifted; the image of the Revolution as a moment of liberation gave way to an emphasis on revolutionary enlightenment and, increasingly, control. However, the shift cannot be adequately understood as a case of "backwardness" forcing policymakers to abandon their revolutionary dreams.[2] Even in the avowedly nonrevolutionary years of the New Economic Policy, the visionary and practical aspects of Soviet policy overlapped and complicated one another. Although by early 1918, Lenin was tempering his vision of the communist future built and run by workers themselves with reminders of the importance of discipline and education,[3] the two potentially incompatible images of revolutionary transformation coexisted through the mid-1920s.

The complex interaction of pragmatic and ideological impulses is particularly striking in the changing Bolshevik approach to children. Improving the material circumstances of children was an urgent necessity. The *besprizorniki* were only the most visible and extreme manifestation of the dangers facing the rising generation as a whole. But through the period of the First Five-Year Plan, solutions to immediate problems could not be separated from the vision of children as the future builders of the communist society. On one level, saving children was vital to the political legitimacy and viability of the Soviet state. In a literal sense, the regime depended on its children. At the same time, the rising generation played a central role in the Bolshevik picture of the process of cultural transformation. Attention to the immediate needs of children did not necessarily preempt or even curtail efforts to remake childhood and families. At the intersection of family and state, the kindergarten worked on the principle that it served not only the child in need of adequate food and supervision but also the child who stood as the icon of the Revolution's future. Realistic assessments of what actual children needed were tempered by the notion that revolution entailed, along with class struggle, generational conflict.

During the Civil War, the intoxicating sense of starting, as Trotsky expressed it, "from the beginning" with "no 'precedents,'"[4] could make even the most utopian project appear both reasonable and necessary. While health care workers argued that the regime's top priority had to be providing children with adequate food and medical care, teachers, who also saw the suffering of children at close range, represented the crisis as an opportunity to revolutionize the experience of childhood. Given the dislocations caused by the war — a growing population of homeless and abandoned children, famine, shortages of the most basic supplies — ensuring minimum standards of health and welfare constituted an ambitious, perhaps unrealistic, goal. Yet for advocates of socialized child care, these same crises required — and made possible — "children's liberation" and the establishment of children's homes to raise all children in clean, safe, and modern environments.

At the heart of the most liberationist conception of the Revolution stood the image of the latent creator, who, once freed from repressive authority, spontaneously and instinctively takes part in collective work and organizes self-regulating communes. Faith in the creative potential of release from oppressive relationships informed the image of the worker as capable of building and directing the socialist future, whether through some type of workers' control in the factory or through rotating responsibility for administrative tasks. Lenin suggested the latter in *State and Revolution*, a work he completed in the heat of the revolutionary year of 1917, when his confidence in spontaneous revolution was at its highest pitch. From this perspective, free upbringing's emphasis on unleashing the creative power of children could be represented as the natural educational corollary of the Revolution.

By contrast, the image of the child as a blank slate or, to borrow Gorky's image, "as a beehive to which various simple obscure people brought the honey of their knowledge,"[5] was connected to the notion that the creation of a socialist society required conscious, directed effort and thorough preparation. Such an understanding of childhood legitimized the tutelary state. The adoption of this definition signaled less a rejection of cultural transformation per se than a growing distrust of the child's (and the worker's) instincts. The conviction that cultural change required training children to be disciplined socialists replaced the vision of the rising generation naturally and spontaneously throwing off the weight of the past. The young child, like the worker, was no longer imagined as capable of building the future on his or her own.

The distrust itself was nothing new. The conviction that workers left to their own devices would, in Lenin's famous phrase, achieve only "trade union consciousness" had been a core tenant of Bolshevism since the beginning, dating back to Lenin's 1902 pamphlet on party organization "What is to Be Done?," which in turn was linked to a longer Russian radical tradition of coupling social revolution and cultural enlightenment. Children's liberation had never precluded the imposition of cleanliness, order, or even the "socialist" values that in 1924 became the organizing principle of life in the kindergarten. The crises of the post–Civil War period may help to explain the ascendancy of the tutelary over the liberationist vision of revolution, but discipline and education (or control and indoctrination) had long existed as revolutionary methods and goals.

Characterizing the NEP as substituting a practical for a utopian policy toward children ignores a shift in the Bolshevik approach to the process of revolutionary transformation that does not fit neatly into these categories. In the aftermath of the Civil War, it became clear that a system of children's homes and kindergartens capable of "liberating" women from the task of child-rearing and children from the authority of adults required resources that the state simply could not muster. Yet the kindergarten retained its role as an agent of "revolutionary" transformation, albeit of a new sort. Rather than eschewing efforts to remake culture as hopelessly utopian, "socialist" upbringing promised pervasive and at the same time efficient, orderly, and cost-effective change. While the new reliance on parents compelled the Bolsheviks to "disavow their proclamations of hostility to the family,"[6] it did not drive them to renounce efforts to remake it. If it was imprudent or impossible to eliminate the family, it, or at least its youngest, most impressionable members, had to be reeducated.

If reassigning primary responsibility for child care to parents could legitimately be represented as "practical," the "socialist" curriculum's basic assumption—that the pliable rising generation could be molded into the reliable vanguard of the Revolution in the home—seems decidedly less scientific and realistic than authorities claimed. Somewhat paradoxically, the NEP and later the preschool campaign kindergartens aimed to win the support of parents even as they stirred up generational conflict within the family by inculcating explicitly "socialist" values. While the decision to defer the socialization of child care to the remote communist future may suggest that Russian "backwardness" dictated the postponement of revolutionary change, the alternative "socialist" upbringing cannot be counted as entirely responsive to cultural or material constraints.

The repudiation of "children's liberation" coincided with an uncoupling of women's emancipation from efforts to restructure relations within the family or to lighten the burden of child care for working mothers. With regard to women, the kindergarten's revolutionary potential was increasingly located in its ability at once to draw women into work outside the home and to transform mothers into "rational" care givers capable of raising their children in the spirit of socialism. Even during the Civil War, amid excited predictions that the family was already withering away, Kollontai and others had represented motherhood as a social duty and had affirmed the existence of a maternal instinct. When new priorities and contingencies returned responsibility for child care to the family, it proved a short step from such premises to defining women's "liberation" as the universalization, rather than the elimination, of the working mother's double shift.

The antiliberationist models of cultural transformation evident in the program of "socialist" upbringing became more pronounced during the First Five-Year Plan, as efforts to mold children and families in the state's image intensified. During the First Five-Year Plan, the socialist link between public upbringing and women's and children's emancipation was severed entirely. Nonetheless, the shoring up of traditional family relationships that can be understood as a pragmatic recognition of parents' continuing role in child-rearing (or at least in disciplining their children) was attached to ambitious efforts to modernize and revolutionize child care practices. Here "revolution" meant something far less inclusive and multivalent than it had during the Civil War. Centrally planned cultural transformation required the rejection of the pedagogical eclecticism and tolerance that had already been curtailed by the "socialist" curriculum of the mid-1920s.

Yet the happy child as the icon of socialist transformation remained. On the level of pedagogy, the continued emphasis on the child's happiness made it possible for teachers to adapt traditional practices for use in the socialist kindergarten. For all its hostility to "bourgeois" education, the "socialist" program did not renounce the progressive dictum that the school experience must be a joyful one so much as recast it in a way that collapsed the present and future needs of children. The insistence on the absolute overlap of the child's happiness and the interests of the industrializing state made it possible to imagine the Stalinist revolution from above as the legitimate heir of the heroic, euphoric spirit of the Civil War years. The army of the young was once again on the march; the Soviet state once again was pictured as standing on the side of the rising generation against all that was old and out-of-date. Linking class conflict and revolutionary transformation to intensified generational conflict had deep symbolic resonance and at least a veneer of social reality, since the working class was being rejuvenated by an influx of young people. Yet behind the co-opted rhetoric, the center of gravity had shifted. Rather than opening up uncharted horizons, both class and generational conflict were linked to ends defined in advance by the state. Recognizing no distinction between the interests of the individual child and the classlike interests of the rising generation as interpreted by the party, the Stalinist Revolution could deploy the Revolution's most liberationist image—happy children building the future—in its war on the revolutionary dreamers.

Postscript

Three Childhoods

If you ask me, "Did this happen?" I will reply, "No."
If you ask me, "Is this true?" I will say, "Of course."
　　　—Elena Bonner, *Mothers and Daughters*

This study has relied primarily on the observations of teachers as the basis for conclusions about children's experiences of the Revolution. While teachers viewed themselves, and often appear to us, as sensitive observers, their pictures of childhood have obvious limitations. The adults who so carefully collected and preserved children's words and work imagined that they were capturing the true perceptions of the rising generation, yet once embedded in the adult narrative, the children's words ceased to be their own. As Barbara Beatty has noted in her study of American preschool education, "young children are the most silent and silenced of historical actors."[1] Teachers hoping to demonstrate the reality of a "new generation" of children imbued with the ideals of the Soviet state or simply free from the constraints of the past clearly adapted the child's words to a Soviet script. Moreover, their "scientific" agenda tended to ignore the relation between the internal development of the child and his or her awareness of the world. By the mid-1920s, children's childishness was the least remarkable thing about them. Depending upon teachers' assessments means accepting, at least in part, their notion of the rising generation as a social category, a quasi-class that was likely to understand the world in predictable and regular ways.

Reminiscences of childhood pose problems of their own. By the time the children themselves could control the recording of their words they were no longer children, and their memories reflect both the child's and the adult's explanations and emotions.[2] Constructed from fragments of memory beyond outside verification, remembrances of childhood can be, as Elena Bonner (Andrei Sakharov's widow) suggests in the epigraph, existentially true but factually inaccurate. Additionally, while politics may only rarely play an important role in many recollections of childhood, in the Soviet case, the Revolution and the revolutionary script with its vision of happy socialist children permeate accounts of childhood.[3] As one of the alumni of Moscow's Model School No. 25 told historian Larry Holmes, "Propaganda gave meaning to our lives."[4] The process of remembering is never wholly internal or individual, and the images and words of the Revolution could function as a sort of prefabricated template of childhood memory.[5]

Perhaps especially for adults whose first memories were of war and revolution, self-definition could not be easily separated from the upheaval of the wider world. Lev Kopelev's memoir echoes the Soviet state's emphasis on the simultaneous birth of the first socialist society and the first socialist generation. Kopelev, who turned five in the revolutionary year of 1917, remembered a time "alive and bursting with youth. Not only with my own tender youth and that of people my age, but with the *youth of the century*."[6] The poet Ol'ga Berggol'ts explicitly places herself among the "children of October." She finds the defining characteristic of her generation in the "happy overlap" of its childhood and the "first years—also childhood!—of our new society."[7] The sense of growing up with the Revolution shaped not only the child's experiences but also the adult's recollections.

Children often lived sheltered from the momentous events surrounding them, and it was frequently the words associated with the Revolution that made the most dramatic, if ambiguous, impact on them. The adults' "nostalgic return," like Kotik Letaev's in Andrei Belyi's novel, "is to the words of childhood as much as to its people and places."[8] The remembered speech of childhood is studded with the linguistic totems of the Soviet state—revolution, reds, socialist construction—that teachers would have taken as evidence of the Soviet imprint on their charges' characters. However, what the adults whom these children became tend to emphasize is the distance between the language of the Revolution and the child's experience. It is precisely in the gaps between images, words, and meanings that many locate childhood.

While they may not provide an accurate or verifiable picture of Soviet childhood, memoirs of childhood underline the limits of the experts' tendency to conceptualize youngsters as "the children of October." This brief review of a select number of interesting and suggestive recollections aims, therefore, not to make a small number of quite exceptional children stand in for their generation, but rather to explore the ways in which children's experiences (or adults' recollections of those experiences) deploy, complicate, contradict, or simply exist apart from the story of childhood produced by the concept of a "first socialist generation." Ultimately, the goal is to provide a number of child's-eye views of the Revolution and to come to some understanding of the process of construct-ing identity in a period of profound instability.

The Revolution, of course, was only the earliest potentially formative experi-ence of a generation that endured more than its share of hardships. For people born in the first thirty years of the twentieth century, who lived through the early decades of Soviet power as children, the experiences of Stalinist prison camps or of World War II could overshadow the Revolution.[9] Ol'ga Berggol'ts's childhood memories of the Civil War (she was born in 1910) are intertwined with her reminiscences of the nine hundred-day siege of Leningrad. Moreover, the presumption that Soviet childhood was a happy time may have militated against deeply personal accounts, as if Soviet childhoods are all happy in the same way. It is perhaps predictable, then, that among the richest memoirs of So-viet childhood are those of dissidents—Lev Kopelev (born in 1912) and Elena Bonner (born in 1923)—although even they have happy memories. In dis-cussing these memoirs, I have tried to distinguish the adult doing the writing (Kopelev, Bonner, Berggol'ts) from the child whose story is being told (Lyova, Lusia, Lialia), although the distinction between the author and the life often seems artificial and has a tendency to collapse.[10]

Ol'ga Berggol'ts: A Tale of Light

In October 1917, Ol'ga, or as she was called, Lialia, was seven years old and living in Petrograd. On the night of what turned out to be the Bolshevik seizure of power, she became alarmed by the bright pink glow of fires burning in what she thought must be a nearby quarter of the city. Her nanny assured her that there was nothing to worry about: "It's far away, the burning embers won't fly to us, don't be afraid." Walking with her mother the next morning, Lialia vis-ited the still-smoking ruins of the previous night's fire and saw armed workers wearing leather jackets and bandoleers packed into trucks speeding down Shlis-sel'burg Prospekt. But what seems to have impressed her at least as much as the dramatic scene was, along with the name "Lenin," the other "awesome, beauti-ful words" on everyone's lips: "decree," "Sovnarkom," "revolution" (Berggol'ts 149–50). Berggol'ts does not say what she took these strange, and apparently wonderful, new words to mean.

Much later, during the wartime siege of Leningrad, Berggol'ts found that re-calling those "legendary" words made it possible to feel once again the thrill and hope of the early days of the Revolution. Discovering the faded remains of a slogan remembered from 1917—"Guard the revolution!"—moved her to tears, "happy sobs"(174). Her emotional attachment to Soviet propaganda was perhaps not so unique. More mundane slogans, recalled under even crueler conditions, could rekindle the excitement of being a child at an extraordinary time. Evgeniia Ginzburg, just ten in the revolutionary year 1917, remembers looking back on her youth from a Stalinist prison in 1938. She and her cell mate "recall happy childhood memories—for in that dawn of the Revolution we had such a childhood as no one has ever had before or since." The memory of "that famous poster bearing the picture of an enormous louse, and summoning us to the fight against typhus, is now sheer poetry to us," bringing to mind more innocent times, personally and politically.[11] Words heard for the first time as a child evoked for the adult the legendary, romantic dimensions of the Revolution. Here the teachers' fondest hopes seemed to be realized, but probably not in a way they imagined.

Although the immediate result of the Revolution for Lialia and her family was dislocation and separation, Berggol'ts remembers the years of childhood and Civil War—the two are inseparable for her—as happy ones. Ol'ga's father, a doctor, who had served in the war against Germany, continued his military service in the Red Army until the famous attack across the ice at Kronstadt in 1921. Lialia and her younger sister moved with their mother to Uglich to escape the famine and the war. There they finally settled in an ancient monastery that Berggol'ts remembers in lyrical terms.

The nostalgia for the "land of childhood" is largely of the magical variety so common in memoirs of childhood.[12] The return to the cathedral's five blue cupolas becomes the central image in the happiest of Berggol'ts' recurring dreams (10). She recalls playing in the dense garden where the tsarevich Dmitrii was murdered—in 1591, although Lialia seemed to understand it as an event much nearer in time. In the wake of the "dethronement of our Petrograd tsar," Lialia had learned that being the tsarevich "was not exactly good," but she sympathized with the young and tragic Dmitrii nonetheless (179).

Her memories are not without their dark side. The war years were ones of privation and fears. The monastery itself could be a frightening place where, but for the presence of her dog Tyzik, the dead might rise from their graves. Berggol'ts recalls one harrowing night alone with her sister, when the oil lamp went out, and the girls' only match broke as they tried to relight it (7-9). And always there was the desire to return to Petrograd, a place her mother said the family had fled because of the famine but that Lialia associated with more prosperous times and sausage (7). Yet Berggol'ts characterizes her childhood as "happy," so often, in fact, that the author feels the need to apologize for the excessive use of the word (174).

With the end of the Civil War, the family returned to Petrograd. The reunion in Uglich with her barely recognizable father was awkward; he patted the girls on the head without letting go of his duffel bag (12). The trip itself was a series of noisy stations and starving, faceless people (19–20). But once again, Berggol'ts recalls revolutionary drama and hope. She identifies a conversation overheard on the train to Petrograd as the source of her powerful and persistent faith in the Revolution. A description of the planned hydroelectric plant at Volkhovstroi filled ten-year-old Lialia with pride, and this "tale of light" (*skazka o svete*) became in the darkest days of World War II a source of hope in the bright Soviet future. Beneath its patina of pro forma patriotism, the story about electrification was deeply personal. The promise of perpetual electric light resonated for Lialia because she linked it with the elimination of the cold and hunger of the Civil War years and, more specifically, with that fearful night she had spent in darkness (23–30).

With the tale of light, Berggol'ts's memories become more political. She recalls singing at a demonstration organized by the school and remembers experiencing each song as "the real truth." Lialia longed "to die for the Revolution" and envied those already old enough to do so (153). Ultimately, the focus of this political nostalgia is Lenin. The effusive devotion to Lenin can be understood, at least in part, as a function of the memoir's publication in the wake of the denunciation of Stalin at the Twentieth Party Congress in 1956. Berggol'ts denies the cult of Stalin by emphasizing the cult of Lenin, reaffirming her membership in a unique generation that "from earliest childhood" held Lenin it its heart (151). She pictures Lenin as the center of the child's conception of the Revolution—the same role assigned to Stalin, albeit with more mixed emotions, in the "precocious autobiography" of her younger peer, the poet Evgenii Evtushenko.[13] Moreover, by recalling youthful enthusiasm for Lenin's revolution, Berggol'ts separates the true spirit of the party from Stalin's crimes, much as Khrushchev did in his "secret" speech. Yet Berggol'ts's memories of Lenin seem too deeply linked to her own sense of identity to be dismissed as purely expedient fabrications or embellishments. She understands Lenin's death in primarily personal terms as marking the divide between childhood and youth—for herself and her entire generation (154).

Standing in the snow with the whistles of the Nevskii gate district's factories blaring in deafening, mournful homage to Lenin, fourteen-year-old Lialia decided to join the Komsomol, despite her grandmother's opposition to its atheism and her mother's worries about the boys. After her friend Valia also decided on the spot to join the Komsomol, Lialia went further and, "almost suffocating with a strange new happiness," pledged herself to become "a professional revolutionary. Like Lenin" (156). Almost immediately, the political commitment became linked to Lialia's aspirations as a poet. She wrote a poem in Lenin's honor that succeeded in bringing her to tears and that became her first published piece—on the wall newspaper at her father's workplace. The poem marked the end of her childhood; it was signed "Ol'ga" rather than "Lialia." Standing in front of her work, torn between pride and embarrassment, Ol'ga amended her vow. She would become a "professional revolutionary-poet" (162). Leaving the land of childhood, the passions that Berggol'ts views as giving meaning to the sacrifices of World War II were already forged. It seems more than a coincidence that she dates her devotion to Lenin and to poetry in precisely the same way— "from earliest childhood" (151, 163). Berggol'ts presents the two together as the key to her identity.

Lev Kopelev: Red D'Artagnan

For five-year-old Lyova the events of 1917 in Kiev were confusing and violent, at once "frightening, mysterious, and attractive" (Kopelev 7). Kopelev begins his account of childhood with a staccato description of a political demonstration, half seen and poorly understood. "Suddenly a commotion. Noise. Nanny shoves me into a doorway. . . . From under Nanny's elbow I see tricolored and red flags. . . . All around, people are saying: 'There goes Kerensky'" (1). Lyova did not know what to make of it all or of the puzzling political disagreements that divided the household. His nanny, a Russian Orthodox woman who secretly took Lyova to church and taught him that his parents "belonged to the bad faith of the Yids," loved the tsar and reverently showed the little boy postcards of the royal family while making the sign of the cross (3). "Great-Gramps," an "actual hero" with two Saint George medals, also stood against Kerensky. But Lyova's grandfather characterized Kerensky as "a good man—for freedom, for justice," and "Papa and Mama, apparently, agree with Grandpa, but don't want to say anything clear about it: 'Wait till you grow up'" (1–2).

Soon the rapid flow of events made the confusion irrelevant, as Kerensky's name disappeared from the adults' conversations, replaced by a series of new names—Lenin, Trotsky, the Hetman, Petlyura, Denikin. In a city held successively by Reds, Germans, Ukrainian nationalists, Reds, Whites, Reds again, Poles, and once again Reds, it was difficult for adults, let alone five-year-olds, to make sense of the shifting political scene. The Revolution entered Lyova's childhood in the form of the "terrible sounds of war" and the menacing yet irresistible words that filtered through the door of the nursery. "Some words would stand out: . . . 'attacking . . . retreating . . . pogrom . . . hunger . . . executions . . . Cheka . . . counterespionage . . . ration . . . search parties . . . '" Danger lurked in "ominous, frightening combinations of words." When the rumble of cannons reverberated nearby, the children were taken into the windowless bathroom, "but even there sharp cracks—shots—were sometimes heard" (7). A change in power meant machine gun fire and a visit from the upstairs neighbors, who came down to play cards and sing in the relative safety of the Kopelev's first floor apartment. The day of the Whites' entrance into the city, Lyova's parents were arrested; they were released the next morning. When the Reds retook the city from the Whites, rumors of pogroms sent the family to a crowded cellar for two days.

Lyova attached his own meanings to the new and fascinating vocabulary associated with these events. Sometimes he connected words to his observations or to the elliptical definitions provided by adults. Sometimes he linked, in personal and idiosyncratic ways, familiar things and people to the abstract language of the Revolution. He imagined the "revolution" that entered his consciousness in 1917 as "throwing a postcard tsar off his throne, and also something brighter, but shameful—the bare bottom of mustachioed Leshchinsky [the local forest ranger] being whipped by a bunch of shaggy muzhiks—and finally, something terrible, painful: squashed puppies," left behind when the family fled the countryside for Kiev and inadvertently stepped on (5). He "didn't understand what the word 'hostage' meant, but it invariably inspired a feeling of overwhelming horror, as did the words 'execution' and 'atrocities'" (10). Lyova understood the "terrible word 'pogrom'" as "a black and blue word," spoken with real terror by his mother (6). Kopelev remembers envisioning the "White movement" as "marching soldiers in white shirts and other soldiers in white Circassian coats atop white horses." "The iron organization of the Reds" he associated with the elaborate picture of "many iron staircases like the ones at the back of our house, which turned fiery cold in the frost and gripped your fingers, supporting cannons, machine guns and men in red shirts" (12).

The Civil War, which ended when Lyova was eight, left him with "no political convictions" (13). What attracted him was the romance, pageantry, and martial glory of war. In all the years that the city was occupied by troops, Lyova was "impressed by a 'real general' only once: a lilac great-coat with raspberry lining and golden epaulets with zigzags" (13). He initially opposed Soviet power on the grounds that Lenin and Trotsky were not legendary military leaders. He and his friend Seryozha "knew for a fact that the great men were Alexander the Great, Peter the Great, [Generalissimo Prince Alexander] Suvorov, and Napoleon" (16). When their friend Senya argued otherwise, Lyova and Seryozha turned to the eighty-two "deluxe volumes" of the Brockhaus and Efron encyclopedia that with its gilded pages, maps, and coats of arms seemed the highest possible authority. Still, Lyova was drawn to the mysterious agent of the Cheka, who lived in the Kopelev's apartment for a short while and whom his mother, fearing typhus and political contamination, ordered him to avoid. "It goes without saying," Kopelev confesses, "that I tried to stick my nose into the forbidden room every chance I got" (14). When the Reds took Kiev for the final time, a commander under Semen Budenny captured Lyova's imagination, and the boy was thrilled to find that the young officer had actually seen both Lenin and Trotsky (19). Nonetheless, eight-year-old Lyova's allegiance was to the

great men who "remained in the past, in bronze, in colored pictures under ciga-
rette paper" (17).

The Bolsheviks began to rise in Lyova's estimation when, between the ages of
nine and ten, his devotion to martial adventure, "my inclinations toward vio-
lence, my interest in horrifying books" became tempered with an "acute sense
of pity" (24). Kopelev provides no systematic analysis of the shift, but it seems
to have occurred on several levels more or less simultaneously. In the summer of
1922, Lyova "fell in love as one only can between nine and ten, after reading
Walter Scott's *Ivanhoe* and A. K. Tolstoy's *Prince Serebryany . . .* and just finding out where babies come from"(24). Lyova's newfound sense of pity also had
a more political side, thanks to his "confirmed Populist" tutor Lydia Lazarevna.
From her he "truly *heard*" for the first time words such as "ideal," "human-
ism," "the good of the people" (26). By the time Lyova learned enough arithmetic and geography to enter what his mother referred to as "the bum Soviet
school" (25) in the autumn of 1923, he had assimilated his tutor's idealism. At
about the same time, Lyova became a boy scout—a "wolf cub." His second
scoutmaster, whom Kopelev identifies as a Young Communist, taught another
sort of idealism, more violent than his tutor's: scouts who "laughed at Ukrainian inscriptions, signs and posters were fools and counterrevolutionaries. You
had to propagandize them, re-educate them or bash them in the chops" (29).
What finally cemented Lyova's communism was reading, in the spring of 1923,
Wilhelm Liebknecht's *The Commune*. Lyova wept "burning tears" over the
"heroism and terrible fate of the Parisian Communards. . . . And I decided then
and there that I was a confirmed communist" (34).

Lyova did not distinguish the various strands of his new revolutionary outlook, and it remained decidedly romantic. The "grandiose and heroic" words
learned from his friend Seryozha—sword knot, caparison, mount—remained
for Lyova as much a part of the Revolution as the bureaucratic acronyms of the
Soviet state and his tutor's idealism. He agonized over abandoning Napoleon
and Peter the Great as heroes (62-64). In his preadolescent reveries, Lyova was
part swashbuckler, part man of the people—pursuing pirates, discovering un-
known islands, constructing barricades in Paris and Berlin. He grafted the Revolution to more traditional subjects of childhood fancy. "On that January
night" that he learned of Lenin's death, Lyova "traveled to Lenin from revolutionary England, having won the heart of the king's daughter, as some sort of
Red D'Artagnan, and Lenin appointed me Narkomvoenmor (People's Commissar of the Army and Navy) of England, in command of the entire fleet," calling
the young hero "a true revolutionary—an idealist!" (54). Later, Lyova imagined Stalin "like one of those heroes in Dumas, Dickens, or Jules Verne: stern in
appearance, somewhat uncouth, tight-lipped, but secretly kind eccentrics, self-
lessly devoted to their duty—to the king, the lady of their heart, a child or

friend whose guardian they were" (68–69). His was a rather catholic understanding of the Revolution.

Lyova's enthusiasm for the martial, if not downright gory, side of the Revolution and his devotion to the "great men" of history tended to produce many lies. Kopelev remembers himself as lying "a lot and with real inspiration" (15), making up elaborate tales of being an eyewitness to the Revolution and to revolutionary leaders. Lyova told stories of street fighting he had supposedly witnessed that "involved a soldier's blue guts pouring out of his belly" (15). He so embroidered his brief talk with the young commander in Budenny's army that as an adult he "cannot unravel the fine threads of truth from all that got stuck in my memory" (19). Among Lyova's most ornate lies was one about seeing Trotsky speak in the square by the bronze Bogdan Khmelnitsky in Kiev. Unable to see above the crowd, eight-year-old Lyova envied "to death" the children perched on the tail of Bogdan's horse who had a clear view. So in the frequent retelling, Lyova put himself among them and explained his inability to remember a word Trotsky said as the result of "intense excitement and childish stupidity" (19–20).

Closer to home, Lyova's "political activity" (31) produced conflict with his parents and grandparents and, more painfully, ambivalence about his identity as a Jew. Lyova's father threatened, "If I see you with any red rag, I'll beat you so hard you won't be able to sit down," and the cautious Lyova initially hid his political convictions (31). He did occasionally slip, but his "loss of God," "the most significant event of 1923, the twelfth year of my life" (49), initially caused barely a ripple in the family. Kopelev relates that he never believed in the "Jewish God of my grandmother and grandfather," but instead in the "Orthodox God" and then the "Lutheran God" of his successive nannies (42). Thus Lyova's rejection of God, while galvanizing his political convictions, had little impact on his uncertain sense of himself as a Jew. His parents' efforts to give him a Jewish education had been uniformly unsuccessful. Nonetheless, Lyova acutely felt his estrangement from the Polish Catholic friends he made during his summers in the country, and he had no ready answer when an adult "would suddenly ask with an unfriendly laugh: 'Hey, you, sonny boy, who d'ya belong to—the Polacks, Russkies or Yids?'" (37). He felt equally a stranger among the small town Jewish boys with bare feet and payess, who in any case would not believe that Lyova, trying to make his German sound Yiddish, was really Jewish. "They were related to me in a way," Kopelev remembers thinking. "But I felt ashamed of them, and even more painfully, I felt ashamed of this feeling of shame" (40).

It was only when he turned thirteen and his grandparents began to agitate for his bar mitzvah that Lyova began to grapple with the relationship between his communist and Jewish identities. His grandfather, who believed that "you should not renounce your own race and people," tried to persuade Lyova to memorize one prayer and one short speech. But Lyova, having taken the "solemn pledge of the young Leninist Pioneer," refused to cooperate, and "Grandpa decided not to argue about it and proposed a deal." In exchange for reading one prayer rendered in Russian letters, Lyova would receive a "real new bicycle" (69–70).

The offer immediately became the subject of intense debate among the troop of young Pioneers. The boys for the most part were in favor of Lyova's reading the prayer and taking the bike—"that's business." Tolya, "a secret smoker, roughneck, and master of mother oaths" argued that not only could everyone learn to ride the bicycle, but that it would be "useful to the Red Army" (70); both the message and the messenger appealed to Lyova. But most of the girls stood for a vision of the Revolution more in line with Lyova's tutor's; to take the bicycle would be a humiliating and "dirty" betrayal of principle. In the end, Lyova accepted his mother's way out, spending his birthday "sick" in bed, forfeiting the bicycle, but avoiding any direct confrontation with his grandfather, who "congratulated me sadly and without affection" (72). The dejected Lyova, who could not view himself "as a valorous champion of atheism," apparently remained silent in the face of his grandfather's admonitions to respect an ancient religion, even if one does not believe in it (72). Lyova left childhood much less certain of his convictions or his identity than did Ol'ga.

Elena Bonner: Daughter of the Revolution

Bonner grew up in the elite inner circle of the communist party without the romantic revolutionary dreams of Lev and Ol'ga. For her, the Revolution was always close to home. Luska's mother was a devoted party member, and her stepfather Gevork Alikhanov was a prominent Comintern official. Luska (a nickname that came from the Armenian "Lusik") often took for granted the perks her family enjoyed—large apartments, extra food rations [14]—but she always had a clear sense of her parents' important connections to the Revolution. When the family lived in Leningrad, "boss of the city" Sergei Kirov lived in the same building, and three-year-old Luska understood his importance, if only because he was the only resident who had a car pick him up and drive him home. Kirov, who had a "personal relationship" with her parents, once gave Luska a ride in his car as the other children looked on, presumably with envy—of the ride if not her illustrious traveling companion. Sometimes Kirov would single her out, with a pat on the head or a brief word, from the other children playing near the building's entrance. "That gave me a sense (age doesn't matter) of my eliteness" (Bonner 30). Later, when the family moved to Moscow, seven-year-old Lusia (no longer Luska in Moscow) "liked Red Square, though it didn't give me aesthetic pleasure, as in Leningrad, but ideological. The Kremlin, the Mausoleum, Lenin—these names filled me with the delight of being part of it," or at least of her parents being "indelibly tied to it all" (107).

Luska's desire to feel her "eliteness" led her to construct all sorts of lies. When she spotted luminaries at the military parades on November 7 and May 1, Luska applauded "loud and long" with everyone else, although, as Bonner remembers it, "I found nothing special about them" (107). Nonetheless, Lusia never returned from a solo walk to Red Square without telling "everyone about it, adding a lie about seeing" Civil War commanders Semen Budenny or Clement Voroshilov. Around the time that Kirov was killed, Lusia reported having "seen Stalin himself" (107). While the adult she became denied feeling any excitement in the presence of the Revolution's leaders, Luska understood that seeing these men was somehow important, or at least interesting enough to lie about.

While her parents exposed Luska to the language and leaders of the Revolution from an early age, she rarely learned what they intended. Sometimes the ideas were simply beyond her understanding, and she assigned to them her own meanings. When her parents said that they were writing brochures on "questions of Party construction," three-year-old Luska concluded, and continued to believe for a "long while," that "the Party built houses" (40). A little older, Luska informed her father's friend Villi Brodsky that he was no longer welcome in their home. She explained that when she was outside with her nanny "everybody was walking around shouting, 'Get rid of Brodsky.'" The misunderstanding made Brodsky and her father laugh; "Get rid of Trotsky," they corrected (48–49). Only later, Bonner relates, did she learn who Trotsky was. As Berggol'ts notes, pronunciation often preceded understanding.[15]

Complicating her parents' task was the influential presence of Luska's strong-willed, anti-Bolshevik Grandma Tanya, or as Luska called her, Batanya. The differences between the grandmother's and the mother's ways of life were visible and palpable. Batanya covered her tables with fine tablecloths. Her flatware matched (251). It was Batanya who went with Luska to the theater, taking advantage of the tickets that Luska's parents received as party members but were too busy to use (45). Batanya wore a silk coat; she dressed Luska in a velvet dress (320, 45). Ruth Bonner, on the other hand, covered her tables with oilcloth (95). She shaved Lusia's head in the summer, as some sort of health measure (317). The beauty of the Luxe hotel in Moscow where the family lived delighted Lusia and irritated her mother (93).

The "bourgeois" pleasures appealed to Luska, perhaps in part because they aggravated her mother. If Lyova's rebelliousness led toward communism, hers led away from it. Only when three-year-old Luska threatened to make a scene did her mother relent and buy her a potted flower, the sort of object that Bonner characterizes as "almost a criminal offense in my mother's strict communist 'antibourgeois' world" (35). Luska understood, at least, that her mother did not approve. At five, Luska demanded a Christmas tree. Her stepfather patiently explained that the tree "was bourgeois and 'atavistic,'" taking care to define "atavism," as if a reasoned elucidation of the revolutionary principles involved would alter Luska's desires. The result was that Luska "knew full well how 'anti-party' my desire was, but that merely increased my longing." Her "maximalist" parents eventually gave in (57). In 1930, when the annual Mardi Gras festivities were banned, Batanya met Luska's tears with the explanation, "filled with dislike," that "you can thank your mommy and daddy for this." Angry at both her parents and her grandmother, Luska threw into the garbage the money she had been saving to buy rubber balls, Chinese lanterns, and other trinkets (77–78).

The primary battlefield between Batanya and Luska's parents was in the arena of literature, and there, Bonner suggests, the grandmother largely triumphed. Batanya's books were always "in opposition to what my parents gave me" (73). Luska read *Little Women*, *Little Lord Fauntleroy*, Dickens, Sir Walter Scott, and Pushkin at a time when the poet was not part of the Soviet canon. Still for Luska, who, like Lyova, found in books all sorts of possible identities, the Soviet stories approved by her parents had a certain appeal. Sometime around the age of seven, Luska read *Red Devils*, and she "envied those kids who had fought in the Civil War and regretted not having been born then and dying with them for the Revolution." Bonner remembers thinking, "I could have been like them" (107). A few years later, Luska risked the communist wrath of her mother by reading the forbidden works of Lydia Charskaia and Anastasiia Verbitskaia. She imagined herself as Charskaia's Princess Nina Dzhavakha (203–204). Bonner meticulously catalogs the books she was reading at a given moment, as if her bibliography holds the key to her identity. Whether consciously or not, she echoes Osip Mandelstam's assertion that "a *raznochinets* needs no memory—it is enough for him to tell of the books he has read, and his biography is done."[16]

Compared to her family and books, the kindergarten and the school played a relatively small role in shaping Luska's vision of the world. Especially with regard to school, Bonner's fondest and most vivid memories are not of teachers or curriculum, but of the friends she made. She characterizes her first years of school in the early 1930s as "an era of experimentation with education" that the pupils experienced primarily as the constant transfer from one inadequate building to another (110–111). It seemed to Lusia that in the second grade the pupils did no studying at all, since one representative answered for each group of ten children. Not until fourth grade (1933) did exams appear; "before that, there seemed to have been no record kept of our work" (117).

As the daughter of a Bolshevik mother who was committed to revolutionary child-rearing methods and who, as Bonner remembers it, had little interest in fussing over her children, Luska attended kindergarten from the age of three. The kindergarten at the Astoria hotel in Leningrad gave Luska one of her first opportunities to interact with children her age. There she experienced her first crush and heard a radio for the first time. Her classmates introduced her to new words, often poorly understood, that expanded Luska's horizons. Bonner, who uses her recollections of the state of her vocabulary as the most accurate representation of childhood time and as the primary gauge of her mentality at any given moment, remembers hearing the name "Esenin" for the first time from some fellow pupils at the Astoria kindergarten. At first she "thought it was a given name, Eseni, and didn't understand." The adult's voice intervenes at this point to explain that Sergei Esenin was a poet who committed suicide (in 1925). Often hearing the name in the grownups' conversation at home, Luska began to sense "that something very bad had happened and that people were sad and disapproving, even afraid" (29–30). But not until a few years later, after witnessing a woman jump to her death in St. Isaac's square, did the then six-year-old Luska put the linguistic puzzle together, associating the story heard in the kindergarten with what she had just seen and with her mother's use of the word "suicide" (43).

While she remembers the Astoria kindergarten as a pleasant place where the children had "several airy rooms, nothing was dirty, there were lots of toys, and the children were always clean and neatly dressed," Bonner depicts the kindergarten she attended in Moscow in 1927 (while her parents were taking "Marxism Courses" there) as "cramped, with dim, gray light" (60). Instead of individual towels, all the children shared a single one that was perpetually wet. The toilet "was filthy and it stank" (60). A long string of illnesses—measles, German measles, mumps—cut the experience short.

Tutored by Batanya in Leningrad the following year, the already literate Luska attended a Leningrad kindergarten in the fall of 1930. This time she experienced the kindergarten as "absolutely useless . . . since we didn't hold a pen or even a pencil in all that time, and there were no notebooks, or books, just a teacher talking and sometimes drawing on the board" (80). When it became clear to the teacher that Luska could read, she went "terribly embarrassed" to Batanya (Luska's parents were working at the party's Central Asia Bureau) to suggest that Batanya go to the school to get her granddaughter promoted to the first grade (81). After only a few days in the first grade, Luska again became seriously ill, this time with scarlet fever. The illness, which kept Luska in the hospital for over two months, forced the return of Ruth Bonner.

Through a long series of childhood illnesses, Luska felt acutely that her mother cared for her only when she was sick, and even then grudgingly. The memoir overflows with examples of what Luska perceived as her mother's coldness. Bonner remembers her mother characterizing her as "useless," "a weakling," "ugly" (66, 61, 46). When, during Lusia's bout of the mumps, her mother compared her unfavorably to her younger brother Egorka, "a golden child" who never got sick, Lusia "blew up," and her mother "ran out of the room with the words, 'I could just kill her'" (62). Returning from the dentist after having had a tooth extracted, Lusia informed her mother that she was "gushing blood." Lusia chose the expression specifically for its power to "overcome Mama's heartlessness," but it succeeded in eliciting only a curt, "I don't see." Her mother "wouldn't even hold my hand" on the way home (66). Lusia called Alikhanov "Papa," and never thought of him "as an evil stepfather," or indeed as a stepfather at all. But she suspected her mother's true identity and "watched her closely for signs" that she was really a wicked stepmother (46-47).

At some ill-defined point, Bonner, by then no longer a child, came to understand her mother's emotional distance in terms of politics. What as a child she understood as heartlessness or indifference, she attributes as an adult to her mother's party membership: "In their milieu being a 'crazy mother' must have been considered nonsense" (42). In retrospect, Bonner no longer sees her mother as a wicked stepmother but instead as "a party worker, antibourgeois and maximalist, who never allowed herself to use a tender word to Egorka or me." When she steps back to consider the full sweep of their relationship, Bonner concludes that only with the "difficult, almost impossible step" of turning in her party card did her mother "fully g[i]ve herself to us, her warm, living love, which was higher than any abstract ideas and principles." Her mother eventually became, much to Bonner's amazement, "a 'crazy' grandmother and great-grandmother" (89–90). Still, the "Forbidden" sign apparently posted by the party prevented Bonner from holding her dying mother in her arms. It was a dream of kissing her mother, an action neither would have "imagined or permitted" when Ruth Bonner was alive, that opened the floodgates of childhood memory (10–11).

The end of that childhood can be dated precisely to "the night of May 27, 1937, on the Moscow Boulevard ring, by the statue of Pushkin" (307), where Lusia, who had spent the night alone on the street, barred from her apartment and turned away from her aunt's after Alikhanov's arrest, realized that she no longer felt ashamed. Her mother's arrest followed shortly thereafter; with that "our era began" (306). But while Bonner views herself as less an heir of the Revolution than of the purges, she also understands the betrayed (or perhaps tragically misguided) ideals of October as responsible for her difficult and distant relationship with her mother. Bonner may not number herself, as both Kopelev and Berggol'ts seem to, among the "children of October," but she too makes sense of the Revolution in generational terms. Echoing, feminizing, and expanding Turgenev's "fathers and sons," Bonner examines not only the relationship of the revolutionary daughter and the older generation but also that of the revolutionary mother and her daughter. In the memoir's final paragraph, Bonner finds the consequences of the Revolution in the guilt Ruth Bonner felt "because her fate ricocheted into her mother's life" and the guilt she herself feels "toward my mother for my life and happiness" (333). She ends by universalizing her conclusions, suggesting both wider generational conflict and the hope of reconciliation: "Mothers and daughters! Mothers and daughters."

What is perhaps most striking in these accounts is that while they recount much pain and sorrow, their authors attest to happy childhoods. That the dissidents Bonner and Kopelev represent their childhoods as happy is particularly surprising, an apparent endorsement of the regime they came to oppose. Bonner fully appreciates the awkward political ramifications of her happy memories. She imagines the "critics, both left and right would really let me have it for that happy childhood," a phrase she expects will be linked to "the poster in the school lobby: 'Thank you, Comrade Stalin, for our happy childhood" (320). Her own narrative can be understood as an effort to sunder this connection. Bonner often locates childhood happiness in her paradoxical status as a member of the Soviet elite and as the beneficiary of Batanya's efforts to provide her with a non-Soviet (if not anti-Soviet) childhood. Bonner remembers finding pleasure in both the "ideological" grandeur of Red Square and in an "anti-party" Christmas tree. Kopelev's happy childhood constitutes part of what he characterizes as the "education of a true believer," but the incidents he retells with the greatest relish have little to do with the stock Soviet images of childhood. While Bonner found happiness in the velvet dresses and opera tickets supplied by her grandmother, Kopelev imagined himself as a revolutionary in the rather unorthodox guise of "Red D'Artagnan."

Berggol'ts's "tale of light" seems to fit the Soviet stereotype more closely: a child sent into raptures by the promise of the bright socialist future. Yet her frequent and earnest insistence on her childhood happiness often works to complicate and qualify the iconic image of the happy Soviet child. In Berggol'ts's account what made childhood happy was not the Soviet system itself so much as the coincidence of the moment in which she viewed the world as magical and the drama of revolution. Recognizing a mirror image of her warm memories in the nostalgia for Leningrad of a child survivor of the deadly winter of 1941–1942 in the besieged city, Berggol'ts suggests that childhood happiness may have more to do with the child's inner life than with the wider Soviet world. Berggol'ts, Bonner, and Kopelev present happy revolutionary childhoods that are often at odds with the sanitized propaganda poster notion of happy childhood as a gift from the Soviet state.

Children clearly "felt" the Revolution, but often in ways that adults did not predict and could not control. Permeated with the language of the Revolution and the sense of belonging to a unique generation, these memories of childhood suggest both that children made their own kind of sense of the momentous events surrounding them and that they viewed the Revolution—or the adults they became represented the Revolution—as a vital element in their self-identification. That children lied about having spotted Trotsky or Stalin may bespeak a more insidious—and therefore more ominous—intrusion of the state into childhood than Pavlik Morozov's extraordinary act. Children who lie in the name of the Revolution may be a fittingly sinister epigram for Stalinism. Still, the understandings behind the lies could be worlds away from those adults hoped to inculcate. For Lyova, the Revolution was part of a grand heroic epic that reached back to Alexander the Great. The more blasé Lusia understood the status associated with the leaders of the Revolution, and perhaps hoped her lies might impress the mother who put the party before her children. Lialia, who identified the idealism of the Revolution with Lenin and the dream of electrification, seems to have perceived the world in the "correct" way. Yet even her understanding of the Revolution was intimate and personal, linked to her poetic sensibility in ways that potentially transcended or ignored the party line. Children may have experienced the Revolution as a profound generational split, but their lives were more varied, and their understandings of the Revolution more personal, than their designation as the "children of October" allowed. Their remembered reality corresponds neither with the vision of the rising generation as spontaneously freed from the weight of the past nor with the picture of the child unproblematically remade in the image of the state.

Notes

Introduction

1. The equation of public laundries and dining rooms with public child care was common. See, for example, activists quoted in Elizabeth Wood, *The Baba and the Comrade: Gender and Politics in Revolutionary Russia* (Bloomington: Indiana University Press, 1997), 62, 79, 86, 100, 160, 207, as well as Chapters 1 and 2 in this volume. Wendy Goldman traces the "origins of the Bolshevik vision" in *Women, the State, and Revolution: Soviet Family Policy and Social Life, 1917–1936* (Cambridge, England: Cambridge University Press, 1993), 1–58. Foundational texts in the Marxist canon include Karl Marx and Frederick Engels, *The German Ideology* (New York: International Publishers, 1970); Engels, *The Origin of the Family, Private Property, and the State* (Chicago: C. H. Kerr and Co., 1902); and August Bebel, *Women and Socialism* (New York: Socialist Literature Co., 1910).

2. Alan M. Ball, *And Now My Soul Is Hardened: Abandoned Children in Soviet Russia, 1918–1930* (Berkeley: University of California Press, 1994), xiii, 40, 80.

3. Lynn Mally, *Culture of the Future: The Proletkult Movement in Revolutionary Russia* (Berkeley: University of California Press, 1990), 180–81.

4. Hugh Cunningham, "Histories of Childhood," *American Historical Review* 103 (Oct. 1998): 1195, 1196.

5. Lynn Hunt, *The Family Romance of the French Revolution* (Berkeley: University of California Press, 1994), xiv, 196. Wood, *The Baba and the Comrade*, 13.

6. Carolyn Steedman's study of the child figure Mignon proceeds "on the assumption that it is helpful to make an analytic separation between real children, living in the time and space of particular societies, and the ideational and figurative force of their existence" but adds that "this is a cognitive dislocation that is extremely difficult to perform"; see *Strange Dislocations: Childhood and the Idea of Human Interiority, 1790–1830* (Cambridge, Mass.: Harvard University Press, 1995), 5.

7. For a fuller discussion of this point and an example of how age categories can be problematized, see Gillian Weiss, "'A Very Great Nuisance': Young Children and the Construction of School Entry in South Australia, 1851–1915," *History of Education Review* 22 (1993): 1–17.

8. Wood focuses primarily on nurseries, but also mentions the Zhenotdel's interest in preschools, see *Baba and the Comrade*, 79–93. For activists, part of the appeal of nurseries over preschools seems to be have been that nurseries did not require trained teachers. On the ways in which providing for (largely school-age) *besprizorniki* forced a "retreat" from socialized child-rearing, see Goldman, *Women, the State, and Revolution*, 59–100. On primary and secondary education, see Larry Holmes, *The Kremlin and the Schoolhouse: Reforming Education in Soviet Russia, 1917–1931* (Bloomington: Indiana University Press, 1991). On secondary education, see James C. McClelland, "The Utopian and the Heroic: Divergent Paths to the Communist Educational Ideal," in *Bolshevik Culture: Experiment and Order in the Russian Revolution*, ed. A. Gleason, P. Kenez, and R. Stites (Bloomington: Indiana University Press, 1985), 114–130. On postsecondary education, see Michael David-Fox, *Revolution of the Mind: Higher Learning among the Bolsheviks, 1918–1929* (Ithaca, NY: Cornell University Press, 1997).

9. Allison James, Chris Jenks, and Alan Prout, *Theorizing Childhood* (New York: Teachers College Press, 1998), 178.

10. James et al., *Theorizing Childhood*, 177. The authors suggest, "Childhood's middle years — from four to ten years old — are comparatively little studied" because "by researching those who have few words and those who have many, the 'problem' of linguistic competence is seemingly reduced."

11. Wood, *Baba and the Comrade*, 3. See, for example, Richard Stites, *The Women's Liberation Movement in Russia: Feminism, Nihilism, and Bolshevism* (Princeton, N.J.: Princeton University Press, 1978), 317–76; Beatrice Farnsworth, "Bolshevik Alternatives and the Soviet Family: The 1926 Marriage Law Debate" in *Women in Russia*, ed. Dorothy Atkinson et al. (Stanford, Calif.: Stanford University Press, 1977), 139–65; Goldman, *Women, The State, and Revolution*; Barbara Evans Clements, "The Effects of the Civil War on Women and Family Relations," in *Party, State, and Society in the Russian Civil War: Explorations in Social History*, ed. Diane Koenker et al. (Bloomington: Indiana University Press, 1989), 105–20.

12. In addition to the sources cited in note 11, see Gail Warshofsky Lapidus, "Sexual Equality in Soviet Policy: A Developmental Perspective," in *Women in Russia*, 115–138; and Leon Trotsky, *The Revolution Betrayed: What Is the Soviet Union and Where Is It Going?* (New York: Pathfinder Press, 1972), 144–157. Trotsky argues both that "society proved too poor and too little cultured" for the "plans and intentions of the Communist Party " to be realized in many areas, and perhaps especially in the sphere of everyday life (145) and that the renewed support of patriarchy reflected "the need of the bureaucracy for a stable hierarchy of relations, and for the disciplining of youth" (153). Elizabeth Waters emphasizes that "focus on family reform was sharpest at times of political ferment"; see "The Bolsheviks and the Family," *Contemporary European History* 4 (1993): 275–291 (quotation, 276). Relevant documents may be found in Rudolf Schlesinger, ed. *The Family in the USSR: Documents and Readings* (London: Routledge and Kegan Paul, 1949).

13. Ball, *And Now My Soul Is Hardened*, 197–199.

14. Harry Hendrick, "Constructions and Reconstructions of British Childhood: An Interpretive Survey, 1800 to the Present" in *Constructing and Reconstructing Childhood: Contemporary Issues in the Sociological Study of Childhood*, ed. Allison James and Alan Prout (London: Falmer Press, 1990), 35–59; Hugh Cunningham, *The Children*

of the Poor: Representation of Childhood Since the Seventeenth Century (Oxford, England: Blackwell, 1991). In an excellent study of working-class childhood, Anna Davin accepts the definition of childhood as a "period of dependence and subordination," arguing that its duration "is not fixed (not even by the biological benchmarks of puberty or mature growth) . . . nor is its content"; see Growing Up Poor: Home, School, and Street in London 1870–1914 (London: Rivers Oram, 1996), 2.

15. Martin Woodhead, "Psychology and the Cultural Construction of Children's Needs," in Constructing and Reconstructing Childhood, 60–77. On the "emotional tawdriness that 'child' and 'childhood' bring into play," see Steedman, Strange Dislocations, 9. For a sensitive discussion of how "today's assumptions" complicate a discussion of "hardships which to us seem extreme but which many children took for granted," see Davin, 8–9. On current studies of children that approach them, much as the Bolsheviks did, as "social actors," see James et al., Theorizing Childhood, and Alan Prout and Allison James, "A New Paradigm for the Sociology of Childhood? Provenance, Promise, and Problems" in Constructing and Reconstructing Childhood, 7–34.

16. James et al., Theorizing Childhood, 42.

Chapter 1

1. Svetlana Boym, Common Places: Mythologies of Everday Life in Russia (Cambridge, Mass.: Harvard University Press, 1994), 91.

2. Allan Bloom, "Introduction," in Jean-Jacques Rousseau, Emile, or On Education, trans. Allan Bloom (New York: Basic Books, 1979), 28, 29. Similarly, John Locke's Some Thoughts Concerning Education (1693) can be understood as of a piece with his political philosophy.

3. Bloom, "Introduction," 28. On the efforts of Johann Pestalozzi and Maria and Richard Edgeworth to raise their children according to Rousseau's precepts, see Barbara Beatty, Preschool Education in America: The Culture of Young Children from the Colonial Era to the Present (New Haven, Conn.: Yale University Press, 1995), 9–13.

4. On the international diffusion of the kindergarten see Roberta Wollons, ed., Kindergartens and Cultures: The Global Diffusion of an Idea (New Haven, Conn.: Yale University Press, 2000).

5. Beatty, Preschool Education in America, 41, 49.

6. On the conceptualization of "childhood experience in terms of the 'stages and scripts' in which space and time are closely interwoven," see Allison James, Chris Jenks, and Alan Prout, Theorizing Childhood (New York: Teachers College Press, 1998), 41.

7. Beatty, Preschool Education in America, 12, 40. Michael Steven Shapiro, Child's Garden: The Kindergarten Movement from Froebel to Dewey (University Park: Penn State University Press, 1983), 20.

8. Friedrich Froebel, Mother's Songs, Games and Stories: Illustrations and Music, trans. Frances Lord and Emily Lord (London: W. Rice, 1886). Beatty, Preschool Education in America, 39–47; on "children's kitsch," 46; Shapiro, Child's Garden, 20–25.

9. Beatty, Preschool Education in America, 79.

10. Anna Davin, Growing Up Poor: Home, School, and Street in London, 1870–1914 (London: Rivers Oram, 1996), 116.

11. Lawrence Cremin, *The Transformation of the School: Progressivism in American Education, 1876–1957* (New York: Vintage Books, 1964), 126–38, 152–56; Denison Deasey, *Education Under Six* (New York: St. Martin's Press, 1978), 38–39, 83–88, 175; Elizabeth Dale Ross, *The Kindergarten Crusade: The Establishment of Preschool Education in the United States* (Athens: Ohio University Press, 1976), 67–82. By the end of the first decade of the twentieth century, many U.S. public schools included one-year, half-day kindergartens, and the kindergarten lost some of its radicalizing potential, especially compared to nursery schools that remained outside the public school system; see Beatty, *Preschool Education in America,* 130–133.

12. Beatty, *Preschool Education in America,* 115.

13. Ann Taylor Allen, "Gardens of Children, Gardens of God: Kindergartens and Day-Care Centers in Nineteenth-Century Germany," *Journal of Social History* 19 (Spring 1986): 443.

14. Ann Taylor Allen, "'Let Us Live with Our Children': Kindergarten Movements in Germany and the United States, 1840–1914," *History of Education Quarterly* 28 (Spring 1988): 38, 29. See also Allen, "Gardens of Children," 439. For a similar politicization of the kindergarten in a different cultural context, see Mark D. Szuchman, "Childhood Education and Politics in Nineteenth-Century Argentina: The Case of Buenos Aires," *Hispanic American Historical Review* 70 (Feb. 1990): 131–132. In France, the Third Republic transformed the church-run *salles d'asile* into the secular *écoles maternelles,* and implemented "republican pedagogy," methods that owed much to the kindergarten; see Frédéric Dajez, *Les origines de l'école maternelle* (Paris: Presses Universitaires de France, 1994), 158–172; quotation, 169.

15. Allen, "Gardens of Children," 440–441. Friedrich Froebel's nephew Karl Froebel and Karl's wife Johanna taught kindergarten pedagogy and linked the kindergarten to utopian socialist ideals, feminism, and unorthodox religious beliefs. See also Allen, "'Let Us Live,'" 26–27.

16. The quotation from Froebel's open letter to the "Wives and Maidens of Germany" (1840) in which he elaborates the kindergarten's role in restoring "the primordial union of womanly life and motherly life with childhood" may be found in Beatty, 48–49, *Preschool Education in America,* and in Shapiro, *Child's Garden,* 25; see also *Froebel's Letters on the Kindergarten,* trans. and ed. Emilie Michaelis and H. Keatley Moore (London: Swan Sonnenschein, 1891), 59, 63–64, 158–159.

17. Seth Koven and Sonya Michel, "Womanly Duties: Maternalist Politics and the Origins of Welfare States in France, Germany, Great Britain, and the United States, 1880–1920," *American Historical Review* 95 (Oct. 1990): 1079, 1091. See also Ann Taylor Allen, "Spiritual Motherhood: German Feminists and the Kindergarten Movement, 1848–1911," *History of Education Quarterly* 22 (Fall 1982): 319–339; Beatty, *Preschool Education in America,* 47–51.

18. Clara Zetkin attacked Lily Braun's "simultaneous embrace of maternalism and socialism"; see Koven and Michel, "Womanly Duties," 1087–1091 (quotation, 1091, n. 61).

19. Allen, "'Let Us Live,'" 39. August Bebel took this approach to the kindergarten in *Women and Socialism.*

20. Quoted in Allen, "'Let Us Live,'" 38.

21. Davin, *Growing Up Poor,* 93. On conservative opposition to the kindergarten as subversive of the family, see Allen, "Gardens of Children," 442–444.

22. Jacques Donzelot, *The Policing of Families*, trans. Robert Hurley (New York: Pantheon, 1979). Ann F. La Berge, "Medicalization and Moralization: The Crèches of Nineteenth-Century Paris," *Journal of Social History* 25 (Fall 1991): 65–87; Siân Reynolds, "Who Wanted the Crèches? Working Mothers and the Birth-Rate in France 1900–1950," *Continuity and Change* 5 (1990): 173–197. Ellen Ross, *Love and Toil: Motherhood in Outcast London, 1870–1918* (New York: Oxford University Press, 1993), 195–221; Roger Cooter, ed., *In the Name of the Child: Health and Welfare, 1880–1940* (New York: Routledge, 1992); Deborah Dwork, *War Is Good for Babies and Other Young Children: A History of the Infant and Child Welfare Movement in England, 1898–1918* (London: Tavistock Publications, 1987). Richard A. Meckel, *Save the Babies: American Public Health Reform and the Prevention of Infant Mortality, 1850–1929* (Baltimore: Johns Hopkins University Press, 1990). Rosa Ballester and Emilio Balaguer, "La infancia como valor y como problema en las luchas sanitarias de principios de siglo en España," *Dynamis* 15 (1995): 177–192. Robert Van Krieken, "Towards 'Good and Useful Men and Women': The State and Childhood in Sydney, 1840–1890," *Australian Historical Studies* 23 (Oct. 1989): 405–425.

23. Beatty (*Preschool Education in America*) characterizes a nursery school in Boston's North End in 1922 as claiming "success in changing the problematic habits of the poor," 149. The second quotation comes from a 1911 petition of the Indianapolis Free Kindergarten Society to the state legislature, quoted in Allen, "'Let Us Live,'" 41.

24. Carolyn Steedman, *Childhood, Culture and Class in Britain: Margaret McMillan, 1860–1931* (New Brunswick, N.J.: Rutgers University Press, 1990), 46.

25. Davin, *Growing Up Poor*, 93. On peasant resistance to modern methods of child care in Russia, see Nancy M. Frieden, "Child Care: Medical Reform in a Traditionalist Culture," in *The Family in Imperial Russia: New Lines of Historical Research*, ed. David L. Ransel (Urbana: University of Illinois Press, 1978), 236–259.

26. Peter C. Pozefsky, "Love, Science, and Politics in the Fiction of *Shestidesiatnitsy* N. P. Suslova and S. V. Kovalevskaia," *The Russian Review* 58 (July 1999): 361. See also Irina Paperno, *Chernyshevsky and the Age of Realism: A Study in the Semiotics of Behavior* (Stanford, Calif.: Stanford University Press, 1988), 4–20.

27. For an overview, see L. N. Litvin, ed., *Istoriia doshkol'noi pedagogiki* (Moscow: Prosveshchenie, 1989), 175–191, 210–228.

28. Rudy Koshar, "Foucault and Social History," *American Historical Review* 98 (April 1993): 360. The article is a response to Laura Engelstein, "Combined Underdevelopment: Discipline and the Law in Imperial and Soviet Russia," *American Historical Review* 98 (April 1993): 338–353. Engelstein's contention that "in Russia, both the reign of law and the ascendance of bourgeois discipline remained largely hypothetical" (348), together with Koshar's response that it may be more accurate to approach Russia as a "heightened and intensified version of [Western] society" than as its conceptual opposite, provides a way of framing the contrast between the politics of childhood in Russia and the West.

29. Litvin, *Istoriia doshkol'noi pedagogiki*, 155–158.

30. Ibid., 156.

31. E. N. Vodovozova, *Na zare zhizni: memuranye ocherki i portreti* (Moscow: Khudozhestvennaia literatura, 1987), 2: 275–279; quotation, 278.

32. Ibid., 278–279.

33. Vodovozova, *Umstvennoe razvitie detei pervogo proiavleniia soznaniia do vos'miletnogo vozrasta: kniga dlia vospitatelei*, 3d ed. (St. Petersburg: Tip. F. S. Sushchinskago, 1876). See also Litvin, *Istoriia doshkol'noi pedagogiki*, 181–187.

34. Vodovozova, *Na zare zhizni*, 2: 275; Vodovozova, *Umstvennoe razvitiie*, 45–48; V. I. Vodovozov, "Detskie sady v Germanii," *Zhurnal ministerstva narodnogo prosveshcheniia* 96 (1857): 111. On Vodovozov, see Nicholas Hans, *The Russian Tradition in Education* (London: Routledge and Kegan Paul, 1963), 134–138.

35. L. N. Tolstoy, "On Popular Education," in *The Complete Works of Count Tolstoy*, trans. Leo Wiener (Boston: D. Estes and Co., 1904), 272.

36. Litvin, *Istoriia doshkol' noi pedagogiki*, 155. By contrast, in the United States the "final showdown between orthodox Froebelianism and progressive kindergarten pedagogy" occurred only in the early twentieth century; see Beatty, *Preschool Education in America*, 116.

37. Vodovozova, *Umstvennoe razvitie*, 49.

38. Vodovozov, "Detskie sady v Germanii," 105; K. D. Ushinskii and V. I. Vodovozov, *Domashnoe vospitanie: rukovodstvo dlia roditelei i vospitatelei k vospitaniiu i obucheniiu detei s prilozheniem rukovodstvo k Frebelskim obrazovetel'nym igram* (St. Petersburg: Tip. K. K. Retgera, 1883), 66. On Ushinskii, see Hans, *The Russian Tradition in Education*, 65–85.

39. Hans outlines the elements of the "tradition"—"social attitude," "secular education," "scientific-utilitarian bias," "universal and European bias," and "productive work as part of education"—in his final chapter in *The Russian Tradition in Education*, 150–171.

40. K. D. Ushinskii, "A General View on the Emergence of Our Public Schools," in *Selected Works*, ed. A. I. Piskunov (Moscow: Progress, 1975), 360.

41. Vodovozova was a student at Smolny when Ushinskii was inspector there. Vodovozov collaborated with Ushinskii, and when the latter was dismissed, Vodovozov resigned. Vodovozova, *Na zare zhizni*; Hans, *The Russian Tradition in Education*, 135.

42. Elizabeth Wood, *The Baba and the Comrade: Gender and Politics in Revolutionary Russia* (Bloomington: Indiana University Press, 1997), 13.

43. Historians have found in the concept of a "generation" of the 1860s a convenient means of distinguishing the radicalism of the 1860s from that of the 1840s. For an example of this general usage, see Nicholas Riasanovsky, *A History of Russia*, 4th ed. (New York: Oxford University Press, 1984), 381.

44. D. I. Pisarev, "Bazarov," *Sochineniia* (Moscow: Gosudarstvennoe izdatel'stvo Khudozhestvennoi literatury, 1955), 2: 7–50.

45. Paperno, *Chernyshevsky and the Age of Realism*, 4–40. Andrzej Walicki's argument that "Dobroliubov's favorite theme was the problem of 'two generations,' or more accurately of the two social forces involved in the reform movement," grants the ubiquity of generational rhetoric, while reading it as code for more "meaningful" social categories; see *A History of Russian Thought: From the Enlightenment to Marxism* (Stanford, Calif.: Stanford University Press, 1979), 206.

46. Vodovozova, *Na zare zhizni*, 2: 87.

47. For an overview of the pedagogical writings of both, see Hans, *The Russsian Tradition in Education*, 107–128; biographical information, 109, 112.

48. N. A. Dobroliubov, "O znachenii avtoriteta v vospitanii," in *Stat'i, retsenzii, iunosheskie raboty, aprel' 1853–iiul' 1857* (Moscow: Gosudarsivennoe izdatel'stvo detskoi literatury, 1961), 498.

49. Quoted in Hans, *The Russian Tradition in Education*, 97.

50. P. Kapterev, *Novaia russkaia pedagogika, ee glavneishie idei, napravlenii i deiateli* (St. Petersburg: Izdatel'stvo zhurnala Russkaia shkola, 1897), 53–54.

51. Ushinskii and Vodovozov, *Domashnoe vospitanie*, 66.

52. Vodovozova, *Na zare zhizni*, 2: 85. On the centrality of natural science, especially physiology, to the radical world view, see Posefsky, "Love, Science, and Politics," 362–363.

53. Vodovozova, *Na zare zhizni*, 2: 88.

54. Ben Eklof, *Russian Peasant Schools: Officialdom, Village Culture, and Popular Pedagogy, 1861–1914* (Berkeley: University of California Press, 1986), 271.

55. Jeffrey Brooks, *When Russia Learned to Read: Literacy and Popular Culture, 1861–1917* (Princeton, N.J.: Princeton University Press, 1985), 35–58. On the traditional methods and curriculum of Russian schools and the perceived threat of innovation, see James McClelland, *Autocrats and Academics: Education, Culture, and Society in Tsarist Russia* (Chicago: University of Chicago Press, 1979). Allen Sinel, *The Classroom and the Chancellery: State Educational Reforms in Russia under Count Dmitry Tolstoi* (Cambridge, Mass.: Harvard University Press, 1973). Eklof, *Russian Peasant Schools*, 262–277. Engelstein, "Combined Underdevelopment," 348. On the fears of the rebellious younger generation in the wake of 1905 see Stephen Frank, "'Simple Folk, Savage Customs'? Youth, Sociability, and the Dynamics of Culture in Rural Russia, 1865–1914," *Journal of Social History* 25 (Summer 1992): 726, 727. Frank, "Confronting the Domestic Other: Rural Popular Culture and its Enemies in Fin-de-Siècle Russia" in *Cultures in Flux: Lower–Class Values, Practices, and Resistance in Late Imperial Russia*, ed. Stephen Frank and Mark Steinberg (Princeton, N.J.: Princeton University Press: 1994), 86–91; Laura Engelstein, *The Keys to Happiness: Sex and the Search for Modernity in Fin-de-Siècle Russia* (Ithaca, N.Y.: Cornell University Press, 1992), 264–266.

56. Beatty, *Preschool Education in America*, 120.

57. K. N. Venttsel', *Teoriia svobodnogo vospitanie i ideal'noyi detskii sad* (Moscow, 1915), 5–6. See also R. H. Hayashida, "The Pedagogy of Protest: Russian Progressive Education on the Eve of Revolution," *Slavic and East European Education Review* 2 (1978): 11–30.

58. Venttsel', *Teoriia*, 8.

59. Ibid., 22.

60. Ibid., 22.

61. Ibid., 23, 24.

62. Ibid., 4.

63. Ibid., 10–11.

64. Venttsel', "K voprosu o prakticheskom osushchestvlenii 'doma svobodnogo rebenka,'" (1908), Nauchnyi Arkhiv Akademii Pedagogicheskikh Nauk SSSR (hereafter APN SSSR), f. 23, op. 1, d. 73, l. 4, 8; Venttsel', *Teoriia*, 18. On the assumption that "children 'naturally' prefer fun over responsibility and that this should be indulged if possible," see Davin, *Growing Up Poor*, 6.

65. Venttsel', *Detskii dom* (Moscow, 1915), 3–6.

66. Quoted in Hayashida, "The Pedagogy of Protest," 16.

67. Venttsel', "K voprosu," l. 2.

68. Venttsel', *Detskii dom*, 1.

69. Venttsel', *Teoriia*, 25, 23.

70. Ibid., 26, 25.

71. M. Kh. Sventitskaia, *Detskii sad: praktika, svedeniia i plany zaniatii* (Moscow, 1912), 2–5.

72. Litvin, *Istoriia doshkol'noi pedagogiki*, 216–217. On the Montessori method's cool reception in the United States, see Shapiro, *Child's Garden*, 178–180.

73. M. Ia. Morozova and E. I. Tikheeva, *Sovremennyi detskii sad: ego znachenie i oborudovanie* (St. Petersburg, 1914), 47–48, 33.

74. Richard Stites, *The Women's Liberation Movement in Russia: Feminism, Nihilism, and Bolshevism, 1860–1930* (Princeton, N.J.: Princeton University Press, 1978), 29–49.

75. Vodovozova, *Na zare zhizni*, 2: 88–89, 32.

76. D. I. Pisarev, "Zhenskie tipy v romanakh i povestiakh Pisemskogo, Turgeneva i Goncharova," in *Sochineniia* (Moscow: Gosudarstvennoe Izdatel'stov Khudozhestvennoi literatury, 1955), 233, 238; Dobroliubov, "Kogda zhe pridet nastoiashchii den'?" in *Izbrannye* (Moscow: Gosudarstvennoe Izdatel'stvo detskoi literatury, 1961), 212.

77. Ushinskii and Vodovozov, *Domashnoe vospitanie*, 3.

78. Kapterev, *Pedagogicheskii protsess* (St. Petersburg: Tipo.-lit. B M. Vol'fa, 1905), 114–25.

79. Vodovozova, *Na zare zhizni*, 2: 274–75.

80. Litvin, *Istoriia doshkol'noi pedagogiki*, 191. Konradi criticized Vodovozova's approach to early childhood education as too structured. On Konradi's work in higher education, see Stites, *The Women's Liberation Movement*, 75–76.

81. Vodovozova, *Na zare zhizni*, 2: 88.

82. Litvin, *Istoriia doshkol'noi pedagogiki*, 196–99. E. Kalacheva, "Narodnyi detskii sad v S. Peterburge," *Trudovaia pomoshch* 7 (May 1898): 84–86.

83. Barbara Beatty brought the similarity between Russian kindergartens and American nursery schools to my attention. On the nursery school, see Beatty, *Preschool Education in America*, 132–168. On crèches see note 22 above. On contemporary British infants' schools, see Davin, *Growing Up Poor*, 85–95, and Jewell Lochead, *The Education of Young Children in England* (New York: Teachers College, 1932). Frieden, "Child Care" (253–254) describes summer nurseries organized by local governments as a means of reducing child mortality.

84. Beatty (*Preschool Education in America*) notes that in the United States, "the distinction between preschool education and child care . . . represents a very real historical division. Until recently, preschools and day nurseries were though of as very different kinds of institutions, with different purposes and clienteles, staffed by people with different occupational identities, allegiances, and training," xi. Allen presents the secular, liberal kindergarten movement as the opponent of church-run day care centers; see "Gardens of Children," 434–437.

85. Morozova and Tikheeva, *Sovremennyi detskii sad*, 32.

86. Ibid., 31.

87. *Detskaia smertnost' i sotsial'naie usloviia. 8 diagramm s prilozheniem obiasnitel'nago teksta* (Petrograd: Muzei truda, 1916), 1. These rates were significantly higher than averages in the United States, where "somewhere between 15 and 20 percent of all American infants born in the second half of the nineteenth century died before they could celebrate their first birthdays"; see Meckel, *Save the Babies*, 1.

88. V. Ia. Kanel', *Vopros vospitaniia v svete sotsial'noi gigieny* (Moscow: Praktich-eskiia znaniia, 1918), 12, 19.

89. Sventitskaia, *Detskii sad*, 3–4, 2.

90. Morozova and Tikheeva, *Sovremennyi detskii sad*, 31–32.

91. E. Kalacheva, "Narodnyi detskii sad v S.- Peterburge," *Trudovaia pomoshch* 7 (May 1898), 88.

92. Ibid., 90–91.

93. Venttsel', *Detskii dom*, i.

94. L. Skatkin, "Vneshkol'naia rabota s det'mi v g. Moskve," *Pedagogicheskiia izvestiia* 1 (1917), 40.

95. Kapterev, *Novaia russkaia pedagogiia*, 68–86. Educating the public about preschool education became one of the highest priorities of the Preschool Department of Narkompros after 1917.

96. Frieden, "Child Care," 238, 246–247.

97. Ross, *Love and Toil*, 201–206. Davin, *Growing Up Poor*, 133–142; Beatty, *Preschool Education in America*, 72–100, 136–142. Donzelot, *The Policing of Families*, 18–23; Meckel, *Save the Babies*, 6; La Berge, "Medicalization and Moralization," 67. The half-day kindergarten that eventually became part of U.S. public school systems assumed that most middle-class parents did a good job of raising children; see Deasey, *Education Under Six*, 138.

98. Engelstein, "Combined Underdevelopment," 348. Frieden ("Child Care") points out that the "Ministry of Interior regarded educational work among the illiterate as a most suspicious activity," 241.

99. Nadezhda Krupskaia, *Pedagogicheskie sochineniia v shesti tomakh* (Moscow: Pedagogika, 1979), 1: 9–14, 105–113, 152–54, 277. However, socialists seem not to have actually opened a single day care center. Soviet historians, who might be expected to play up such efforts, make no mention of socialist-run kindergartens; see M. F. Shabaevaia, ed., *Istoriia doshkol'noi pedagogiki v Rossii* (Moscow: Prosveshchenie, 1976); Litvin, *Istoriia doshkol'noi pedagogiki*, 199–200.

100. Karl Marx, "The German Ideology" in *The Marx–Engels Reader*, ed. Robert Tucker (New York: W. W. Norton, 1978), 156–57; "Manifesto of the Communist Party" ibid., 487–88; Friedrich Engels, *The Origin of Family, Private Property, and the State*, ibid., 744–746; Lenin, "The Development of Capitalism in Russia" in *The Lenin Anthology*, ed. Robert Tucker (New York: W. W. Norton, 1975), 681.

101. Nadezhda, Krupskaia, "Zhenshchina — rabotnitsa," *Sochineniia*, 1: 11.

102. Ibid., 12.

103. Ibid., 13.

104. Nadezhda, Krupskaia, "Sem'ia i shkola," *Sochineniia*, 1: 111; "Sleduet li obuchat' mal'chikov 'bab'emy delu'?" *ibid*, 1: 40–41.

105. Krupskaia, Zhenshchina — rabotnitsa," 1: 14.

106. Krupskaia, "Itogi s"ezda po narodnomu obrazovaniiu," *Sochineniia*, 1: 148.

107. Kapterev, *Novaia russkaia*, 33. McClelland, *Autocrats and Academics*; Sinel, *The Classroom and the Chancellery*.

108. D. A. Lazurkina, "V svete Otdela Doshkol'nogo Vospitaniia," *Narodnoe prosveshchenie* (hereafter *NP*) 19 (1918), 11.

Chapter 2

1. Alan Ball, "The Roots of *Besprizornost'* in Soviet Russia's First Decade," *Slavic Review* 51 (Summer 1992): 264–266. *Besprizornik* is usually translated as "homeless child" or "waif." The term was also applied to children with homes who suffered neglect (*beznadzornost'*) as a result of being left without supervision during the work day.

2. Tsentral'nyi Gosudarstvennyi Arkhiv RSFSR (hereafter TsGA RSFSR), f. 2306, op. 12, d. 136, l. 56; Wendy Goldman, *Women, the State and Revolution: Soviet Family Policy and Social Life, 1917–36* (Cambridge, England: Cambridge University Press, 1993), 67.

3. Richard Stites, *Revolutionary Dreams: Utopian Vision and Experimental Life in the Russian Revolution* (New York: Oxford University Press, 1989), 39. For a similar assessment more clearly tied to children, see Barbara Evans Clements, "The Effects of the Civil War on Women and Family Relations," in *Party, State, and Society in the Russian Civil War: Explorations in Social History*, ed. Diane Koenker et al. (Bloomington: Indiana University Press, 1989), 105.

4. Aleksandra Kollontai, " 'Krest materinstva' i sovetskaia respublika" Nauchnyi Arkhiv Akademii Pedogicheskikh Nauk SSR (hereafter APN SSSR), f. 18, op. 2, d. 198, l. 2.

5. "Dokladnaia zapiska, 1918," TsGA RSFSR, f. 413, op. 2, d. 327, ll. 22–23; Kollontai, "'Krest materinstva'," l. 4.

6. "Dokladnaia zapiska, 1918," ll. 25, 4–6.

7. V. Ia. Kanel', *Vopros vospitaniia v svete sotsial'noi gigieny* (Moscow: Prakticheskiia znaniia, 1918), p. 50; Vera Lebedeva, *Okhrana materinstva i mladenchestva v sovetskoi trudovoi respublike* (Moscow, 1921), 51.

8. Narodnyi Kommissariat po Prosveshcheniiu, Doshkol'nyi Otdel, *Spravochnik po doshkol'nomu vospitaniiu* (Moscow, 1919), 82, 46.

9. "Instruktsiia po vedeniiu ochaga i detskogo sada," *NP* 6–7 (Jan.–Feb. 1919), 84.

10. "Doklad tov. D. A. Lazurkinoi: 'O novykh zadachakh doshkol'nogo vospitaniia v novykh formakh obshchestvennoi zhizni,'" in *Pervyi Vserossiiskii S"ezd po doshkol'nomu vospitaniiu: Doklady, protokoly, rezoliutsii* (Moscow: Gosudarstvennoe izdatel'stvo, 1921), 13.

11. V. Iakovleva, "Organizatsiia dela doshkol'nogo vospitaniia," *NP* 19 (Nov. 1918), 5.

12. Narodnyi Kommissariat po Prosveshcheniiu, *Spravochnik*, 29.

13. Lebedeva, *Okhrana*, 51; TsGA RSFSR, f. 2306, op. 12, d. 136, l. 19.

14. On tuition, see Z. Lilina, *Sotsial'no–trudovoe vospitanie: itog chetyrekhletnei raboty s oktiabr'skoi revoliutsii 1917 g. do oktiabria 1921 g.* (Petersburg: Gosudarstvennoe izdatel'stvo, 1921), 36. On wages, see S. A. Smith, *Red Petrograd: Revolution in the Factories, 1917–18* (Cambridge, England: Cambridge University Press, 1983), 47–48.

15. L. N. Litvin, ed. *Istoriia doshkol'noi pedagogiki* (Moscow: Prosveshchenie, 1989), 199.

16. A. Elizarova, "Osnovy sotsial'nogo vospitaniia," *NP* 21–22 (Apr.–May 1920), 4.

17. TsGA RSFSR, f. 2306, op. 12, d. 69, l. 89.

18. Sheila Fitzpatrick, *The Commissariat of Enlightenment: Soviet Organization of Education and the Arts Under Lunacharskii, Oct. 1917–21* (Cambridge, England: Cambridge University Press, 1970), 227.

19. TsGA RSFSR, f. 2306, op. 13, d. 32, l. 25.

20. TsGA RSFSR, f. 2306, op. 12, d. 136, l. 12.

21. TsGA RSFSR, f. 1575, op. 5, d. 14, l. 12.

22. "Obzor polozheniia doshkol'nogo vospitaniia po dannym otchetov na oktiabr' 1919," NP 16–17 (Nov.–Dec. 1919), 12.

23. Preschool teachers frequently complained about the low priority Narkompros gave their department. See, for example, Dora Lazurkina, "K voprosu o detskom sade, kak podgotovitel'noi stupeni k shkole," NP 22 (Dec. 1918), 6; R. Prushitskaia, "Razvitie pedagogicheskoi raboty Doshkol'nogo Otdela," NP 18–20 (Jan.–March 1920), 23; TsGA RSFSR, f. 2306, op. 12, d. 69, l. 27.

24. "Svodka anket polozhenii dela doshkol'nogo vospitaniia za 1918 g. (po guberniiam)," TsGA RSFSR f. 2306, op. 12, d. 56, ll. 2-1450b.

25. "Obzor polozheniia doshkol'nogo vospitaniia," 92–94.

26. TsGA RSFSR, f. 2306, op. 12, d. 106, ll. 16–19.

27. Narodnyi Kommissariat po Prosveshcheniiu, Spravochnik, 20, 47; "Proekt organizatsii doshkol'nogo podotdela narodnogo obrazovaniia," NP 9–10 (Apr.–March 1919), 19, 22; "Podgotovka rabotnikov prosveshcheniia," NP 18–20 (Jan.–March 1920), 13; R. Prushitskaia, "Razvitie," 23.

28. Narodnyi Kommissariat po Prosveshcheniiu, Spravochnik, 18.

29. Ibid., 45. The same general instructions were reprinted in various issues of NP and Biulleteni Otdela Doshkol'nogo Vospitaniia (hereafter Biulleteni).

30. Ibid., 42–46; TsGA RSFSR, f. 2306, op. 12, d. 136, l. 190b; TsGA RSFSR, f. 1575, op. 7, d. 82, l. 146.

31. TsGA RSFSR, f. 1575, op. 7, d. 60, ll. 7–8.

32. TsGA RSFSR, f. 1575, op. 7, d. 82, ll. 146–1460b; ibid., op. 5, d. 14, l. 12.

33. TsGA RSFSR, f. 1575, op. 7, d. 57, l. 17.

34. TsGA RSFSR, f. 2306, op. 12, d. 106, ll. 27, 32. For reports of the work weeks of teachers in children's homes, see TsGA RSFSR f. 1575, op. 7, d. 60, ll. 6–2560b.

35. Teacher shortages constituted a constant refrain in preschool department publications and meetings. NP devoted an entire issue to problem of teacher training—June–July 1919. The teacher shortage was a central theme of the Third All-Russian Congress of Preschool Teachers in 1920; see TsGA RSFSR, f. 2306, op. 12, d. 106.

36. TsGA RSFSR, f. 2306, op. 12, d. 69, l. 96.

37. TsGA RSFSR, f. 2306, op. 12, d. 104, l. 63.

38. Paul-Louis Hervier, 800 enfants Russes autour du monde: un pèlerinage de deux ans (Paris: Editions de la Nouvelle Revue, 1921).

39. Boris Sokoloff, Sauvez les enfants! (Les enfants de la Russie soviétique) (Prague: Volia Rossii, 1921), 32, 18, 10, 28. In a similar vein, see Vladimir Zenzinov, Deserted: The Story of the Children Abandoned in Soviet Russia (London: H. Joseph, 1931); Vospominaniia 500 russkikh detei (Prague: Izdatel'stvo Pedagogicheskago biuro, 1924).

40. Lebedeva, Okhrana, 54–64. See also Klara Zetkin, Sotsial'noe obespechenie materi i rebenka v Rossii (Moscow: Izdatel'stvo Polit. Otdela 2-i armii Vostochnogo fronta, 1919); Aleksandra Kollontai, Sem'ia i kommunisticheskoe gosudarstvo (Moscow-Petrograd: Kommunist, 1918); E. P. Radin, Chto delaet sovetskaia vlast' dlia okhrany zdorov'ia detei, 2nd ed. (Moscow: Izdatel'stvo pamiati V. M. Bonch-Bruevich, 1920).

41. Fedor Gladkov, Cement, trans. A. S. Arthur and C. Ashleigh (New York: Frederick Ungar, 1960), 34, 38, 40.

42. Kollontai, *Sem'ia i kommunisticheskoe gosudarstvo*; Radin, *Chto delaet sovet-skaia vlast' dlia okhrany zdorov'ia detei*; Zetkin, *Sotsial'noe obespecheniie materi i rebenka v Rossii*.

43. TsGA RSFSR, f. 2306, op. 12, d. 69, l. 26; V. Iakovleva, "Organizatsiia postoiannykh i peredvizhnykh bibliotek po doshkol'nomu vospitaniiu," *NP* 11–12 (June–July 1919), 47.

44. Elena Krichevskaia, *Sovety materiam po vospitaniiu detei: opyt pedagogicheskoi konsul'tatsii* (Moscow: Izd. "Okhrana materinstva i mladenchestva," 1927), 9–10.

45. "Glavsotsvos otdel opytno-pokazatel'nykh uchrezhdenii," TsGA RSFSR, f. 1575, op. 4, d. 72, l. 89; "Otchet o mladshei i starshei gruppakh d. sada Krasno-Malokhovskoi, 1923 g.," TsGA RSFSR, f. 1575, op. 4, d. 80, l. 19.

46. TsGA RSFSR, f. 1575, op. 4, d. 72, ll. 88, 90.

47. N. Al'medingen-Tumin, "Obshchestvennoe i semeinoe doshkol'noe vospitanie," in *Doshkol'noe delo* (Petrograd, 1922), 157.

48. TsGA RSFSR, f. 2306, op. 12, d. 136, l. 19.

49. Lilina, *Sotsial'no–trudovoe vospitanie*, 34.

50. Kanel', *Vopros vospitaniia*, 53, 43.

51. Narodnyi Kommissariat po Prosveshcheniiu, *Spravochnik*, 69.

52. TsGA RSFSR, f. 1575, op. 4, d. 72, l. 90.

53. E. Arkin, "Polovaia zhizn' v rannem detsve," *Biulleteni* 9–10 (1921), 15.

54. TsGA RSFSR, f. 1575, op. 4, d. 72, ll. 93–94.

55. "Materialy ob Iaroslavskom gub. opytnom ochage 'Zvezdochka,' 1923 g.," TsGA RSFSR, f. 1575, op. 4, d. 373, l. 3.

56. Narodnyi Kommissariat po Prosveshcheniiu, *Spravochnik*, 57.

57. Kanel', *Vopros vospitaniia*, 9.

58. "O doshkol'noi rabote v Basmanno-Lefortovskom raione," *NP* 29 (Apr. 1919), 21.

59. Krichevskaia, *Sovety materiam po vospitaniiu detei*, 19–21; TsGA RSFSR f. 1575, op. 4, d. 72, l. 119; TsGA RSFSR f. 1575, op. 4, d. 80, l. 23.

60. TsGA RSFSR, f. 1575, op. 4, d. 72, l. 88; 23.7 percent of the fathers were illiterate.

61. Nadezhda Krupskaia, "K voprosu o sotsialisticheskoi shkole," *NP* 1–2 (1918), 41; Kanel', *Vopros vospitaniia* 50; TsGA RSFSR, f. 2306, op. 12, d. 69, l. 23.

62. "Doklad tov. D.A. Lazurkinoi: 'O novykh zadachakh,' " 9.

63. Kollontai, " 'Krest materinstva'," l. 5.

64. TsGA RSFSR, f. 2306, op. 13, d. 39, l. 2.

65. Dora Lazurkina, "K voprosu ob obshchestvennom vospitanii," *NP* 9–10 (Apr.–May 1919), 8.

66. Lilina, *Sotsial'no–trudovoe vospitanie*, 24.

67. TsGA RSFSR, f. 1575, op. 4, d. 80, ll. 20, 260b.

68. Krichevskaia, *Sovety materiam*, 9–10, 19–21, 31.

69. Lazurkina, "K voprosu ob obshchestvennom vospitanii," *NP* 9–10 (Apr.–May 1919), 8.

70. Kanel', *Vopros vospitaniia*, 54.

71. A. E. Kamentsev, "Doshkol'noe vospitanie," *NP* No. 9–10 (Apr.–May 1919), 9.

72. "Doklad tov. D.A. Lazurkinoi: " 'O novykh zadachakh,' " 9.

73. This is a common assertion in preschool literature. See, for example, "Organizatsiia postoiannykh i peredvizhnykh bibliotek po doshkol'nomu vospitaniiu," *NP* 11–12

(June–July 1919), 48; Kanel', *Vopros vospitaniia*, 8; Lilina, *Sotsial'no–trudovoe vospitanie*, 34; Narkomzdrav, Otdel Okhrany Materinstva i Mladenchestva, *Sputnik po okhrane materinstva i mladenchestva* (Moscow: OMM, 1921), 57; Krupskaia, "K voprosu," 40–41.

Chapter 3

1. Barbara Evans Clements, "The Effects of the Civil War on Women and Family Relations," in *Party, State, and Society in the Russian Civil War: Explorations in Social History*, ed. Diane Koenker et al. (Bloomington: Indiana University Press, 1989), p. 105.

2. "Doklad tov. D. A. Lazurkinoi: 'O novykh zadachakh doshkol'nogo vospitaniia v novykh formakh obshchestvennoi zhizni," in *Pervyi Vserossiiskii s"ezd po doshkol'nomu vospitaniiu: Doklady, protokoly, rezoliutsii* (Moscow: Gosudarstnennoe izdatel'stvo, 1921) pp. 8–9.

3. Nadezdha Krupskaia, "K voprosu o sotsialisticheskoi shkole," *Narodnoe prosveshchenie* (hereafter *NP*) 1–2 (1918), 41.

4. "Opytno-pokazetl'nyi dom rebenka pri Doshkol'nom Otdele Narkomprosa," *Biulleteni Otdela Doshkol'nogo Vospitaniia* (hereafter *Biulleteni*) 5–6 (1921), p. 11.

5. Arkhiv Akademii Pedagogicheskikh Nauk SSSR (hereafter APN SSSR), f. 18, op. 2, d. 208, l. 4.

6. Tsentral'nyi Gosudarstvennyi Arkhiv RSFSR (hereafter TsGA RSFSR), f. 1575, op. 4, d. 3, l. 2.

7. TsGA RSFSR, f. 2306, op. 12, d. 106, l. 790b.

8. TsGA RSFSR, f. 2306, op. 12, d. 69, l. 940b.

9. Narkompros, *Statisticheskii ezhegodnik: sostoianie narodnogo obrazovaniia v RSFSR za 1923–24 god* (Moscow: Izdatel'stvo "Doloi negramotnost'," 1925), 327.

10. For the 1923–1924 school year, 92.7 percent of preschool teachers were female, with some areas reporting no male teachers at all. The teaching staff at children's homes was 72.2 percent female. There was a bit more balance in the schools, where 65.2 percent of the teachers were female. The situation in the preschools remained essentially unchanged through the mid-1920s. Narkompros, *Statisticheskii ezhegodnik: sostoianie narodnogo obrazovaniia v RSFSR za 1923–24 god* (Moscow: Izdatel'stvo "Doloi negrmotnost'," 1925), 325; Narkompros, *Statisticheskii sbornik po narodnomu prosveshcheniiu v RSFSR 1926 g.* (Moscow: Gosizdat, 1927), 126. On female party membership see Gail Lapidus, "Sexual Equality in Soviet Policy: A Developmental Perspective" in *Women in Russia*, ed. Dorothy Atkinson, Alexander Dallin, and Gail Lapidus (Stanford, Calif.: Stanford University Press, 1977), 120.

11. Narkompros, *Narodnoe prosveshchenie v RSFSR v tsifrakh za 15 let sovetskoi vlasti (kratkii statisticheskii sbornik)* (Moscow-Leningrad: Gosudarstvennoe uchebnopedagogicheskoe izdatel'stvo, 1932), 31.

12. Narkompros, *Statisticheskii sbornik po narodnomu prosveshcheniiu v RSFSR 1926 g.*, 127. Preschool teachers and schoolteachers had similar levels of education. While more school teachers (9.9 percent) than preschool teachers (4.4 percent) had some type of higher education, fewer preschool teachers had only a primary education (18.4 percent, versus 25.2 for schoolteachers). Preschool teachers in Siberia were more likely than their colleagues in the schools to have had some type of higher education. Ibid., 326.

13. TsGA RSFSR, f. 1575, op. 7, d. 60, ll. 6-2560b; TsGA RSFSR, f. 2306, op. 12, d. 106, l. 800b. See also *Biulleteni* 5–6 (1921), 12; TsGA RSFSR, f. 1575, op. 4, d. 3, l. 3. A survey of children's homes in the Russian Federation in 1926–1927 found that 64.8 percent of the children were orphans; 85.2 percent were orphans or "half orphans." No information was available for 11.9 percent of the children. See *Kul'turnoe stroitel'stvo Soiuza Sovetskikh Sotsialisticheskikh Respublik: K dokladu A. V. Lunacharskii no 2–i sessi Tsentral'nogo Ispolnitl'nogo Komiteta Soiuza SSSR IV sozyva* (Leningrad: Gosudarstevennoe izdatel'stvo, 1927), 41.

14. E. K. Krichevskaia, "Vospitanie detei v uchrezhdeniiakh O. M. M.," *Materialy pervogo vserossiiskogo soveshcheniia po okhrane materinstva i mladenchestva* (Moscow: OMM, 1921), p. 109.

15. Here I am adapting a distinction made by Lynn Hunt in her examination of the French revolutionaries' "creative efforts to reimagine the political world" in terms of family relations. She distinguishes between the family "as some kind of modal social experience" and "as an imaginative construct of power relations"; see *The Family Romance of the French Revolution* (Berkeley: University of California Press, 1994), xiv, 196. In arguing that the discourse on family can provide new insight into political divisions, I am influenced by Joan Scott's suggestion that the "concerns of political history and women's history can be joined around an analysis of gender in political discourse"; see "Rewriting History," in *Behind the Lines: Gender and the Two World Wars*, ed. Margaret Randolph Higonnet et al. (New Haven, Conn.: Yale University Press, 1987), 30.

16. Narkompros, *Spravochnik po doshkol'nomu vospitaniiu* (Moscow, 1919), p. 48.

17. TsGA RSFSR, f. 2306, op. 12, d. 69, l. 13.

18. TsGA RSFSR, f. 1575, op. 5, d. 12, l. 45.

19. TsGA RSFSR, f. 2306, op. 12, d. 136, l. 57.

20. TsGA RSFSR, f. 2306, op. 12, d. 104, l. 64.

21. TsGA RSFSR, f. 2306, op. 12, d. 107, l. 10b.

22. TsGA RSFSR, f. 2306, op. 12, d. 69, ll. 19–20.

23. TsGA RSFSR, f. 1575, op. 7, d. 86, l. 85.

24. M. Kh. Sventitskaia, "Doshkol'niki v detskom gorodke," *NP* 21–22 (Apr.–May 1920), 74.

25. A. Elizarova [Lenin's sister], "Osnovy sotsial'nogo vospitaniia," *NP* 21–22 (Apr.–May 1920), 7. Similar attitudes prevailed at Narkomsobes; see TsGA RSFSR, f. 413, op. 2, d. 327, l. 130b. Boris Sokoloff presents the debate over mixed-age homes in *Sauvez les enfants! (Les enfants de la Russie sovietique)*, (Prague: Volia Rosii, 1921), p. 32.

26. TsGA RSFSR, f. 1575, op. 7, d. 14, l. 1370b. See note 13, this chapter.

27. E. I. Tikheeva, *Organizatsiia detskogo sada i detskogo doma* (Moscow, 1923), 93, 105–106, 91–92, 5.

28. Elizarova, "Osnovy sotsial'nogo vospitaniia," 5, 8.

29. TsGA RSFSR, f. 2306, op. 12, d. 106, l. 790b.

30. TsGA RSFSR, f. 1575, op. 7, d. 60, l. 9.

31. Quoted in Wendy Goldman, *Women, the State, and Revolution: Soviet Family Policy and Social Life, 1917–1936* (Cambridge, England: Cambridge University Press, 1993), 53.

32. Jane Burbank, "Lenin and the Law in Revolutionary Russia," *Slavic Review* 54 (Spring 1995): 39.

33. TsGA RSFSR, f. 2306, op. 12, d. 104, l. 209.

34. *Pervyi Vserossiiskii S"ezd po doshkol'nomu vospitaniiu: Doklady, protokoly, rezoliutsii* (Moscow: Gosudarstvenno izdatel'stvo, 1921), 19

35. TsGA RSFSR, f. 2306, op. 12, d. 104, l. 209, 64.

36. *Pervyi Vserossiiskii S"ezd*, 26.

37. "Zadachi sotsial'nogo vospitaniia," *NP* 8 (March 1919), 4.

38. TsGA RSFSR, f. 2306, op. 12, d. 136, l. 20.

39. *Materialy pervogo vserossiiskogo soveshchaniia po okhrane materinstva i mladenchestva, 1920 g.*, pp. 39–40.

40. Laurie Bernstein, "The Evolution of Soviet Adoption Law," *Journal of Family History* 22 (April 1997): 206.

41. TsGA RSFSR, f. 1575, op.7, d. 35, ll. 260b, 250b-26; biographical information on Shleger can be found in L. N. Litvin, ed., *Istoriia doshkol'noi pedagogiki* (Moscow: Prosveshchenie, 1989), 224–28.

42. TsGA RSFSR, f. 2306, op. 12, d. 69, l. 3.

43. TsGA RSFSR, f. 2306, op. 13, d. 39, l. 4.

44. TsGA RSFSR, f. 1575, op. 5, d. 14, l. 7.

45. *Rabotnitsa–mat'* (St. Petersburg: Zhizn' i znanie, 1917), p. 20.

46. R. Prushitskaia, "Razvitie pedagogicheskoi raboty," *NP* 19–20 (Jan.–March 1920), 25.

47. TsGA RSFSR, f. 1575, op. 7, d. 4, l. 25.

48. Ibid., l. 250b.

49. TsGA RSFSR, f. 1575, op. 7, d. 35, ll. 250b-26.

50. Narkomzdrav, *Sputnik po Okhrane materinstva i mladenchestva* (Moscow: OMM, 1921), 53–54; Ekaterina Arbore-Ralli, *Mat' i ditia v sovetskoi Rossii* (Moscow, 1920), 29.

51. "Plan organizatsii vystavki po doshkol'nomu vospitaniiu pri Tsentral'nom D/s No. 2 g. Saratova," APN SSSR f. 18, op. 2, d. 140, ll. 12-120b.

52. TsGA RSFSR, f. 2306, op. 12, d. 136, l. 20.

53. TsGA RSFSR, f. 2306, op. 12, d. 56, l. 2.

54. TsGA RSFSR, f. 1575, op. 5, d. 14, l. 8.

55. Ibid.

56. TsGA RSFSR, f. 2306, op. 12, d. 106, l. 790b.

57. Narkomzdrav, *Materialy pervogo vserosiiskogo sovveshcheniia po okhrane materinstva i mladenchestva* (Moscow: OMM, 1920), 36–37; APN SSSR f. 18, op. 2, d. 198, l. 2.

58. TsGA RSFSR, f. 1575, op. 7, d. 18, l. 490b. On the connection of the Zhenotdel to children's institutions, see also Archives of the Smolensk Oblast' (hereafter Smolensk), National Archives, Washington, DC, WKP 207. Elizabeth Wood, *The Baba and the Comrade: Gender and Politics in Revolutionary Russia* (Bloomington: Indiana University Press, 1997), 79–93.

59. M. Vilenskaia, "Doshkol'naia rabota v derevne," *NP* 2 (Feb. 1926), 100–101. See also M. Vilenskaia et al., ed, S. *Tretii Vserossiiskii S"ezd po doshkol'nomu vospitaniiu* (Moscow: G.M.P.T., 1925), 10, 17–18.

60. Richard Stites, *Revolutionary Dreams: Utopian Vision and Experimental Life in the Russian Revolution* (New York: Oxford University Press, 1989), 108.

61. TsGA RSFSR, f. 2306, op. 12, d. 69, l. 7.

62. A. Gelina, "Detskie ploshchadki," *NP* 9–10 (Apr.–May 1919), 25; see also TsGA RSFSR, f. 1575, op. 4, d. 3, l. 3.

Chapter 4

1. The terms "glorification" and "suspicion" are used by Moshe Lewin, "Leninism and Bolshevism: The Test of History and Power," in *The Making of the Soviet System: Essays in the Social History of Interwar Russia* (New York: Pantheon Books, 1985), 194. Gail Lapidus contrasts an early "libertarian" approach to women's emancipation with the "instrumental" approach of the 1930s that emphasized "the ways in which role change might be utilized as an important political and economic resource"; see "Sexual Equality in Soviet Policy: A Developmental Perspective" in *Women in Russia*, ed. Dorothy Atkinson et al. (Stanford, Calif.: Stanford University Press, 1977), 117–118. Barbara Evans Clements similarly distinguishes between the Zhenotdel leadership's insistence on "woman-centered" local initiative (*samodeiatel'nost'*) and their male colleagues' centralizing, technocratic visions that seemed to make one variant of the liberationist impulse the special property of women; see "The Utopianism of the Zhenotdel," *Slavic Review* 51 (Summer 1992): 485–496.

2. Jane Burbank makes a similar point in "Lenin and the Law in Revolutionary Russia," *Slavic Review* 54 (Spring 1995): 41.

3. See "The State and Revolution" in *The Lenin Anthology*, ed. Robert C. Tucker (New York: W. W. Norton, 1975), 374, 383–384.

4. Lenin, "The Tasks of the Youth Leagues," in ibid., 661–674.

5. Larry Holmes, *The Kremlin and the Schoolhouse: Reforming Education in Soviet Russia, 1917–31* (Bloomington: Indiana University Press, 1991), 7–11. Ekaterina Nikolaevna (Vel'iusheva) Ianzhul, *Trudovoe nachalo v shkolakh Evropy: izdanie tret'e* (Moscow: Izdatel'stvo zhurnala "Na rodnyi uchite," 1918–19), 21; D. Lazurkina, "K voprosu o detskom sade, kak podgotovitel'noi stupeni k shkole," *NP*, 22 (Dec. 1918), 6–7.

6. In developing this picture, I have drawn on a wide range of archival and published sources. Reports from the schools, including the results of surveys sent by the Preschool Department to children's homes or kindergartens, provide accounts of activities, typical schedules, and descriptions of the institution and its teachers. Many of the following include accounts from several institutions: Tsentral'nyi Gosudarstvennyi Arkhiv RSFSR (hereafter TsGA RSFSR), f. 1575, op. 4, dd. 276, 301; ibid., op. 5, dd. 2, 12, 13, 14; ibid., op. 7, dd. 2, 8, 23, 35, 57, 60, 82; TsGA RSFSR f. 2306, op. 12, dd. 107, 136. Arkhiv Akademii Pedagogicheskikh Nauk SSSR (hereafter APN SSSR), f. 18, op. 2, dd. 118, 135, 208. An important part of the curriculum at teacher training courses was visiting and then analyzing working institutions. Materials from courses often include accounts of a number of kindergartens and children's homes; see TsGA RSFSR, f. 2306, op. 12, dd. 49, 69, 73, 129. Teachers often described the programs of their kindergartens and the problems they encountered at conferences; see TsGA RSFSR, f. 1575, op. 7, dd. 11, 35; TsGA RSFSR, f. 2306, op. 12, dd. 104, 106. See also *Pervyi Vserossiiskii S"ezd po doshkol'nomu vospitaniiu: Doklady, protokoly, rezoliutsii* (Moscow: Gosudarstvennoe izdatel'stvo, 1921). The pedagogical press carried reports from both central and

provincial institutions. A. Gelina, "Detskie ploshchadki," *NP*, No. 9–10 (May–June 1919), 25; "Dom rebenka," *Biulleteni Otdela Doshkol'nogo Vospitaniia* (hereafter *Biulleteni*), 5–6 (Jan.–March 1921), 15–16; M. Kh. Sventitskaia, "Doshkol'niki v detskom gorodke," *NP* 21–22 (April–May 1920), 73–74. V. Diushen, "Otchet o detskom gorodok im. III Internatsionala," *NP* 21–22 (April–May 1920), 67–71. A. P. Vygotskaia, "Postanovka gramoty v detskom sadu," *NP* 6–7 (1919), 60–63.

7. TsGA RSFSR, f. 1575, op. 5, d. 14, 1. 11.

8. See, for example, the reactions of Elena Bonner (at a slightly later period), in *Mothers and Daughters* (New York: Vintage Books, 1993), 29, 60–61; also Lev Kopelev, *The Education of a True Believer* (New York: Harper and Row, 1978), 28–29, on the social element in Communist youth groups.

9. *Pervyi Vserossiiskii S"ezd*, 17.

10. TsGA RSFSR, f. 2306, op. 13, d. 39, l. 3.

11. Lazurkina, "K voprosu o detskom sade," 6.

12. *Pervyi Vserossiiskii S"ezd*, 17.

13. TsGA RSFSR, f. 2306, op. 13, d. 39, l. 3.

14. TsGA RSFSR, f. 2306, op. 12, d. 69, l. 24ob.

15. Narodnyi Kommissariat po Prosveshcheniiu, Doshkol'nyi Otdel, *Spravochnik po doshkol'nomu vospitaniiu* (Moscow, 1919), 69.

16. Ibid., 35–36; "Instruktsiia po vedeniiu ochaga i detskogo sada," *NP* 6–7 (Jan.–Feb. 1919), 84–85.

17. TsGA RSFSR, f. 2306, op. 12, d. 69, l. 13.

18. TsGA RSFSR, f. 1575, op. 5, d. 13, l. 118.

19. TsGA RSFSR, f. 2306, op. 12, d. 136, l. 19; ibid., d. 69, l. 15.

20. Narodnyi Kommissariat po Prosveshcheniiu, *Spravochnik*, 33, 37; Gelina, "Detskie ploshchadki," 24.

21. TsGA RSFSR, f. 2306, op. 12, d. 69, l. 17.

22. Ibid., l. 16ob.

23. TsGA RSFSR, f. 2306, op. 12, d. 136, l. 43.

24. TsGA RSFSR, f. 2306, op. 12, d. 69, l. 24ob.

25. TsGA RSFSR, f. 1575, op. 7, d. 11, l. 3.

26. "Dom rebenka," *Biulleteni* 5–6 (1921), 16.

27. Sventitskaia, "Doshkol'niki v detskom gorodke," 73.

28. TsGA RSFSR, f. 2306, op. 12, d. 69, l. 25.

29. TsGA RSFSR, f. 2306, op. 12, d. 107, l. 100b; ibid., d. 69, l. 3.

30. Narodnyi Kommissariat po Prosveshcheniiu, *Spravochnik*, 54, 9.

31. TsGA RSFSR, f. 2306, op. 12, d. 136, ll. 33–41ob; ibid., d. 69, l. 26.

32. Ianzhul, *Trudovoe nachalo v shkolakh*, 23.

33. A. E. Kamentsev, "Doshkol'noe vospitanie," *NP* 9–10 (Apr.–May 1919), 12–13; see also TsGA RSFSR, f. 2306, op. 12, d. 69, l. 3.

34. "Doklad tov. D. A. Lazurkinoi: 'O novykh zadachakh doshkol'nogo vospitaniia v novykh formakh obshchestvennoi zhizni,'" in *Pervyi Vserossisskii S"ezd*, 10; Lazurkina, "K voprosu o zadachakh vospitaniia," *Biulleteni* 5–6 (Jan.–March 1921), 2; APN SSSR, f. 23, op. 1, d. 31, l.102.

35. Pavel Blonskii, "O naibolee tipichnykh pedagogicheskikh oshibakh pri organizatsii trudovoi shkoly," *NP* 13–14 (Aug.–Sept. 1919), 63.

36. Richard Stites, *Revolutionary Dreams: Utopian Vision and Experimental Life in the Russian Revolution* (New York: Oxford University Press), 147–64.

37. TsGA RSFSR, f. 1575, op. 7, d. 35, l. 1.

38. TsGA RSFSR, f. 2306, op. 12, d. 69, l. 6.

39. TsGA RSFSR, f. 1575, op. 7, d. 35, l. 17.

40. A. Elizarova, "Osnovy sotsial'nogo vospitaniia s tochki zreniia kommunizma," *NP* 21–22 (Apr.–May 1920), 3.

41. Narodnyi Kommissariat po Prosveshcheniiu, *Spravochnik*, 42–43, 31, 49.

42. "Doklad tov. D. A. Lazurkinoi," 10.

43. Narodnyi Kommissat po Prosveshcheniiu, *Spravochnik*, 49–51. On the importance of physical surroundings for free upbringing, see also K. N. Venttsel', *Detskii dom*, (Moscow, 1915), 2.

44. V. Iakovleva, "Organizatsiia dela doshkol'nogo vospitaniia," *NP* 19 (Nov. 1918), 5.

45. TsGA RSFSR, f. 2306, op. 12, d. 69, l. 7; Narodnyi Kommissariat po Prosveshcheniiu, *Spravochnik*, 33.

46. Nadezhda Krupskaia, "K voprosu o sotsialisticheskoi shkole," *NP* 1 (1918), 40.

47. TsGA RSFSR, f. 1575, op. 7, d. 35, l. 190b.

48. TsGA RSFSR, f. 2306, op. 12, d. 69, ll. 6, 8–9.

49. TsGA RSFSR, f. 2306, op. 12, d. 136, l. 19.

50. Allison James, Chris Jenks, and Alan Prout, *Theorizing Childhood* (New York: Teachers College Press, 1998), 90.

51. "Instruktsiia po vedeniiu ochaga i detskogo sada," 85. See also TsGA RSFSR, f. 2306, op. 12, d. 69, l. 5.

52. TsGA RSFSR, f. 2306, op. 12, d. 69, l. 19.

53. TsGA RSFSR, f. 2306, op. 12, d. 69, l. 950b.

54. TsGA RSFSR, f. 1575, op. 7, d. 35, l. 6.

55. Z. I. Lilina, *Sotsial'no–trudovoe vospitanie: Itog chetyrkhletnei raboty s oktiabr'skoi revoliutsii 1917 g. do oktiabria 1921 g.* (St. Petersburg: Gosudarstvennoe izdatel'stvo, 1921), 38; see also TsGA RSFSR, f. 2306, op. 12, d. 69, l. 13.

56. TsGA RSFSR, f. 2306, op. 12, d. 69, l. 13.

57. Lilina, *Sotsial'no–trudovoe vospitanie*, 26. In a survey of Moscow children's homes in 1920, only two reported using "reprimands" as a form of discipline. The rest relied on conversations, "moral influence," meetings, and isolating "naughty" pupils to maintain order. TsGA RSFSR, f. 1575, op. 7, d. 60.

58. TsGA RSFSR, f. 2306, op. 12, d. 69, ll. 930b–940b, 13; see also M. Kh. Sventitskaia, "Doshkol'niki v detskom gorodke," *NP* 21–22 (Apr.–May 1920), 74.

59. TsGA RSFSR, f. 2306, op. 12, d. 136, l. 19.

60. A. Elizarova, "Osnovy sotsial'nogo vospitaniia," *NP* 21–22 (Apr.–May 1920), 4.

61. "K voprosu ob obshchestvennom vospitaniia," *NP* 9–10 (Apr.–May 1919), 8; see also V. Iakovleva, "Organizatsiia dela doshkol'nogo vospitaniia," *NP* 19 (Nov. 1918), 5.

62. Narodnyi Kommissariat po Prosveshcheniiu, *Spravochnik*, 30–31.

63. Iakovleva, "Organizatsiia dela doshkol'nogo vospitaniia," 5.

64. V. Ia Kanel', *Vopros vospitaniia v svete sotsial'noi gigeny* (Moscow: Prakticheskiia znaniia, 1918), 77.

65. A. P. Vygotskaia, "Postanovka gramoty v detskom sadu," *NP* 6–7 (1919), 60–63.

66. TsGA RSFSR, f. 1575, op. 7, d. 35, l. 2.

67. Narodnyi Kommissariat po Prosveshcheniiu, *Spravochnik*, 36–38; A. Gelina, "Detskie ploshchadki," *NP* 9–10 (May–June 1919), 25.

68. Narodnyi Kommissariat po Prosveshcheniiu, *Spravochnik*, 50–53.

69. Merle Curti, *The Social Ideas of American Educators* (New York: C. Scribner's Sons, 1935), 409, 419–420 (Hall); 452 (James); 490 (Thorndike); 521 (Dewey).

70. K. N. Kornilov, "K psikhologii detskoi igry v kukly," in *Rebenok i igrushka*, ed. N. A. Rybnikov (Moscow, 192–), 36–38. The pre-Revolutionary study can be found in Kornilov, "K psikhologii detskoi igry v kukly," *Vestnik vospitaniia* 2 (1916). A popularized version of the research advised mothers to allow their daughters to play with dolls even until age sixteen; V. V. K., "Pis'ma materiam: igra v kukly," *Zhenskoe delo* 12 (July 1918), 2–3.

71. E. A. Arkin, "Polovaia zhizn' v rannem detstve," *Biulleteni* 9–10 (July–Oct. 1921), 10.

72. "Iz nabliudenii v detskom sadu 2/II-1920 g.," TsGA RSFSR, f. 1575, op. 5, d. 2, l. 28ob.

73. "Nabliudenie v detskom sadu praktikantki A. Kondrat'evoi, 1919 g.," ibid., l. 5ob.

74. Ibid., l. 43.

75. "Protokol konferentsii s kursantkami," TsGA RSFSR, f. 2306, op. 12, d. 69, ll. 91ob-92.

76. Z. I. Lilina, *Pervoe maia: prazdnik truda—prazdnik detei* (Petersburg, 1921).

77. TsGA RSFSR, f. 1575, op. 7, d. 60, ll. 6-256ob.

78. TsGA RSFSR, f. 1575, op. 7, d. 35, l. 19.

79. "Izuchenie detei," *Biulleteni* 9–10 (1921), 4; TsGA RSFSR, f. 1575, op. 7, d. 8, l. 2; ibid., d. 35, l. 26ob; ibid., op. 5, d. 13, l. 118.

80. "Instruktsiia po vedeniiu ochaga i detskogo sada," 85.

81. TsGA RSFSR, f. 1575, op. 5, d. 13, l. 118; TsGA RSFSR, f. 2306, op. 12, d. 69, l. 13; "Dom rebenka," *Biulleteni* 5–6 (1921), 15.

82. TsGA RSFSR, f. 1575, op. 7, d. 57, l. 6.

83. TsGA RSFSR, f. 2306, op. 12, d. 106, l. 30ob.

84. TsGA RSFSR, f. 2306, op. 12, d. 69, l. 2.

85. Lilina, *Sotsial'no-trudovoe vospitanie*, 38.

86. "Doklad tov. D. A. Lazurkinoi," 10.

87. "Protokoly zasedenii III vserossiiskoi konferentsii," TsGA RSFSR, f. 2306, op. 12, d. 104, l. 64.

88. TsGA RSFSR, f. 2306, op. 12, d. 136, l. 19.

89. Narodnyi Kommissariat po Prosveshcheniiu, *Spravochnik*, 37.

90. Lilina, *Sotsial'no–trudovoe vospitanie*, 41–43.

91. Dora Lazurkina, "K voprosu ob organizatsii kursov po doshkol'nomu vospitaniiu," *NP* 11–12 (June–July 1919), 37; TsGA RSFSR, f. 2306, op. 12, d. 106, l. 110ob.

92. *Pervyi Vserossiiskii S"ezd*, 29; Dora Lazurkina, "Ocherednaia zadacha," *Biulleteni* 3–4 (Aug.–Dec. 1920), 1.

93. "Doklad tov. D. A. Lazurkinoi," 11.

94. "Materialy doshkol'nykh kursov po podgotovke gubernskikh instruktorov (osen' 1920 goda)," TsGA RSFSR, f. 2306, op. 12, d. 73, l. 2; "Instruktorskie kursy po doshkol'nomu vospitaniiu (otkryty v Moskve 15 oktiabria 1920 g.), *Biulleteni* 3–4 (Aug.–Dec. 1920), 7–8.

95. "Iz praktiki kursov po doshkol'nomu vospitaniiu," *NP* 11–12 (June–July 1920), 40.

96. TsGA RSFSR, f. 2306, op. 12, d. 73, ll. 5–6.

97. On the relative autonomy of the Petrograd intelligentsia during the Civil War years and its interest in bringing highbrow culture to the masses, see Katerina Clark, *Petersburg, Crucible of Cultural Revolution* (Cambridge, Mass.: Harvard University Press, 1995), 100–121.

98. TsGA RSFSR, f. 2306, op. 12, d. 104, l. 221; "Podgotovka doshkol'nykh rabotnikov," *Biulleteni* 3–4 (Aug.–Dec. 1920), 2–3.

99. "Materialy doshkol'nykh kursov po podgotovke gubernskikh instruktorov," TsGA RSFSR, f. 2306, op. 12, d. 73, l. 2.

100. Narodnyi Kommissariat po Prosveshcheniiu, *Spravochnik*, 20–21.

101. TsGA RSFSR, f. 2306, op. 12, d. 106, l. 59.

102. "Rabota Moskovskogo gubernskogo doshkol'nogo podotdela za 1919 g.," TsGA RSFSR, f. 2306, op. 12, d. 69, l. 86ob.

103. TsGA RSFSR, f. 2306, op. 12, d. 106, l. 23.

104. *Statisticheskii ezhegodnik: sostoianie narodnogo obrazovaniia v RSFSR za 1923–24 god* (Moscow: Izdatel'stvo "Doloi negramotnost'," 1925), 325. In 1926, the percentage of female preschool teachers was 97.1 percent; see *Statisticheskii sbornik po narodnomu prosveshcheniiu v RSFSR 1926 g* (Moscow: Gosizdat, 1927), 126.

105. TsGA RSFSR, f. 2306, op. 12, d. 106, l. 23.

106. Klara Zetkin, "Okhrana materinstva i mladenchestva, 1918 g.," APN SSSR, f. 18, op. 2, d. 199, l. 5; "Obshchaia zhizn' kratkosrochnykh kursov po podgotovke rukovoditel'nits na ploshchadki dlia detei doshkol'nogo vozrasta, 1919 g.," TsGA RSFSR, f. 2306, op. 12, d. 69, l. 7; "Otchet o rabote gubernskogo praktikuma po doshkol'nomu i preddoshkol'nomu vospitaniiu, 8/III-25/IV 1926 g.," APN SSSR, f. 18, op. 2, d. 120. Two-thirds of the teachers in Petrograd for the 1916–1917 school year were female; see TsGA RSFSR, f. 2306, op. 12, d. 136, l. 64ob.

107. "Doklad tov. D. A. Lazurkinoi," 11.

108. Venttsel', *Teoriia svobodnogo vospitaniia i ideal'nyi detskii sad*, 20.

109. TsGA RSFSR, f. 1575, op. 5, d. 13, l. 60ob.

110. TsGA RSFSR, f. 1575, op. 7, d. 35, ll. 27ob-28.

111. K. N. Venttsel', "Sotsializm i svobodnoe vospitanie, 1918 g.," APN SSSR, f. 23, op. 1, d. 31, l. 108.

112. "Deklaratsiia po doshkol'nomu vospitaniiu," TsGA RSFSR, f. 2306, op. 13, d. 39, l. 2.

113. TsGA RSFSR, f. 1575, op. 7, d. 35, l. 2.

114. *Pervyi Vserossiiskii S"ezd*, 20.

115. P. Blonskii, "Marksizm kak metod resheniia pedagogicheskikh problem," *NP* 21–22 (Apr.–May 1920), 9.

Chapter 5

1. Beatrice Farnsworth, "Bolshevik Alternatives and the Soviet Family: The 1926 Marriage Law Debate," in *Women in Russia*, ed. Dorothy Atkinson et al. (Stanford,

Calif: Stanford University Press, 1977), 141, 149–54; Wendy Goldman, *Women, the State, and Revolution: Soviet Family Policy and Social Life* (Cambridge, England: Cambridge University Press, 1993), 90–100.

2. "Introduction: NEP Russia as a 'Transitional' Society," in *Russia in the Era of NEP*, ed. Sheila Fitzpatrick, et al. (Bloomington: Indiana University Press, 1991), 4. Richard Stites makes a similar point, see *Revolutionary Dreams: Utopian Vision and Experimental Life in the Russian Revolution* (New York: Oxford University Press), 40.

3. "Dokladnaia zapiska, 1923 g.," Tsentral'nyi Gosudarstvennyi Arkhiv RSFSR (hereafter TsGA RSFSR), f. 1575, op. 7, d. 14, l. 105. Similar figures are reported in "Otchet doshkol'nogo otdela za 1922 god," ibid., l. 14; see also N. Al'medingen-Tumin, "Obshchestvennoe i semeinoe doshkol'noe vospitanie," *Doshkol'noe delo* (Petrograd, 1922), 154.

4. TsGA RSFSR, f. 2306, op. 12, d. 136, l. 120b; "Kratkii otchet o tekushchei rabote Doshkol'nogo Otdela," *NP* 6–7 (1919), 83. For 1918 figures, see D. Lazurkina, "K smete Otdela Doshkol'nogo Vospitanie," *NP* 19 (16 Nov. 1918), 11–12.

5. The salaries of primary teachers also became the responsibility of the localities; see TsGA RSFSR, f. 1575, op. 7, d. 14, l. 103, 106.

6. *Statisticheskii ezhegodnik: sostoianie narodnogo obrazovaniia v RSFSR za 1923–24 god* (Moscow: Izdatel'stvo "Doloi negramotnost'," 1925), 329–330.

7. *Narodnoe prosveshchenie v RSFSR v tsifrakh za 15 let sovetskoi vlasti (kratkii statisticheskii sbornik)* (Moscow: Gosudarstvennoe uchebno-pedagogicheskoe izdatel'stvo, 1932), 37; Narkompros, *Narodnoe prosveshchenie v osnovnykh pokazateliakh: statisticheskii sbornik* (Moscow-Leningrad: Gosizdat, 1928), 111.

8. TsGA RSFSR, f. 1575, op. 7, d. 40; M. Vilenskaia et al. eds., *Tretii Vserossiiski S"ezd po doshkol'nomu vospitaniiu* (Moscow: G.M.P.T., 1925), 64–67.

9. TsGA RSFSR, f. 1575, op. 7, d. 40; *Statisticheskii ezhegodnik* (1925), 329, 330.

10. Narkompros, *Narodnoe prosveshchenie v osnovnykh pokazateliakh: statisicheski isbornik* (Moscow: Gosizdat, 1928), 110, 111. Outside the RSFSR, the local share was closer to 60 percent of education funding by 1932; see Narkompros, *Narodnoe prosveshchenie v tsifrakh* (1932), 134.

11. "Rasporiazheniia po Narkomprosu Zaveduiushchemu Gubono," TsGA RSFSR, f. 1575, op. 7, d. 14, l. 81.

12. "Tsirkular vsem gub. otdelam narodnogo obrazovaniia," TsGA RSFSR, f. 1575, op. 7, d. 14, l. 107, 119.

13. Narkompros, *Narodnoe prosveshchenie v osnovnykh pokazateliakh* (1928), 156. If funding for children's homes, which served older children as well, is included, the Soviet figure goes up to 46 percent, raising it above Egypt, India, and Spain. In England (for 1923–24), over 77 percent of the education budget went to primary education; in the United States (1922), just over 60 percent.

14. Narkompros, *Narodnoe prosveshchenie v tsifrakh* (1932), 38.

15. A. V. Surovtseva, "K zakrepleniiu minimal'noi seti doshkol'nykh uchrezhdenii," *NP* 3 (1923), 17; TsGA RSFSR, f. 1575, op. 7, d. 14, ll. 1190b–120. On the situation in the schools, see Larry Holmes, *The Kremlin and the Schoolhouse: Reforming Education in Soviet Russia, 1917–1931* (Bloomington: Indiana University Press, 1991), 27–29.

16. "Protokol zasedaniia kollegii doshkol'nogo otdela: Doklad o doshkol'nom dele v Moskovskoi gub.," TsGA RSFSR, f. 1575, op. 7, d. 86, ll. 73–740b.

17. "Dokladnaia zapiska," ibid., d. 14, ll. 1370b, 105.

18. Ibid., l. 137.

19. Letter to ARA, 14 June 1922, ARA Russian Operations, box 10, folder 1, Hoover Archives, Stanford University.

20. M. Vilenskaia, "Blizhaishie zadachi doshkol'noi raboty," *NP* 5 (May 1927), 44; M. Epshtein, "Osnovye cherty proizvodstvennogo plana Glavsotsvosa na 1926–27 g. O kolichestve i kachestve," *NP* 1 (Jan. 1927), 5–12.

21. Ibid; Arkhiv Akademii Pedagogicheskikh Nauk SSSR (hereafter APN SSSR), f. 18, op. 2, d. 139, l. 85. Vilenskaia, "Blizhaishie zadachi," 44.

22. *Rezoliutsii po dokladam II–go vserossiiskogo s"ezda po doshkol'nomu vospitaniiu (25 noiabria do 2 dekabria 1921 g.)* (Moscow, 1921), 9.

23. "Otchet opytno-pokazatel'nogo doshkol'nogo D/Doma imeni Krupskoi za 1925 god," TsGA RSFSR, f. 1575, op. 7, d. 46, l. 4.

24. "Organizatsiia detskoi zhizni vokrug truda. Rabota saratovskogo opytnogo detsada No. 11," APN SSSR f. 18, op. 2, d. 139, l. 1550b.

25. H. O. Eversole to Dr. Haven Emerson, 28 Feb. 1923, ARA Russian Operations, box 19, folder 4, Hoover Archives.

26. M. Vilenskaia, et al., eds, *Tretii vserossiiskii s"ezd*, 7.

27. The results of this work are the subject of Chapter 6.

28. A. Lunacharskii, "V nov' k starym zadacham!" *NP* 3 (1923), 3; "Tsirkular vsem Gubono," TsGA RSFSR, f. 1575, op. 7, d. 14, l. 113; Tezarovsnaia, "O stroitel'nom materiale," *Biulleteni* 9–10 (1921), 16–18.

29. N. Al'medingen-Tumin, "Sovremennaia doshkol'naia rabota," in *Doshkol'noe delo* (Petrograd, 1922), 23; M. Vilenskaia et al., eds, *Tretii vserossiiskii s"ezd*, 53–55.

30. "Set' doshkol'nykh uchrezhdenii (sadov i ochagov) na 1923–24 uch. god (na aprel' 1923 g.)," TsGA RSFSR, f. 1575, op. 7, d. 14, l. 209; "Opytnye pokazatel'nye uchrezhdenii," ibid., d. 40, ll. 130b–14.

31. M. Vilenskaia et al., eds, *Tretii vserossiiskii s"ezd*, 49–50.

32. *Kul'turnoe stroitel'stvo Soiuza Sovetskikh Sotsialisticheskikh Respublik: K dokladu A. V. Lunacharskogo na 2-i sessii Tsentral'nogo Ispolnitel'nogo Komiteta Soiuza SSR IV sozyva* (Lennigrad: Gosudarstvennoe izdatel'stvo, 1927), diagram 16.

33. Gosudarstvennyi muzei-vystavka po narodnomu prosveshcheniiu, *Sbornik diagramm: Kul'turnoe stroitel'stva soiuza sovetskikh sotsialisticheskikh respublik* (Moscow: Gosudarstvennoe izdatel'stvo, 1929), 41; Tsentral'noe statisticheskoe upravlenie SSSR, *Vsesoiuznaia perepis' naseleniia 1926 goda*, vol. 17 (Moscow: Izdanie Ts. S. U Soiuza SSR, 1929), 46.

34. "Instruktskiia o poriadke vzimaniia platy za obuchenie v uchrezhdeniiakh sotsvosa," TsGA RSFSR, f. 1575, op. 7, d. 14, l. 97.

35. "Rezoliutsii II-go Vserossiiskogo S"ezda Zav. Gubsotsvosa," ibid., l. 1190b.

36. "K materialam komissii po doshkol'noi politike," TsGA RSFSR, f. 1575, op. 7, d. 14, l. 152.

37. M. Vilenskai, et al., eds, *Tretii vserossiiskii s"ezd*, 60–61, 76–77; see also Goldman, *Women, the State, and Revolution,* 96.

38. TsGA RSFSR, f. 1575, op. 7, d. 14, l. 152.

39. M. Vilenskaia, et al., eds, *Tretii vserossiiskii s"ezd*, 100, 105, 87–88.

40. "Material programmnoi komissii, 1923 g.," TsGA RSFSR, f. 1575, op. 7, d. 14, l. 150; Al'medingen-Tumin, "Obshchestvennoe vospitanie," 154–155.

41. See chapter 2.

42. M. Vilenskaia, et al., eds, *Tretii vserossiiskii s"ezd*, 8, 10; see also Goldman, *Women, the State, and Revolution*, 76.

43. "Instruktivnoe pis'mo po podgotovke k provedeniiu doshkol'noi raboty v gorode i derevne letom 1927 goda," TsGA RSFSR, f. 1575, op. 7, d. 94, l. 27. See also "Rasporiazheniia po narkomprosu zaveduiushchemu Gubono," ibid., d. 14, l. 85.

44. *Statisticheskii ezhegodnik* (1925), 102; *Kul'turnoe stroitel'stvo* (1927), diagram 19.

45. *Statisticheskii ezhegodnik* (1925), 102–103.

46. *Kul'turnoe stroitel'stvo*, diagram 17. Similar figures for the 1925–1926 school year can be found in "Statistika uchrezhdenii doshkol'nogo vospitaniia," in *Pedagogicheskaia entsiklopediia*, vol. 2, ed. A. G. Kalashnikov (Moscow: Rabotnik prosveshcheniia, 1929), 113–114. On the question of categorizing white-collar workers, see Daniel Orlovsky, "The Hidden Class: White-Collar Workers in the Soviet 1920s," in *Making Workers Soviet: Power, Class, and Identity*, ed. Lewis H. Siegelbaum and Ronald Grigor Suny (Ithaca, N.Y.: Cornell University Press, 1994), 220–252.

47. Goldman, *Women, the States, and Revolution*, 109–118.

48. "Protokol roditel'skogo sobraniia III-go Detskogo Sada," TsGA RSFSR, f. 1575, op. 7, d. 76, ll. 9–11.

49. Elena Krichevskaia, *Sovety materiam po vospitaniiu detei: opyt pedagogicheskoi konsul'tatsii* (Moscow: Izd. "Okhrana materinstva i mladenchestva", 1927), 10; "Otchet o mladshei i starshei gruppakh d. sada Krasnovo-Malokhovskoi, 1923 g.," TsGA RSFSR, f. 1575, op. 4, d. 80, l. 16; "Glavsotsvos otdel opytno-pokazatel'nykh uchrezhdenii," ibid., d. 72, l. 88.

50. M. Vilenskaia et al., eds, *Tretii vserossiiskii s"ezd*, 459.

51. "Konferentsii doshkol'nykh rabotnikov 8/XII/24," APN SSSR, f. 18, op. 2, d. 120, l. 59ob.

52. M. Vinenskaia et al., eds, *Tretii vserossiiskii s"ezd*, 457.

53. TsGA RSFSR, f. 1575, op. 4, d. 80, l. 38. See also ibid., d. 72, ll. 119–120.

54. "Detskii sad Krasnovo-Malokhovskii, 1922–23 gg.," TsGA RSFSR, f. 1575, op. 4, d. 301, l. 18.

55. APN SSSR, f. 18, op. 2, d. 136, ll. 3–4.

56. Elena Bonner, *Mothers and Daughters*, trans. Antonina W. Bouis (New York: Vintage Books), 42.

57. M. Kh. Sventitskaia, *Nash detskii sad (Iz opyta doshkol'noi raboty Detskogo Gorodka imeni III Internatsionala pri Narkomprose v Moskve)* (Moscow, 1924), 193.

58. TsGA RSFSR, f. 1575, op. 4, d. 80, ll. 10, 16–17, 37.

59. "Protokol roditel'skogo sobraniia VI-go Detskogo Sada," TsGA RSFSR, f. 1575, op. 7, d. 76, ll. 4–40b.

60. Ibid., ll. 40b–50b.

61. "Protokol roditel'skogo sobraniia III-go Detskogo Sada," TsGA RSFSR, f. 1575, op. 7, d. 76, ll. 8–80b.

62. TsGA RSFSR, f. 1575, op. 7, d. 76, ll. 50b–7, 80b.

63. TsGA RSFSR, f. 1575, op. 7, d. 76, ll. 5, 9–90b.

64. Al'medingen-Tumin, "Obshchestvennoe vospitanie," 160. See also E. I. Tikheeva, *Organizatsiia detskogo sada i detskogo doma* (Moscow, 1923), 42–45.

65. TsGA RSFSR, f. 1575, op. 4, d. 301, l. 19.

66. "Otchet v rabote ob"edinennogo kollektiva doshkol'nykh rabotnikov," APN SSSR, f. 18, op. 2, d. 147.

Chapter 6

1. Richard Stites, *Revolutionary Dreams: Utopian Vision and Experimental Life in the Russian Revolution* (New York: Oxford University Press, 1989), 135–140, 167–189, 190–204, quotation from 225.

2. Robert Tucker, "Lenin's Bolshevism as a Culture in the Making," in *Bolshevik Culture: Experiment and Order in the Russian Revolution*, ed. Abbott Gleason, Peter Kenez, and Richard Stiles (Bloomington: Indiana University Press, 1985), 32.

3. Elizabeth Waters calls the moment of the debate on the 1926 marriage code a "watershed"; see "The Bolsheviks and the Family," *Contemporary European History* 4 (1993):288.

4. Goldman, *Women, the State, and Revolution: Soviet Family Policy and Social Life, 1917–1936* (Cambridge, England: Cambridge University Press, 1993), 247. Goldman emphasizes different political implications than I have stressed here. Noting that debate on the marriage code "paralleled" critical debates on industrialization, Goldman pictures it as largely isolated from the "larger political struggle within the Party" (222). She illustrates the point with the example of Alexander Beloborodov and Evgenii Preobrazhenskii, leftists with regard to economic policy who disagreed on the family. Goldman locates the larger significance of the marriage code debate in its reproduction of the "headlong collision between the socialist-libertarian tradition and the conditions of the time" (231). I prefer to understand the failure of divisions on policy toward family and children to reproduce divisions on economic policy not as evidence that family constituted a largely self-contained sphere of policy, but as suggesting that the political issues were more complicated and multivalent than the notion of an opposition between pragmatic gradualism and utopian vision allows.

5. M. Vilenskaia et al., eds., *Tretii Vserossiiskii S"ezd po doshkol'nomu vospitaniiu* (Moscow: G.M.P.T., 1925), 117. "Otchet opytno-pokazatel'nogo doshkol'nogo d/doma imeni Krupskoi za 1925 god," Tsentralsnyi Gosudarstvennyi Arkhiv RSFSR (hereafter TsGA RSFSR), f. 1575, op. 7, d. 46, l. 5; "Proizvodstvennyi plan d. sada im M. N. Kovalenskogo, 1924–25 gg.," ibid., d. 40, ll. 45–47; A. V. Surovtseva, "Blizhaishie zadachi v oblasti doshkol'nogo vospitaniia," *NP* 3 (1923), 16.

6. S. Lebedev, "Izuchenie detei v doshkol'nykh uchrezhdeniiakh," *Biulletenii Otdela Doshkol'nyo Vospitani'ia* (hereafter *Biulleteni*) 9–10 (July–Oct. 1921), 1; "Razvitie doshkol'nogo dela v RSFSR," TsGA RSFSR f. 1575, op. 7, d. 14, ll. 84–840b; *Rezoliutsii po dokladam II–go vserossiiskogo s"ezda po doshkol'nomu vospitaniiu (25 noiabria do 2 dekabria 1921 g)* (Moscow, 1921), 1.

7. L. N. Litvin, ed. *Istoriia doshkol'noi pedagogiki* (Moscow: Proveshchenie, 1989), 264–65; Larry Holmes, *The Kremlin and the Schoolhouse: Reforming Education in Soviet Russia* (Bloomington: Indiana University Press, 1991), 30–36.

8. Lawrence Cremin, *The Transformation of the School: Progressivism in American Education* (New York: Vintage Books, 1964), 216–219; Holmes, *The Kremlin and the Schoolhouse,* 30–40; R. Prushitskaia, "Doshkol'noe vospitanie i programmy GUS'a," *NP* 2 (1924), 26–27.

9. M. Vilenskaia et al., eds., *Tretii Vserossiiskii S"ezd*, 117.

10. "Otchet opytno-pokazatel'nogo doshkol'nogo d/doma imeni Krupskoi za 1925 god," TsGA RSFSR, f. 1575, op. 7, d. 46, l. 5; "Proizvodstvennyi plan d. sada im M. N. Kovalenskogo, 1924–25 gg.," ibid., d. 40, ll. 45–47.

11. M. Vilenskaia et al., eds., *Tretii Vserossiiskii S"ezd*, 194–96; Vilenskaia, "K III s"ezdu," *NP* No. 8 (1924), 137.

12. M. Vilenskaia et al., eds., *Tretii Vserossiiskii S"ezd*, 75–76.

13. Sventitskaia, *Nash detskii sad (iz opyta doshkol'noi raboty Detskogo Gorodka imeni III Internatisionala pri Narkomprose v Moskve)* (Moscow, 1924), 17.

14. Tikheeva, *Organizatsiia detskogo sada i detskogo doma* (Moscow, 1923), 10, 60.

15. M. Vilenskaia et al., eds., *Tretii Vserossiiskii S"ezd*, 112, 132–137.

16. "Instruktsii vedeniia doshkol'nogo uchrezhdeniia, 13/II/23," Arkhiv Akademii Pedagogicheskikh Nauk SSSR (hereafter APN SSSR), f. 18, op. 2, d. 118, l. 24.

17. "Trud i igra v doshkol'nomu vozraste," ibid., d. 122, l. 50.

18. APN SSSR f. 18, op. 2, d. 120, includes several schedules from 1926; see below for more on specific topics.

19. "Proizvodstvenny plan d. sada im. M. N. Kovalenskogo, 1924–25 gg.," TsGA RSFSR, f. 1575, op. 7, d. 40, ll. 45–47.

20. "Doklad ob Iaroslavskom gubernskom opytnom ochage, 1922 g.," TsGA RSFSR f. 2306, op. 12, d. 129, ll. 20b, 8.

21. "Detskii sad imeni Polonskogo, 1922 g.," TsGA RSFSR, f. 1575, op. 7, d. 9, ll. 4–40b.

22. The combined percentage in the primary and secondary schools for 1924–1925 was 6.2. In 1926–1927, the percentage of Party and Komsomol members and candidates in the preschools (10.6) fell behind the primary schools (14.2), but not the secondary schools (8.3); see *Narodnoe prosveshchenie v RSFSR v tsifrakh za 15 let sovetskoi vlasti (kratkii statisticheskii sbornik)* (Moscow: Gosudarstvennoe uchebno-pedagogicheskoe izdatel'stvo, 1932), 31.

23. A. V. Surovtseva, "Blizhaishie zadachi v oblasti doshkol'nogo vospitaniia," *NP* 3 (1923), 16.

24. "Ekskursii, 1924 g.," TsGA RSFSR, f. 1575, op. 7, d. 41, ll. 2–20b.

25. "Plan raboty za period mai, iiun' (starshei gruppy), 1926 g," APN SSSR, f. 18, op. 2, d. 120, ll. 37–41.

26. "D/dom pri tsentral'noi biblioteke v g. Moskva," TsGA RSFSR, f. 1575, op. 7, d. 90, ll. 39–400b. The pupils' work covers ll. 104–181.

27. Sventitskaia, *Nash detskii sad*, 195, 197, 192, 193.

28. On the impact of pedology in the schools later in the decade, see Sheila Fitzpatrick, *Education and Social Mobility in the Soviet Union, 1921–1934* (Cambridge, England: Cambridge University Press, 1979), 19–22, 139–143.

29. "Otchet o rabote doshkol'nogo otdela 1-oi opytnoi stantsii po narodnomu obrazovaniiu pri NKP (Krasnopresenskii raion) za 1922/23 g.," TsGA RSFSR, f. 1575, op. 4, d. 72, ll. 53–530b, 790b; "Izuchenie rebenka," APN SSSR, f. 18, op. 2, d. 140, l. 880b.

30. "Protokol zasedaniia kollegii doshkol'nogo otdela Glavsotsvosa Narkomprosa, 7/II/1923 g.," TsGA RSFSR, f. 1575, op. 7, d. 86, l. 84; "Protokol pedagogichsekogo zasedaniia detskogo sada i doshkol'nogo detskogo doma gorodka im. III Internatsionala, 20/II/1925 g.," ibid., d. 40, ll. 2–20b.

31. S. S. Molozhavyi, "Metody izucheniia rebenka," in M. Vilenskaia et al., eds., *Tretii Vserossiiskii S"ezd*, pp. 277–98; APN SSSR f. 18, op. 2, d. 140, ll. 86–86ob.

32. "Zapis' nabliudeniia za trudom detei starshei gruppy (7 let) Tsentral'nyi d/sad No. 2 za osennii period 1927/28 uch. goda po skheme Molozhavogo," APN SSSR, f. 18, op. 2, d. 140, ll. 95–105; "Izuchenie detei," ibid., l. 86ob.

33. "Rabota saratovskogo opytnogo detsada No. 11, 1927 g.," APN SSSR, f. 18, op. 2, d. 159, l. 165; ibid., d. 140, ll. 87, 90.

34. APN SSSR, f. 18, op. 2, d. 140, ll. 56–56ob.

35. "Organizatsiia detskoi zhizni vokrug trud. Rabota saratovskogo opytnogo detsada No. 11," APN SSSR, f. 18, op. 2, d. 139, ll. 158ob, 154ob.

36. APN SSSR, f. 18, op. 2, d. 139, ll. 154ob–155ob.

37. Ibid.

38. APN SSSR, f. 18, op. 2, d. 140, l. 96ob; ibid., d. 139, l. 165.

39. Ibid., ll. 154ob, 165.

40. "Organizatsiia detskoi zhizni," l. 165; APN SSSR, f. 18, op. 2, d. 159, l. 96ob.

41. Ibid., ll. 154ob, 156.

42. M. Vilenskaia et al., eds., *Tretii Vserossiiskii S"ezd*, 129.

43. Kornei Chukovskii, *From Two to Five*, trans. Miriam Morton (Berkeley: University of California, 1968), 116–118.

44. M. Vilenskaia et al., eds., *Tretii Vserossiiskii S"ezd*, 128–29, 179–80; Chukovskii, *From Two to Five,* characterizes the new stories as focusing on diesels and radio, 116.

45. "Protokol zasedanii kollegii doshkol'nogo otdela Glavsotsvosa pri Narkomprose, 27/XII 1923 g.," TsGA RSFSR, f. 1575, op. 7, d. 86, l. 30b.

46. See Chapter 4.

47. M. Vilenskaia et al., eds., *Tretii Vserossiiskii S"ezd*, 126–27.

48. APN SSSR, f. 18, op. 2, d. 139, ll. 162ob, 158ob.

49. APN SSSR, f. 18, op. 2, d. 140, ll. 49, 58ob.

50. M. Vilenskaia et al., eds., *Tretii Vserossiiskii S"ezd* , 127.

51. Ibid., 148.

52. Tikheeva, *Organizatsiia*, 50–53, 115.

53. Sventitskaia, *Nash detskii sad*, 148.

54. Ibid., 145–47.

55. Shalok, "Muzei igrushki," *NP* 2 (1924), 62.

56. M. P. Andreeva, "Stroitel'nyi material, izgotovliaemyi Otdelom Uchebnykh Posobii Moskovskogo soiuza kustarnykh artelei," in N. A. Rybnikov, ed. *Rebenok i igrushka* (Moscow, 192–), 17. M. Vilenskaia et al., eds., *Tretii Vserossiiskii S"ezd*, 112, 125.

57. Teachers hoped the newly-enlightened children would inform their parents. See M. Vilenskaia et al., eds, *Tretii Vserossiiskii S"ezd*, 130–31.

58. M. Vilenskaia et al., eds., *Tretii Vserossiiskii S"ezd*, 124, 150.

59. Ibid., 121–22.

60. "Sreda d/uchrezhdenii: 1-ia mladshaia gruppa (3-kh-4-kh letok) Tsentral'nogo detskogo sada No. 2 g. Saratov, 1926/27 ucheb. god," APN SSSR, f. 18, op. 2, d. 140.

61. M. Vilenskaia et al., eds., *Tretii Vserossiiskii S"ezd*, 122, 150.

62. "Raspisanie i kratkie zapisi ekskursii doshkol'nykh rabotnikov, 23/I/1924," TsGA RSFSR, f. 1575, op. 7, d. 41, l. 2.

63. "Konferentsii doshkol'nykh rabotnikov, 1924 g.," APN SSSR f. 18, op. 2, d. 120, ll. 53–54.

64. "Uchet truda shestiletok i semiletok," APN SSSR f. 18, op. 2, d. 140, l. 480b. See also M. Vilenskaia et al., eds., *Tretii Vserossiiskii S"ezd*, 119–20.

65. M. Vilenskaia, "Doshkol'naia rabota v derevne," *NP* 2 (1926):103.

66. Nina Tumarkin, *Lenin Lives! The Lenin Cult in Soviet Russia* (Cambridge, Mass.: Harvard University Press, 1983), 135.

67. "Tsirkular No. 81. Ob izuchenii zhizni i deiatel'nosti t. Lenina v detuchrezhdeni-akh Sotsvosa," APN SSSR, f. 18, op. 2, d. 118, ll. 15–160b.

68. Vilenskaia, "Doshkol'naia rabota v derevne," 104.

69. M. Vilenskaia et al., eds., *Tretii Vserossiiskii S"ezd*, 120.

70. Mariia Markovich, "Pervoe maia u doshkol'nikov," *NP* 3 (1924), 26.

71. "Otchet o mladshei i starshei gruppakh d. sada Krasnovo-Malokhovskoi," TsGA RSFSR, f. 1575, op. 4, d. 80, ll. 10, 37; "Detskii sad Krasnovo-Malokhovskii," ibid., d. 301, ll. 16–17; "Otchet o Iaroslavskom opytnom ochage," ibid., d. 212, l. 50.

72. Sventitskaia, *Nash detskii sad*, 149–52.

73. Markovich, "Pervoe maia," 27, 29–30.

74. Ibid., 27–29.

75. V. Diushen, *Piat' let detskogo gorodka im. III Internatsionala* (Moscow, 1924), 60–63. "Materialy Narkomprosa i OPU (opytno-pokazatel'nykh uchrezhdenii) napravlennye v det sad No. 11 g. Saratova," APN SSSR, f. 18, op. 2, d. 118, l. 28; "Otchet o rabote s det'mi I-oi mladshei gruppy," ibid., d. 140, l. 170b.

76. "Programma-Maksimum dlia perepodgotovki rabotnikov prosveshcheniia," TsGA RSFSR, f. 1575, op. 5, d. 139, ll. 87–890b; "Politicheskaia samopodgotovka rabotnikov prosveshcheniia," ibid., ll. 375–3750b; "Doklad o rabote na Tsentral'nykh Doshkol'nykh Kursakh pri N. K. P.," ibid., d. 58, ll. 28–31.

77. Holmes, *The Kremlin and the Schoolhouse*, 38.

78. "Otchet o letnei rabote doshkol'nykh uchrezhdenii g. Balashova i ego uezda," APN SSSR, f. 18, op. 2, d. 147, l. 8; "Opytnoe zadanie tsentral'nogo opytno-pokaza-tel'nogo detsada No. 2 g. Saratova," ibid., d. 120, l. 52; "Materialy konferentsii doshkol'nykh rabotnikov Saratovskoi gubernii, 3/X/1927 g.," ibid., d. 121, l. 3.

79. M. Vilenskaia et al., eds., *Tretii Vserossiiskii S"ezd*, 123.

80. Ibid., 147.

81. Ibid., 123, 143–44.

82. "Otchet starshei gruppy," APN SSSR, f. 18, op. 2, d. 140, l. 54.

83. APN SSSR, f. 18, op. 2, d. 120, ll. 17–18.

84. APN SSSR, f. 18, op. 2, d. 140, ll. 520b–55.

85. Sventitskaia, *Nash detskii sad*, 28–29, 153–56.

86. Fitzpatrick, *Education and Social Mobility*, 25–29. Smolensk Archive, WKP–402, WKP–404.

87. "Metodicheskoe pis'mo po sviazi s pionerami v doshkol'nykh uchrezhdeniiakh," TsGA RSFSR f. 2306, op. 12, d. 141, ll. 1–4; see also M. Vilenskaia et al., eds., *Tretii Vserossiiskii S"ezd*, 125–26; "Protokol kruzhkov ob"edinennykh zasedanii," APN SSSR, f. 18, op. 2, d. 138, l. 3.

88. M. Vilenskaia et al., eds., *Tretii Vserossiiskii S"ezd*, 107, 130–31; see also, "Ob-shchestvenno-proizvodstvennaia rabota v doshkol'nykh uchrezhdeniiakh," TsGA RSFSR, f. 2306, op. 12, d. 142, l. 20; ibid., d. 141, l. 7.

Chapter Seven

1. Richard Stites, *Revolutionary Dreams: Utopian Vision and Experimental Life in the Russian Revolution* (New York: Oxford University Press, 1989), 226; Fitzpatrick, *The Russian Revolution, 1917–1932* (New York: Oxford University Press, 1984), 121; Robert C. Tucker, "Stalinism as Revolution from Above," in Robert C. Tucker, ed., *Stalinism: Essays in Historical Interpretation* (New York: W. W. Norton, 1977), 82–84.

2. Elizabeth Waters discusses the various interpretations in "The Bolsheviks and the Family" *Contemporary European History* 4 (1993): 290.

3. The distinction between "social" and "human" costs is made by Gail Warshofsky Lapidus, "Sexual Equality in Soviet Policy: A Developmental Perspective," in Dorothy Atkinson, Alexander Dallin, and Gail Warshofsky Lapidus, ed., *Women in Russia,* (Stanford, Calif.: Stanford University Press, 1977), 126.

4. Ibid.

5. Perel', *Doshkol'noe vospitanie* (Moscow, 1932), 27, 34–35; M. E. Makhlina et al., ed., *Doshkol'noe vospitanie v Leningrade za 15 let, 1917–32* (Moscow-Leningrad: Uchpedgiz, 1932), 36.

6. Nadezhda Krupskaia, "O pionerdvizhenii na dannom etape," *Pedagogicheskie sochineniia v shesti tomakh* (Moscow: Pedagogika, 1979), 4: 412.

7. "O doshkol'nom vospitanii detei," *Pedagogicheskie sochineniia,* 5: 68. On the need for kindergartens on collective farms, see "V zapadnoi oblasti (ot nashego spetsial'nogo korrespondenta)," *NP* 6 (1930), 27–28.

8. Perel', *Doshkol'noe vospitanie,* 27; M. M. Vilenskaia, ed., *Spravochnaia Kniga po doshkolnomu vospitaniiu* (Moscow-Leningrad: Gosudarstvennoe izdatel'stvo, 1928), 6–7.

9. *Doshkol'nyi pokhod* (hereafter *DP*) 11 (1929), 1–2.

10. E. E. Tsyrlina et al., eds., *Materialy IV-go Vserossiiskogo s"ezda po doshkol' nomu vospitaniiu (po stenograficheskomu otchetu)* (Moscow-Leningrad: G. M. P. T., 1929), 16 (Lunacharskii's remark), 19, 23, 26, 69–70, 81, 89–90 (resolutions).

11. E. E. Tsyrlina, "Itogi i perspektivy doshkol'noi raboty v RSFSR," in Tsyrlina et al., eds., *Materialy IV-go,* 19–32. For the discussion of the funding in Ivanovo-Vosnesnek, see 22–23. Orlova, a delegate from Moscow, called health workers "aristocrats," 49. For local funding crises and suggestions on how to cope with them, see the debate on Tsyrlina's speech, 39–89, and throughout the proceedings. Similar complaints can be found in Vilenskaia, *Spravochnaia kniga,* 8–9.

12. Issledovatel'skii institut nauchnai pedagogki Moskva 2 Gosudarstvennyi Universitet, *Narodnoe prosveshchenie v piatletnem plane sotsialisticheskogo stroitel'stvo: ocherki* (Moscow: Rabotnik prosveshcheniia, 1930), 186–87.

13. Teachers' salaries reportedly accounted for about 50 percent of preschool budgets. See Tsyrlina et al., eds., *Materialy IV-go,* 23, 24. In a survey of kindergarten budgets for the 1924–1925 school year, expenditures for salary exceeded expenditures for food only in the cities of Moscow and Leningrad and in three of the fifteen *gubernii* reporting data. In the most extreme cases, kindergartens in the *gubernii* of Gomel' and Pskov spent almost half of their budgets on food. On average, just short of 39 percent of spending went to salary, and about one-third to food. See Narkompros, *Statisticheskii sbornik po narodnomu prosveshcheniiu RSFSR, 1926g* (Moscow: Gosizdat, 1927), 28.

14. Tsyrlina et al., eds., *Materialy IV-go,* 23, 40–41, 87 (quote). On the kindergartens' inability to accommodate all children, see also L. K. Shleger, "Vospitanie

rebenka v sem'e," in *Doshkol'noe vospitnaie*, A. V. Surovtseva, ed. (Moscow-Leningrad: Gosudarstvennoe izdatel'stvo, 1928), 96. On parents' support for preschools, see Vilenskaia, *Spravochnaia kniga*, 7.

15. Tsyrlina et al., eds., *Materialy IV-go*, 24.

16. Ibid., 26–27, 56–61. On efforts to control private kindergartens, see Vilenskaia, *Spravochnaia kniga*, 114–115.

17. *Narodnoe prosveshchenie v RSFSR v osnovnykh pokazateliakh* (1932), 8; Barbara Beatty, *Preschool Education in America: The Culture of Young Children from the Colonial Era to the Present* (New Haven, Conn.: Yale University Press, 1995), 111, 171.

18. Perel', *Doshkol'noe vospitanie*, 27. *Narodnoe prosveshchenie v RSFSR v tsifrakh*, 38–39.

19. Figures on the size of the preschool-age population in these years vary widely. The 1926 census put the number of children between three and seven in the RSFSR at 14,944,341; see *Vsesoiuznaia perepis'*, 17: 50. The 1928 handbook of preschool education estimated the preschool-age population of the USSR at ten million children, 1 percent of whom were served by year-round institutions; see Vilenskaia, *Spravochnaia kniga*, 7. A speaker at the fourth preschool congress in 1929 cited the "latest data" that put the number of preschool-age children, apparently in the USSR, at "about 12 million"; see Tsyrlina et al., eds., *Materialy IV-go*, 21. *Narodnoe prosveshchenie v RSFSR v osnovnykh pokazateliakh* (8) reports percentages that assume a 1930–1931 preschool-age population of 13,802,236. Based on 1939 population statistics that provide numbers of three-, four-, and five- to nine-year-olds, one author proposes an estimated Soviet preschool-age population of about 15.8 million, with 6 percent attending some type of kindergarten; see Dorothea Meeks, *Soviet Youth: Some Achievements and Problems* (London: Routledge and Kegan Paul, 1957), 5–6. In 1988, 56 percent of Soviet children under 7 attended preschool, but in some republics this number fell as low as 10 percent; see N. Grishaeva, "Kooperativnye doshkol'nye uchrezhdeniia v krupnom gorode," in *Perestroika—sem'e, sem'ia—perestroike (stat'i opublikovannye v periodicheskoi pechati)* (Moscow: Mysl', 1990), 227. Comparisons with other nations are complicated by the fact that the Russian system defined the preschool years so broadly. In the last decade of the nineteenth century, one-year kindergartens serving four- to five-year olds were becoming part of the public school system in the United States. By 1915, 8,463 public kindergartens served roughly 12 percent of the American preschool population. Unlike Soviet kindergartens, U.S. kindergartens never aimed to provide full-day childcare. See Michael S. Shapiro, *Child's Garden: The Kindergarten Movement from Froebel to Dewey* (University Park: Penn State University Press, 1983), 146, 172. In Britain, compulsory education began at age five; see Jewell Lochhead, *The Education of Young Children in England* (New York: Teachers College, 1932), 41.

20. Perel', *Doshkol'noe vospitanie*, 27.

21. Tsyrlina et al., eds., *Materialy IV-go*, 74; Makhlina et al., eds., *Doshkol'noe vospitanie v Leningrade za 15 let, 1917–32*, 36; Vilenskaia, *Spravochnaia kniga*, 13–14.

22. Tsyrlina et al., eds., *Materialy IV-go*, 59–60.

23. Ibid., 26, 48–49. Additionally, the congress favored organizing "null" groups connected to primary schools—similar to the one-year U.S. kindergarten—for seven-year-olds, especially in countryside, where children tended to leave school earlier, 25,122. Vilenskaia, *Spravochnaia kniga*, describes work with children in "evening rooms" at clubs and at playgrounds, and "null" groups, 13–18.

24. Tsyrlina et al., eds., *Materialy IV–go*, 30–31, 69. For the 1925–1926 school year, the salaries of teachers in urban preschools (36.38 rubles per month in the average *guberniia*) were lower than those of urban primary school teachers (38.75 rubles) and were almost 30 percent behind those of urban secondary teachers (50.28 rubles), with fairly wide variations between *gubernii*. By 1931, primary school teachers had fallen an additional 10 percent behind secondary teachers. The gap narrowed a bit the following year, but pay differentials remained wider than they had been in 1925–1926. Preschool workers' salaries had been dropped from the published comparisons. Based on the figures from the mid-1920s and on the relative priority of preschool education, it seems safe to assume that preschool teachers earned no more, and probably less, than primary teachers. While the number of people earning (unspecified) qualifications as primary teachers increased by more than four and a half times between 1928 and 1931, the number of newly qualified preschool teachers increased at less than half that rate. See *Statisticheskii sbornik* (1927), 32–33; *Narodnoe prosveshchenie* (1932), 161, 97.

25. Tsyrlina et al., eds., *Materialy IV–go*, 58, 56, 85. Zhenotdel and Komsomol activists might participate in a six-week training course or a "practicum" at a preschool institution; see Vilenskaia, *Spravochnaia kniga*, 19.

26. Tsyrlina et al., eds., *Materialy IV–go*, 85, 26, 39–41, 44–48, 74–77, 80–81. The department adopted the slogans, "through the playground to the kindergarten" and "organizing playgrounds is a way of expanding the network of permanent preschool institutions"; see Vilenskaia, *Spravochnaia kniga*, 16.

27. Quoted in Jessica Smith, *Women in Soviet Russia* (New York: Vanguard Press, 1928), 103. See also Ethel Mannin, "Playtime of the Child in Modern Russia," in *Playtime in Russia*, ed. Hubert Griffith (London: Methuen, 1935), 137–38.

28. Moshe Lewin, *The Making of the Soviet System* (New York: Pantheon Books, 1985), 219–20.

29. S. Frederick Starr, "Visionary Town Planning during the Cultural Revolution," in *Cultural Revolution in Russia, 1928–31*, ed. Sheila Fitzpatrick (Bloomington: Indiana University Press, 1978), 209–212; Stites, *Revolutionary Dreams*, 198–200.

30. *Narodnoe prosveshchenie v piatletnem plane*, 240–241.

31. Nadezhda Krupskaia, "Vazhnyi bytovoi vopros," *Pedagogicheskie sochineniia*, 4: 112–113; Krupskaia, "Gde zhit' detiam v sotsialisticheskom gorode?" ibid., 4: 355.

32. Zlata Ionovna Lilina, *Roditeli, uchites' vospityvat' svoikh detei* (Moscow: Glavlit, 1929).

33. Ibid., 5.

34. Ibid., 7, 9, 4; "Anketa domashniaia sreda rebenka," Tsentral'nyi Gosudarstvennyi Arkhiv RSFSR (hereafter TsGA RSFSR), f. 1575, op. 7, d. 94, ll.280–282ob. Teachers eager for parental contributions to building kindergartens emphasized that parents often spent a great deal of money on their children, but that their spending tended to be "irrational" if not "dangerous"; Tsyrlina et al., eds., *Materialy IV–go*, 45, 63. Vilenskaia, *Spravochnaia kniga*, 23.

35. "Anketa domashniaia sreda rebenka," TsGA RSFSR, f. 1575, op. 7, d. 94, ll. 280–882ob; "Plan raboty detskogo doma stantsii SPON imeni Kominterna na 1927/28 god," in *Doshkol'noe vospitanie* (Moscow-Leningrad: Gosudarstvennoe izdatel'stvo, 1928), 54–57.

36. Alan M. Ball, *And Now My Soul Is Hardened: Abandoned Children in Soviet Russia, 1918–1930* (Berkeley: University of California Press, 1994), 192–195; Wendy

Goldman, *Women, the State, and Revolution: Soviet Family Policy and Social Life,* *1917–1936* (Cambridge, England: Cambridge University Press, 1993), 313–327; Frederic Lilge, *Anton Semyonovitch Makarenko: An Analysis of His Educational Ideas in the Context of Soviet Society* (Berkeley: University of California Press, 1958), 13–14.

37. Carol Eubanks Hayden, "The Zhenotdel and the Bolshevik Party," *Russian History* 3 (1976): 171; see also Richard Stites, *The Women's Liberation Movement in Russia: Feminism, Nihilism, and Bolshevism, 1860–1930* (Princeton, N.J.: Princeton University Press, 1978), 344; Goldman, *Women, the State, and Revolution,* 331–32.

38. Lapidus, "Sexual Equality," 118, 125.

39. Tsyrlina et al., eds., *Materialy IV-go,* 28–29, 50–51, 55, 57, 75. Vilenskaia, *Spravochnaia kniga,* 9–11.

40. *DP* 11 (1929), 8; "Kak organizovat' zhizn' detei v sem'e," *DP* 7–8 (1929), 2; Tsyrlina et al., eds., *Materialy IV-go,* 86–87.

41. "Detskii sad vospityvaet stroitelia novoi zhizni," *DP* No. 11 (1929), 6–7; Shleger, "Vospitanie rebenka v sem'e," 96.

42. "Kooperirovanie materei v dele vospitaniia detei," *DP* 3–4 (Moscow, 1929), 1–2.

43. *DP* 13 (1930), 6–7.

44. Stites, *Women's Liberation Movement,* 385.

45. *DP* 1–2 (1929), 14–16 (emphasis added). On the importance of teaching sexual equality in early childhood, see Tsyrlina et al., eds., *Materialy IV-go,* 17, 101.

46. Quoted in Sheila Fitzpatrick, "Cultural Revolution as Class War" in *The Cultural Front: Power and Culture in Revolutionary Russia,* (Ithaca, N.Y.: Cornell University Press, 1992), 117.

47. The emphasis on health and hygiene is visible in the column "V pomoshch' materi" in *Rabotnitsa* and in the series *Doshkol'nyi pokhod.* Typical titles in *Rabotnitsa* included "Zdorovye deti—zabota vzroslykh," "Kakaia pishchia samaia zdorovaia dlia rebenka-doshkol'nika," No. 1 (1927), 19–20; "O skarlatine," "Ob odezhde rebenka," 2 (1927), 21–22. See also Elena Krichevskaia, *Sovety materiam po vospitaniiu detei: opyt pedagogichsekoi konsul'tatsii* (Moscow, 1927). Shleger, "Vospitanie rebenka v sem'e," 97; "Plan organizatsii vystavki po doshkol'nomu vospitaniiu pri Tsentral'nom D/s No. 2 g. Saratova," Arkhiv Akademii Pedagogicheskikh Nauk (hereafter APN SSSR), f. 18, op. 2, d. 140. The intervention of kindergarten teachers is described in "Plan raboty detsada stantsii SPON imeni Kominterna za 1927/28 g," in *Doshkol'noe vospitanie* (Moscow-Leningrad, 1928), 59.

48. *DP* 12 (1930), 2–5; *DP* 14 (1930), 3–6.

49. Meeks, *Soviet Youth,* 7.

50. *DP* 13 (1930), 6–7; *DP* 5–6 (1929), 7–12.

51. *DP* 7–8 (1929), 8–10.

52. *DP* 7–8 (1929).

53. Meeks cites Soviet sources that note peasants' fears that the kindergarten would confiscate children's crosses, see *Soviet Youth,* 4.

54. *DP* 9 (1929), 6–8.

55. Tsyrlina et al., eds., *Materialy IV-go,* 44–45, 32.

56. "Materialy o rabote Saratovskogo opytno-pokazatel'nogo d. sada No. 11," APN SSSR, f. 18, op. 2, d. 136, ll. 18–18ob. On women's support for the kindergarten program in Azerbaijan, see Tsyrlina et al., eds., *Materialy IV-go,* 73.

57. A. V. Surovtseva, "Plan raboty detsada," in *Doshkol'noe vospitanie,* 58.

58. *DP* 5–6 (1929), 1–2; Z. I. Lilina, *Roditeli uchites' vospityvat' svoikh detei*, 8–20.

59. Moshe Lewin, "Social Relations inside Industry during the Prewar Five-Year Plans, 1928–41," in *The Making of the Soviet System*, 250.

60. Fitzpatrick, "Cultural Revolution as Class War," in *The Cultural Front: Power and Culture in Revolutionary Russia*, 125.

61. Victoria Bonnell, "The Iconography of the Worker in Soviet Political Art," in *Making Workers Soviet*, ed. Lewis Siegelbaum and Ronald Grigor Suny (Ithaca, N.Y.: Cornell University Press, 1994), 366, 363.

62. Richard Stites, *Russian Popular Culture: Entertainment and Society since 1900* (Cambridge, England: Cambridge University Press, 1992), 64, 70.

63. Ella Winter, *Red Virtue: Human Relationships in the New Russia* (New York, 1933), 217.

64. Fitzpatrick, *The Cultural Front*, 102–103. Lev Kopelev recalls one such attack on a French teacher who insisted on Napoleon's heroic status; see *The Education of a True Believer*, trans. Gary Kern (New York: Harper and Row, 1978), 58–60.

65. *DP* 1–2 (1929), 1–2.

66. Tsyrlina et al., eds., *Materialy IV-go*, 99–100, 103–104.

67. Ibid., 103–109. Sample schedules and descriptions of activities can be found in *Pedagogicheskaia entsiklopediia*, 85–96.

68. Tsyrlina et al., eds., *Materialy IV-go*, 137 (on need for "directives"), 138–139, 143–47, 152 (on need to avoid "recipes").

69. Ibid., 99, 100, 163.

70. Perel', *Doshkol'noe vospitanie*, 30, 28; Makhlina et al., eds., *Doshkol'noe vospitanie v Leningrade*, 15, 14.

71. John Dewey, *Impressions of Soviet Russia and the Revolutionary World: Mexico—China—Turkey* (New York: New Republic, 1929), 84–85, 76, 81.

72. Elena Bonner, *Mothers and Daughters*, trans. Antonina W. Bouis (New York: Vintage Books, 1993), 320; Andrew Wachtel, *The Battle for Childhood: Creation of a Russian Myth* (Stanford, Calif.: Stanford University Press, 1990), 152.

73. Winter, *Red Virtue*, 214–15, 238, 241–42; for a picture of children using the conveyor, see 242.

74. Mannin, "Playtime of the Child in Modern Russia," 143–162; quotes from 156, 147.

75. Samuel Marshak, *At Life's Beginning: Some Pages of Reminiscence*, trans. Katherine Hunter Blair (New York: E. P. Dutton, 1964), 26.

76. Kornei Chukovskii, *From Two to Five*, trans. Miriam Morton (Berkeley: University of California Press, 1990), 51.

77. Winter, *Red Virtue*, 229.

78. Chukovskii, *From Two to Five*, 52, 54, 56.

79. Winter, *Red Virtue*, 229.

80. Nadezhda Krupskaia, "XVII partkonferentsiia i zadachi doshkol'nogo vospitaniia," *Pedagogicheskie sochineniia*, 5:194.

81. Tsyrlina et al., eds., *Materialy IV-go*, 158–159, 147.

82. Ibid., 123–26. Lunacharskii argued that the malleability that made children particulary susceptible to the "reactionary" influences of the family also made it possible to free the young generation from such influences. Asserting that the role of instinct and

"biological determinants" had often been exaggerated, Lunacharskii concluded that "the same person, with an absolutely identical biological makeup moved to a another century, in other surroundings, would be totally different," ibid., 16. Vilenskaia, *Spravochnaia kniga*, 116–117. On Komsomol work with preschools, see Smolensk Archive, WKP–405, 406, 407, 415.

83. Yuri Druzhnikov, *Voznesenie Pavlika Morozova* (London: Overseas Publications Interchange, 1988), 139–153. Ethel Mannin, "Playtime of the Child in Modern Russia," 160. See Stites, *Russian Popular Culture*, 68–69. On Morozov and other Stalinist "sons," see Katerina Clark, *The Soviet Novel: History as Ritual* (Chicago: University of Chicago Press, 1985), 114–135.

84. Paul Thorez, *Model Children: Inside the Republic of Red Scarves*, trans. Nancy Cadet (New York: Autonomedia, 1991), 93–94.

85. *The Soviet Novel*, 114, 85; Stites, *Revolutionary Dreams*, 226; Fitzpatrick, *The Russian Revolution*, 121; Tucker, "Stalinism as Revolution from Above," 82–84.

Conclusion

1. I have adopted this terminology from Iurii M. Lotman and Boris A. Uspenskii, "Binary Models in the Dynamics of Russian Culture (to the End of the Eighteenth Century)," in *The Semiotics of Russian Culture*, ed. Alexander Nakhimovsky and Alice Stone Nakhimovsky (Ithaca, N.Y.: Cornell University Press, 1985), 30–66.

2. Here my approach differs from Margaret Stolee's, which casts the development of school policy in terms of an effort—undermined by inauspicious conditions—to translate ideology into practice; see "'A Generation Capable of Establishing Communism': Revolutionary Child Rearing in the Soviet Union, 1917–1928," (Ph.D. diss., Duke University, 1982).

3. Jane Burbank, "Lenin and the Law in Revolutionary Russia," *Slavic Review* 54, no. 1 (Spring 1995), 37–38. Leon Trotsky describes the Lenin of this period as "showing impatience, irony, and sometimes downright bitter mockery" when colleagues were "not talking business"; see *My Life: The Rise and Fall of a Dictator* (London: Thornton Butterworth, 1930), 304.

4. Trotsky, *My Life*, 294.

5. Maxim Gorky, *My Childhood*, tr. Ronald Wilks (London: Penguin Books, 1966), 132.

6. Barbara Evans Clements, "The Effects of the Civil War on Women and Family Relations," in *Party, State, and Society in the Russian Civil War: Explorations in Social History*, ed. Diane Koenker et al. (Bloomington: Indiana University Press, 1989), 118–119.

Postscript: Three Childhoods

1. Barbara Beatty, *Preschool Education in America: The Culture of Young Children from the Colonial Era to the Present* (New Haven, Conn.: Yale University Press, 1995), x.

2. Psychoanalyst Dori Laub describes his childhood memories of the Holocaust as "the memories of an adult" and suggests that "events are remembered and seem to have

been experienced in a way that was far beyond the normal capacity for recall in a young child of my age"; see "An Event Without a Witness: Truth, Testimony, and Survival" in *Testimony: Crises of Witnessing in Literature, Psychoanalysis, and History,* ed. Dori Laub and Shoshana Felman (New York: Routledge, 1992), 76.

3. Richard Coe defines reminiscences of childhood, or at least the best ones, as closer to "the poet's 'truth' rather than the historian's 'accuracy.'" He maintains that except in extreme situations, "politics as such rarely influence the child one way or another." He offers a memoir of childhood in fascist Italy to demonstrate how "ideas drawn from the greater world" can penetrate the child's "small world"; see *When the Grass Was Taller: Autobiography and the Experience of Childhood* (New Haven, Conn.: Yale University Press, 1984), 2, 68, 237. Memoirs of childhood in Nazi-occupied France are also notably attuned to the "greater world." For example see, Saul Friedlander, *When Memory Comes,* trans. Helen R. Lane (New York: Farrar, Straus, Giroux, 1979); Georges Perec, *W ou le souvenir d'enfance* (Paris: Denoël, 1975); Sarah Kofman, *Rue Ordener, Rue Labat,* trans. Ann Smock (Lincoln: University of Nebraska Press, 1996).

4. Larry Holmes, "Part of History: The Oral Record and Moscow's Model School No. 25, 1931–1937," *Slavic Review* 56 (Summer 1997): 297.

5. This view of memory draws on the work of cognitive psychologists, who have pictured memory as operating not like a computer faithfully retrieving inputs as they were entered, but instead like a paleontologist unearthing bone fragments and piecing them together to resemble an imagined dinosaur. With each attempt at reconstruction, bits and pieces of memory have to be brought together, reassembled, given coherency. In the process, memories shift, corrupted by fragments that have over time attached themselves to the original experience. See Daniel Schacter, "Memory Distortion: History and Current Status," in *Memory Distortion: How Minds, Brains, and Societies Reconstruct the Past,* ed. Daniel Schacter (Cambridge, Mass.: Harvard University Press, 1995), 10. Jerome Bruner approaches narratives of the self "as a construction that, so to speak, proceeds from the outside in as well as from the inside out, from culture to mind as well as from mind to culture"; see *Acts of Meaning* (Cambridge, Mass.: Harvard University Press, 1990), 108. See also Philippe Lejeune, *On Autobiography,* trans. Katherine Leary (Minneapolis: University of Minnesota Press, 1989).

6. Emphasis in original. Lev Kopelev, *The Education of a True Believer,* trans. Gary Kern (New York: Harper and Row, 1978), ix.

7. Ol'ga Berggol'ts, *Dnevnye zvezdy* (Leningrad: Sovetskii pisatel', 1959, reprint ed. 1971), 39.

8. Andrew Wachtel, *The Battle for Childhood: Creation of a Russian Myth* (Stanford, Calif: Stanford University Press, 1990), 165.

9. This has been the case for writers as diverse as Alexander Solzhenitsyn (born 1918) and Evgeniia Ginzburg (born 1907), whose memoir *Journey into the Whirlwind* focuses not on her happy childhood but on the gulag. Those who took part in and wrote accounts of the events of October or the Civil War were usually young, and thus in the broadest sense part of the "rising generation," but their pre-Revolutionary childhoods separated them from the children of October. See for example, Eduard M. Dune, *Notes of a Red Guard,* trans. Diane P. Koenker and S. A. Smith (Urbana: University of Illinois Press, 1993); Isaac Babel, *1920 Diary,* tr. H. T. Willetts (New Haven, Conn.: Yale University Press, 1995).

10. Reginald Zelnik makes the distinction, and notes its limits, in his discussion of Vasilii Gerasimov's memoir in *Law and Disorder on the Narova River: The Kreenholm Strike of 1872* (Berkeley: University of California, 1995), 227.

11. Eugenia Ginzburg, *Journey into the Whirlwind*, trans. Paul Stevenson and Max Hayward (San Diego, Calif.: Harcourt Brace Jovanovich, 1967), 233.

12. Coe, *When the Grass Was Taller*, 104–138.

13. Evgeny Evtushenko, "A Precocious Autobiography," in *Yevtushenko's Reader* (New York: E. P. Dutton, 1972), 16–17.

14. Elena Bonner, *Mothers and Daughters*, trans. Antonina W. Bouis (New York: Vintage Books, 1993), 125.

15. Berggol'ts, *Dnevnye zvezdy*, 113.

16. Osip Mandelstam, *The Noise of Time*, trans. Clarence Brown (New York: Penguin Books, reprint ed., 1993), 110. A *raznochinets* was a person of mixed background below the gentry.

Bibliography

Primary Sources

Archives

Archive of the Smolensk Oblast, National Archives, Washington, DC (Smolensk)
Record Group 242
WKP-127, 133, 164, 207, 274, 275, 281, 393, 396, 397, 399–407, 415, 462, 467

Hoover Institution on War, Revolution, and Peace, Stanford University (Hoover)
ARA—Russian Operations
Box 7 Clothing
Box 10 Education
Box 12 Children
Box 19 Health
Box 15 Gomel
Box 33 Moscow
Box 34 Children's Relief
Box 65 Petrograd
Box 96 Saratov
ARA—Ru Unit Historical Div

Nauchnyi arkhiv akademii pedagogichesikh nauk SSSR (APN SSSR)
f. 18, Arkhivnye materialy gosudarstvennykh uchrezhdenii, obshchestvennykh organizatsii i chastnykh lits
op. 2, dd. 123, 124, 135, 137, 138, 145, 149, 198, 199, 208
f. 23, op. 1 Arkhiv Venttsel' Konstantina Nikolaevicha, 1878–1938, dd. 31, 54, 73

Tsentral'nyi Gosudarstvennyi Arkhiv RSFSR (TsGA RSFSR; now GARF)
f. 413, Ministerstvo sotsial'nogo obespecheniia RSFSR op. 2 d. 327
f. 1575, Glavnoe upravlenie sotsial'nogo vospitaniia i politekhnicheskogo obrazovaniia detei (Glavsotsvos)

216

op. 4, Otdel opytno-pokazatel'nykh uchrezhdenii, dd. 3, 72, 80, 211, 212, 276, 301, 373
op. 5, Otdel podgotovki pedagogicheskogo personala, dd. 2, 15, 47, 58, 68, 139, 141
op. 7, Otdel doshkol'nogo vospitaniia, dd. 2, 18, 30, 35, 53, 57, 73, 89
f. 2306, Ministerstvo prosveshcheniia RSFSR
op. 12, Otdel doshkol'nogo vospitaniia, dd. 79, 106
op. 13, Otdel okhrany detstva, dd. 32, 34, 39
op. 14, Otdel doshkol'nogo obespecheniia, dd. 19, 20

Journals

Biulleteni Otdela Doshkol'nogo Vospitaniia Narkomprosa
Doshkol'noe vospitanie
Na putiakh k novoi shkole
Narodnoe prosveshchenie
Novaia shkola
Pedagogicheskie izvestiia
Pedagogichskaia mysl'
Puti kommunisticheskogo prosveshcheniia
Rabotnitsa
Revoliutsia i kul'tura
Vestnik prosveshcheniia

Other Published Sources

Al'medingen-Tumin, N., E. Tikheeva, and Iu. Fausek, eds. *Doshkol'noe delo: sbornik statei.* Petrograd, 1922.
Arbore-Ralle, Ekaterina. *Mat' i ditia v sovetskoi Rossii.* Moscow: Gosudarstvennoe izdatel'stvo, 1920.
Bartram, N. *Muzei igrushki: ob igrushke, kukol'nom teatre,nachatkakh truda i znanii i o knige dlia rebenka.* Leningrad: Academia, 1928.
Bebel, August. *Woman and Socialism.* New York: Socialist Literature Co., 1910.
Berggol'ts, Ol'ga. *Dnevnye zvezdy.* Leningrad: Sovetskii pisatel', 1971.
Bibanova, E. G. *Kak gotovit' iz rebenka v vozraste do 3-kh let budeshchego stroitelia novoi zhizni.* Moscow-Leningrad, 1927.
———. *Trud i tvorchestvo.* Moscow-Leningrad, 1927.
Blonskii, Pavel Petrovich. *Novye programmy GUS'a i uchitel'.* 2d ed. Moscow: Rabotnik prosveshcheniia, 1925.
Bogdanov, V. *Uchitel'stvo i sovetskaia vlast'.* Moscow: Gosudarstvennoe izdatel'stvo, 1919.
Bonner, Elena. *Mothers and Daughters.* Translated by Antonina W. Bouis. New York: Vintage Books, 1993.
Chukovskaia, Lydia. *To the Memory of Childhood.* Translated by Eliza Kellogg Klose. Evanston, Ill.: Northwestern Univ. Press, 1988.
Chukovskii, Kornei. *From Two to Five.* Translated by Miriam Morton. Berkeley: University of California Press, 1968.
Curti, Merle. *The Social Ideas of American Educators.* New York: C. Scribner's Sons, 1935.
Detskaia smertnost' i sotsial'naie usloviia: 8 diagramm s prilozheniem obiasnitel'nago teksta. Petrograd: Muzei truda, 1916.
Dewey, John. *Impressions of Soviet Russia and the Revolutionary World: Mexico—China—Turkey.* New York: New Republic, 1929.

Diushen, V. *Politicheskie prazdniki v shkole i detskom dome: Rukovodstvo dlia pedagogov.* Moscow-Leningrad, 1926.

———, ed. *Piat' let detskogo gorodka imeni III Internatsionala.* Moscow, 1924.

Dobroliubov, N. *Stat'i, retsenzii, iunosheskie raboty aprel' 1853-iiul' 1857.* Moscow: Gosudarstvennoe izdatel'stvo detskoi lieteratury, 1961.

Doshkol'noe vospitanie: teoriia i praktika. Moscow, 1928.

El'iashuk, A. I. *Kak pravil'no vospityvat' sovmestno mal'chikov i devochek v sem'e.* Moscow, 1930.

Epshtein, S. O. *O pionerskoi stengazete.* Kharkov, 1926.

Evtushenko, Evgeny. "A Precocious Autobiography." In *Yevtushenko's Own Reader.* New York: E. P. Dutton, 1972.

Fediaevsky, Vera, and Patty Smith Hill. *Nursery School and Parent Education in the Soviet Union.* New York: E. P. Dutton, 1936.

Field, Alice W. *Protection of Women and Children in Soviet Russia.* New York: E. P. Dutton, 1932.

Froebel, Friedrich. *The Education of Man.* Translated by Josephine Jarvis. New York: A. Lovell and Co., 1886.

———. *A Selection from His Writings by Irene M. Lilley.* Cambridge: Cambridge University Press, 1967.

Fülop-Miller, René. *The Mind and Face of Bolshevism: An Examination of Cultural Life in Soviet Russia.* New York: Knopf, 1928.

Gosudarstvennyi muzei-vystavka po narodnomu prosveshcheniiu. *Sbornik diagramm: Kul'turnoe stroitel'stvo soiuza sovetskikh sotsialisticheskikh respublik,* 2d ed. Moscow and Leningrad: Gosudarstvennoe izdatel'stvo, 1929.

Herzen, Alexander. *My Past and Thoughts.* Translated by Constance Garnett. Berkeley: University of California Press, 1973.

Ianzhul, Ekaterina Nikolevna (Vel'iusheva). *Trudovoe nachalo v shkolakh Evropy: izdanie tret'e.* Moscow: izdatel'stvo zhurnala "Narodyi uchitel'," 1918–19.

Issledovatel'skii institut nauchnoi pedagogki Moskva 2 Gosudarstvennyi Universitet. *Narodnoe prosveshchenie v piatlenem plane sotsialisticheskogo stroitel'stvo: ocherki.* Moscow and Leningrad: Rabotnik prosveshcheniia, 1930.

Kanel', V. Ia. *Vopros vospitaniia v svete sotsial'noi gigieny (Gigiena telesnoi i dushevnoi zhizni rebenka).* Moscow: Prakticheskii znaniia, [1918].

Kapterev, Petr. *Novaia russkaia pedagogika, ee glavneishie idei, napravlenii i deiateli.* St. Petersburg, 1897.

Kilpatrick, William Heard. *Froebel's Kindergarten Principles Critically Examined.* New York: Macmillan, 1916.

Kollontai, Aleksandra. *Obshchestvo i materinstvo.* Petrograd: Zhizn' i znanie, 1916.

———. *Rabotnitsa-mat'.* St. Petersburg: Zhizn' i znanie, 1917.

———. *Sem'ia i kommunisticheskoe gosudarstvo.* Moscow-Petrograd: Kommunist, 1918.

———. *Sotsial'nye osnovy zhenskogo voprosa.* St. Petersburg: Znanie, 1909.

Kopelev, Lev. *The Education of a True Believer.* Translated by Gary Kern. New York: Harper & Row, 1978.

Korosteleva, A. A. *Uchitel' i revoliutsiia.* Moscow: Rabotnik prosveshcheniia, 1925.

Kozhanyi, P. *Rabotnitsa i byt.* Moscow: Voprosy truda, 1926.

Krichevskaia, Elena. *Lektsii po pedagogike rannego vozrasta dlia sester-vospitatel'nits.* Moscow, 1928.

———. *Pis'ma o materinstve.* Petrograd, 1916.

———. *Prakticheskoe rukovodstvo po vospitaniiu detei v pervye 3 goda ikh zhizni.* Moscow, 1922.

———. *Sovety materiam po vospitaniiu detei: Opyt pedagogicheskoi konsul'tatsii.* Moscow: Izd. "Okhrana materinstva i mladenchestva," 1927.

Krupskaia, Nadezhda. *Pedagogicheskie sochineniia v shesti tomakh.* Moscow: Pedagogika, 1979.

Kul'turnoe stroitel'stvo Soiuza Sovetskikh Sotsialisticheskikh Respublik: K dokladu A. V. Lunacharskogo na 2-i sessii Tsentral'nogo Ispolnitel'nogo Komiteta Soiuza SSR IV sozyva. Leningrad: Gosudarstvennoe izdatel'stvo, 1927.

Lebedeva, Vera Pavlovna. *Okhrana materinstva i mladenchestva v sovetskoi respublike.* Moscow, 1918.

———. *Kniga materi.* Moscow, 1926.

Levin-Shchirina, F. S., and D. V. Mendzheritskaia. *Doshkol'noe vospitanie: uchebnoe posobie dlia pedagogicheskikh uchilishch.* Moscow, 1939.

Lilina, Z. I. *Deti revoliutsionery.* Leningrad, 1926.

———. *Nash uchitel' Lenin: Knizhka dlia detei.* Leningrad, 1924.

———. *Ot kommunisticheskoi sem'i k kommunisticheskomu obshchestvu.* St. Petersburg, 1920.

———. *Pervoe maia: prazdnik truda—prazdnik detei.* St. Petersburg, 1921.

———. *Roditeli, uchites' vospityvat' svoikh detei.* Moscow: Glavlit, 1929.

———. *Sotsial'no-trudovoe vospitanie: itog chetyrkhletnei raboty s oktiabr'skoi revoliutsii 1917 g. do oktiabria 1921 g.* St. Petersburg: Gosudarstvennoe izdatel'stvo, 1921.

Makarenko, A. S. *The Collective Family: A Handbook for Russian Parents.* Translated by Robert Daglish. Gloucester, Mass.: Peter Smith, 1973.

Makhlina, M. E., N. A. Tumin-Al'medingen, and O. V. Shirokogorova, eds. *Doshkol'noe vospitanie v Leningrade za 15 let, 1917-32.* Moscow-Leningrad: Uchpedgiz, 1932.

Mannin, Ethel. "Playtime of the Child in Modern Russia." In *Playtime in Russia,* ed. Hubert Griffith. London: Methuen, 1935.

Markovich, Mariia. *Pervoe maia v doshkol'nykh uchrezhdeniiakh.* Moscow: Izdatel'stvo "Rabotnik prosveshcheniia," 1924.

Marshak, Samuel. *At Life's Beginning: Some Pages of Reminiscence.* Translated by Katherine Hunter Blair. New York: E. P. Dutton, 1964.

Minusinskii okruzhnoi pedagogichskii kabinet. *Doshkol'noe vospitanie v kolkhoze.* Minusinsk: Minusinskii okruzhnoi pedagogicheskii kabinet, 1930.

Molozhavyi, S. S., R. E. Orlova, R. I. Prushitskaia, and A.V. Surovtseva, eds. *Doskhol'noe vospitanie.* Moscow-Leningrad: Gosudarstvennoe izdatel'stvo, 1928.

Montessori, Maria. *Dr. Montessori's Own Handbook.* 1914. Reprint, Cambridge, Mass.: Robert Bentley, 1964.

Morozova, M. Ia., and E. I. Tikheeva. *Sovremennyi detskii sad: ego znachenie i oborudovanie.* St. Petersburg, 1914.

Narkompros. *1917-Oktiabr' 1920 (Kratkii otchet).* Moscow: Gosudarstvennoe izdatel'stvo, 1920.

———. *Narodnoe prosveshchenie v osnovnykh pokazateliakh: statisticheskii sbornik.* Moscow: Gosizdat, 1928.

———. *Narodnoe prosveshchenie v RSFSR v osnovnykh pokazetliakh: statisticheskii sbornik (1927/28–1930/31 gg., co vkliucheniem nekotorykh dannykh za 1931/32 g).* Moscow: Gosudarstvennoe uchebno-pedagogicheskoe izdatel'stvo, 1932.

———. *Narodnoe prosveshchenie v RSFSR v tsifrakh za 15 let sovetskoi vlasti (kratkii statisticheskii sbornik).* Moscow: Gosudarstvennoe uchebno-pedagogicheskoe izdatel'stvo, 1932.

————. *Spravochnik po doshkol'nomu vospitaniiu*. Moscow, 1919.

————. *Statisticheskii ezhegodnik: sostoianie narodnogo obrazovaniia v RSFSR za 1923–24 god*. Moscow: Izdatel'stvo "Doloi negramotnost'," 1925.

————. *Statisticheskii ezhegodnik: god vtoroi: sostaoinie narodnogo obrazovaiia v RSFSR (bez avtonomykh respublik) za 1924/25 uch god*. Moscow: Izdatel'stvo adm. org. upr. Narkomprosa, 1926.

Narkomzdrav, Otdel Okhrany Materinstva i Mladenchestva. *Sputnik po okhrane materinstva i mladenchestva*. Moscow: OMM, 1921.

————. *Materialy pervogo vserossiiskogo soveshcheniia po okhrane materinstva i mladenchestva*. Moscow: Izdatel'stvo otdela okhrany materinstvai mladenchestva Narkomzdrava, 1921.

Perel', Ia. A., ed. *Doshkol'noe vospitanie*. Moscow-Leningrad, 1932.

Pervyi Vserossiiskii S"ezd po doshkol'nomu vospitaniiu: doklady, protokoly, rezoliutsii. Moscow: Gosudarstvennoe izdatel'stvo, 1921.

Pistrak, M. M., and R. E. Orlova, eds. *Doshkol'nyi pokhod*. Moscow: Biblioteka Kopeika, 1929–30.

Prushitskaia, Rakhil' Isaakovna. *Doshkol'noe vospitanie i sovremennost'*. Moscow-Petrograd: Izdatel'stvo rabotnik prosveshcheniia, 1923.

Radin, E. P. *Chto delaet sovetskaia vlast' dlia okhrany zdorov'ia detei*. 2d ed. Moscow: Izdatel'stvo pamiati K. M. Bonch-Bruevich, 1920.

Rezoliutsii i tezisy dokladov 1-go vserossiiskogo s"ezda po doshkol'nomu vospitaniiu. Moscow, 1919.

Rezoliutsii po dokladom II-go vserossiiskogo s"ezda po doshkol'nomu vospitaniiu (25 noiabria do 2 dekabria 1921 g). Moscow, 1921.

Rozenberg, V. L. *Nasha sistema vospitaniia v svete marksistskoi psikhologii*. Rostov-Don: Severo-Kavkazskoe kraevoe partiinoe izdatl'stvo "Burevestnik," 1925.

Rozhdestvenskii, Vsevolod. *Stranitsy zhizni*. Moscow: Sovremennik, 1974.

Rybnikov, Nikolai Aleksandrovich. *Detskie igrushki i ikh vybor*. Moscow: Pedalogicheskaia biblioteka Moskovskogo Gorodskogo Pedalogicheskoe Muzeia, 1920.

————. *Kak izuchat' rebenka*. Moscow, 1916.

————, ed. *Igra i igrushka: Pedagogicheskii sbornik*. Moscow-Leningrad: Gosizdat, 1926.

————, ed. *Rebenok i igrushka*. Moscow, 192–.

Schlesinger, Rudolf, ed. *The Family in the USSR: Documents and Readings*. London: Routledge and Kegan Paul, 1949.

Semashko, Nikolai Aleksandrovich. *Novyi byt i polovoi vopros*. Moscow-Leningrad, 1926.

————. *Sem'ia i brak v proshlom i nastoiashchem*. Moscow, 1927.

Sem'ia i novyi byt: Spory o proekte novogo kodeksa zakonov o sem'e i brake. Moscow, 1926.

Smith, Jessica. *Women in Soviet Russia*. New York: Vanguard Press, 1928.

Sokoloff, Boris. *Sauvez les enfants! (Les enfants de la Russie soviétique)*. Prague: Volia Rossii, 1921.

Spravochnaia kniga po doshkol'nomu vospitaniiu. Moscow-Leningrad, 1928.

Strong, Anna Louise. *Children of the Revolution: Story of the John Reed Children's Colony on the Volga*. Seattle: Pigott printing concern, 1925.

Surovtseva, A. V., ed. *Doshkol'noe vospitanie*. Moscow-Leningrad, 1928.

————. *O vospitanii rebenka-doshkol'nika v sem'e*. Moscow-Leningrad: Gosudarstvennoe izdatel'stvo, 1927.

Sventitskaia, M. Kh. *Detskii sad: kratkiia svedeniia i plany zaniatii*. Moscow, 1912.

————. *Nash detskii sad (Iz opyta doshkol'noi raboty Detskogo Gorodka imeni III Internatsionala pri Narkomprose v Moskve)*. Moscow, 1924.

————. *Russkie narodnye skazki dlia malen'kikh detei*. Moscow, 1910.

————. *Skazki i rasskazy*. Moscow, 1923.

Thorez, Paul. *Model Children: Inside the Republic of Red Scarves*. Translated by Nancy Cadet. New York: Autonomedia, 1991.

Tikheeva, E. I. *Organizatsiia detskogo sada i detskogo doma*. Moscow, 1923.

Trotsky, Leon. *My Life: The Rise and Fall of a Dictator*. London: Thorton Butterworth, 1930.

————. *Problems of Everyday Life and Other Writings on Culture and Science*. New York: Monad, 1973.

————. *The Revolution Betrayed*. New York: Pathfinder Press, 1972.

————. *Women and the Family*. New York: Pathfinder Press, 1972.

Tsyrlina, E. E., A. V. Surovtseva, and S. S. Molozhavyi, eds. *Materialy IV-go Vserossiiskogo s"ezda po doshkol'nomu vospitaniiu (po stenograficheskomu otchetu)*. Moscow-Leningrad: Gosudarstvennoe izdatel'stvo, 1929.

Ushinskii, K. D., and V. I. Vodovozov. *Domashnoe vospitanie: rukovodstvo dlia roditelei i vospitatelei k vospitaniiu i obucheniiu detei s prilozheniem rukovodstvo k Frebelskim obrazovatel'nym igram*. St. Petersburg: Tip. K. K. Retgera, 1883.

Venttsel', K. N. *Detskii dom*. Moscow, 1915.

————. *Novye puti vospitaniia i obrazovaniia detei*. Moscow, 1910.

————. *Teoriia svobodnogo vospitaniia i ideal'nyi detskii sad*. Moscow, 1915.

Vilenskaia, M. *Doshkol'noe vospitanie*. Moscow-Leningrad, 1928.

————, ed. *Spravochnaia kniga po doshkol'nomu vospitaniiu*. Moscow-Leningrad: Gosudarstvennoe izdatel'stvo, 1928.

Vilenskaia, M., S. S. Molozhavyi, and R. I. Prushitskaia, eds. *Tretii Vserossiiski S"ezd po doshkol'nomu vospitaniiu*. Moscow: G.M.P.T., 1925.

Vinogradov, N. *Ocherki po istorii idei doshkol'nogo vospitaniia*. Leningrad-Moscow, 1925.

Vodovozova, E. N. *Na zare zhizni: memuarnye ocherki i portrety*. Moscow: Khudozhestvenaia literatura, 1987.

————. *Umstvennoe razvitie detei pervogo proiavleniia soznaniia do vos'miletnogo vozrasta: kniga dlia vospitatelei*. 4th ed. St. Petersburg: Tip. V. S. Balasheva, 1891.

Vospominaniia 500 russkikh detei. Prague: Izdatel'stvo Pedagogicheskago biuro, 1942.

Winter, Ella. *Red Virtue: Human Relationships in the New Soviet Russia*. New York: Harcourt, Brace, and Co., 1933.

Zenzinov, Vladimir. *Deserted: The Story of the Children Abandoned in Soviet Russia*. London: H. Joseph, 1931.

Zetkin, Klara. *Sotsial'noe obespechenie materi i rebenka v Rossii*. Moscow: Izdatel'stvo Polit. otdela 2-i armii Vostochnogo fronta, 1919.

Secondary Sources

Anikin, V. P., V. E. Gusev, and N. I. Tolstoi, eds. *Mudrost' narodnaia: zhizn' cheloveka v russkom fol'klore*. Vol. 1, *Mladenchestvo, detsvo*. Moscow: Khudozhestvenaia literatura, 1991.

Archambault, Reginald. "Introduction." In *Tolstoy on Education*. Translated by Leo Weiner. Chicago: University of Chicago Press, 1967.

Ball, Alan. *And Now My Soul Is Hardened: Abandoned Children in Soviet Russia, 1918–1930*. Berkeley: University of California Press, 1994.

Beatty, Barbara. *Preschool Education in America: The Culture of Young Children from the Colonial Era to the Present*. New Haven, Conn.: Yale University Press, 1995.

Beliaev, V. I. "Shkola, sem'ia i obshchestvennost' (peredovoi opyt 20–30–kh gg.)." *Sovetskaia pedagogika* 12 (Dec. 1984):95–100.

Bonnell, Victoria. "The Iconography of the Worker in Soviet Political Art." In *Making Workers Soviet: Power, Class, and Identity*, ed. Lewis Siegelbaum and Ronald Grigor Suny. Ithaca, N.Y.: Cornell University Press, 1994.

———. "The Representation of Women in Early Soviet Political Art." *Russian Review* 50 (July 1991): 267–288.

Borisova, Z. N. "Osnovy kommunisticheskogo vospitaniia v trudakh N. Krupskoi i ikh realizatsiia v sovetskoi doshkol'noi pedagogike." *Sovetskaia pedagogika* 2 (Feb. 1984): 111–13.

Bowen, James. *Soviet Education: Anton Makarenko and the Years of Experiment*. Madison: University of Wisconsin Press, 1962.

Brooks, Jeffrey. *When Russia Learned to Read: Literacy and Popular Literature, 1861-1917*. Princeton, N.J.: Princeton University Press, 1985.

Burbank, Jane. "Lenin and the Law in Revolutionary Russia." *Slavic Review* 54 (Spring 1995):23–44.

Clark, Katerina. *The Soviet Novel: History as Ritual*. Chicago: University of Chicago Press, 1981.

Clements, Barbara Evans. "The Effects of the Civil War on Women and Family Relations." In *Party, State, and Society in the Russian Civil War: Explorations in Social History*, ed. Diane Koenker et al. Bloomington: Indiana University Press, 1989.

———. "The Utopianism of the Zhenotdel." *Slavic Review* 50 (Fall 1992): 485–496.

Coe, Richard N. *When the Grass Was Taller: Autobiography and the Experience of Childhood*. New Haven, Conn.: Yale University Press, 1984.

Cremin, Lawrence. *The Transformation of the School: Progressivism in American Education, 1876–1957*. New York: Vintage Books, 1964.

Deasey, Denison. *Education Under Six*. New York: St. Martin's Press, 1978.

Dovator, R. L. "Problemy semeinogo vospitaniia v progressivnoi russkoi pedagogike (konets XIX–nachalo XX v.)." *Sovetskaia pedagogika* 12 (Dec. 1985): 91–95.

Druzhnikov, Yuri. *Voznesenie Pavlika Morozova*. London: Overseas Publications Interchange, 1988.

Eklof, Ben. *Russian Peasant Schools: Officialdom, Village Culture, and Popular Pedagogy, 1861–1914*. Berkeley: University of California Press, 1986.

Engelstein, Laura. *The Keys to Happiness: Sex and the Search for Modernity in Fin-de-Siècle Russia*. Ithaca, N.Y.: Cornell University Press, 1992.

Farnsworth, Beatrice Brodsky. "Bolshevik Alternatives and the Soviet Family: The 1926 Marriage Law Debate." In *Women in Russia*, ed. Dorothy Atkinson et al. Stanford, Calif.: Stanford University Press, 1977.

Fitzpatrick, Sheila. *The Commissariat of Enlightenment: Soviet Organization of Education and the Arts Under Lunacharskii, Oct. 1917-21*. Cambridge: Cambridge University Press, 1970.

———. *The Cultural Front: Power and Culture in Revolutionary Russia*. Ithaca, N.Y.: Cornell University Press, 1992.

———. *Education and Social Mobility in the Soviet Union, 1921–34*. Cambridge: Cambridge University Press, 1979.

Frieden, Nancy M. "Child Care: Medical Reform in a Traditionalist Culture." In *The Family in Imperial Russia: New Lines of Historical Research*, ed. David Ransel. Urbana: University of Illinois Press, 1978.

Geiger, H. Kent. *The Family in Soviet Russia*. Boston, Mass.: Harvard University Press, 1968.

Gleason, Abbott. *Young Russia: The Genesis of Russian Radicalism in the 1860s*. Chicago: University of Chicago Press, 1980.

Goldman, Wendy Z. *Women, the State, and Revolution: Soviet Family Policy and Social Life, 1917–1936*. Cambridge: Cambridge University Press, 1993.

Hans, Nicholas. *The Russian Tradition in Education*. London: Routledge and Kegan Paul, 1963.

Hayashida, Ronald Hideo. "The Pedagogy of Protest: Russian Progressive Education on the Eve of the Revolution." *Slavic and European Education Review* 2 (1978): 11–30.

Hayden, Carol Eubanks. "The Zhenotdel and the Bolshevik Party." *Russian History* 3 (1976): 150–73.

Holmes, Larry E. *The Kremlin and the Schoolhouse: Reforming Education in Soviet Russia, 1917–31*. Bloomington: Indiana University Press, 1991.

———. "Part of History: The Oral Record and Moscow's Model School No. 25, 1931–1937." *Slavic Review* 56 (Summer 1997):279–306.

Johnson, R. E. "Family Life in Moscow During NEP." In *Russia in the Era of NEP: Explorations in Soviet Society and Culture*, ed. Sheila Fitzpatrick et al. Bloomington: Indiana University Press, 1991.

Joravsky, David. "The Construction of the Stalinist Psyche." In *Cultural Revolution in Russia*, ed. Sheila Fitzpatrick. Bloomington: Indiana University Press, 1978.

Keirim-Markus, M. B. *Gosudarstvennoe rukovodstvo kul'turoi: stroitel'stvo Narkomprosa (noiabr' 1917–seredina 1918 gg)*. Moscow: Nauka, 1980.

Konius, E. M. *Puti razvitiia sovetskoi okhrany materinstva i mladenchestva (1917–1940)*. Moscow, 1954.

Koven, Seth, and Sonya Michel. "Womanly Duties: Maternalist Politics and the Origins of the Welfare State in France, Germany, Great Britain, and the United States," *American Historical Review* 95 (Oct. 1990):1076–1108.

Kuzin, N. P., M. N. Kolmakova, and Z. I. Ravkin, eds. *Ocherki istorii shkoly i pedagogicheskoi mysli narodov SSSR, 1917–1941 gg*. Moscow: Pedagogika, 1980.

Lewin, Moshe. *The Making of the Soviet System: Essays in the Social History of Interwar Russia*. New York: Pantheon Books, 1985.

———. "Russia/USSR in Historical Motion: An Essay in Interpretation." *The Russian Review* 50 (1991):249–266.

Lilge, Frederic. *Anton Semyonovitch Makarenko: An Analysis of His Educational Ideas in the Context of Soviet Society*. Berkeley: University of California Press, 1958.

Litvin, L. N., ed. *Istoriia doshkol'noi pedagogiki*. Moscow: Proveshchenie, 1989.

Lotman, Iurii M., and Boris A. Uspenskii. "Binary Models in the Dynamics of Russian Culture (to the End of the Eighteenth Century)." In *The Semiotics of Russian Culture*, ed. Alexander Nakhimovsky and Alice Stone Nakhimovsky. Ithaca, N.Y.: Cornell University Press, 1985.

Mally, Lynn. *Culture of the Future: The Proletkult Movement in Revolutionary Russia*. Berkeley: University of California Press, 1990.

McClelland, James C. "The Utopian and the Heroic: Divergent Paths to the Communist Educational Ideal." In *Bolshevik Culture: Experiment and Order in the Russian Revolution*, ed. Abbott Gleason, et al. Bloomington: Indiana University Press, 1985.

McNeal, Robert. *Bride of the Revolution: Krupskaia and Lenin*. Ann Arbor: University of Michigan Press, 1972.

Monoszon, E. I. *Stanovlenie i razvitie sovetskoi pedagogiki, 1917–87*. Moscow: Prosveshchenie, 1987.

"Nachal'naia shkola v RSFSR za 40 let." *Nachal'naia shkola* 10 (1957):3–11.

Paperno, Irina. *Chernyshevsky and the Age of Realism: A Study in the Semiotics of Behavior.* Stanford, Calif.: Stanford University Press, 1988.

Petrova, B. D. *Istoriia meditsiny SSSR.* Moscow, 1964.

Petrovskii, B. V., ed. *50 let sovetskogo zdravookhraneniia, 1917–67.* Moscow: Meditsina, 1967.

Rosenberg, William. "Commentary: The Elements of Social and Demographic Change in Civil War Russia." In *Party, State, and Society in the Russian Civil War: Explorations in Social History,* ed. Diane Koenker, et al. Bloomington: Indiana University Press, 1989.

——. "Introduction: NEP Russia as a 'Transitional' Society." In *Russia in the Era of NEP: Explorations in Soviet Society and Culture,* ed. Sheila Fitzpatrick, et al. Bloomington: Indiana University Press, 1991.

Shabaeva, M. F., ed. *Istoriia doshkol'noi pedagogiki v Rossii: Khrestomatiia:* Moscow. Prosveshchenie, 1976.

Shapiro, Michael Stern. *Child's Garden: The Kindergarten Movement from Froebel to Dewey.* University Park: Penn State University Press, 1983.

Smith, S. A. *Red Petrograd: Revolution in the Factories, 1917–18.* Cambridge: Cambridge University Press, 1983.

Starr, S. Frederick. "Visionary Town Planning during the Cultural Revolution." In *Cultural Revolution in Russia,* ed. Sheila Fitzpatrick. Bloomington: Indiana University Press, 1978.

Stites, Richard. *Revolutionary Dreams: Utopian Vision and Experimental Life in the Russian Revolution.* New York: Oxford University Press, 1989.

——. *Russian Popular Culture: Entertainment and Society Since 1900.* Cambridge: Cambridge University Press, 1992.

——. *The Women's Liberation Movement in Russia: Feminism, Nihilism, and Bolshevism, 1860–1930.* Princeton, N.J.: Princeton University Press, 1978.

Teitelbaum, S. M. "Parental Authority in the Soviet Union." *American Slavic and East European Review* 4 (1945): 54–69.

Tucker, Robert, ed. *Stalinism: Essays in Historical Interpretation.* New York: W. W. Norton, 1977.

Tumarkin, Nina. *Lenin Lives! The Lenin Cult in Soviet Russia.* Cambridge: Harvard University Press, 1983.

Vendrovskaia, R. B. "Vospitanie v protsesse obucheniia: teoriia i praktika 20-kh gg." *Sovetskaia pedagogika* 4 (Apr. 1988):113–17.

Wachtel, Andrew. *The Battle for Childhood: Creation of a Russian Myth.* Stanford, Calif.: Stanford University Press, 1990.

Waters, Elizabeth. "The Bolsheviks and the Family." *Contemporary European History* 4 (1993):275–291.

——. "Teaching Mothercraft in Post-Revolutionary Russia." *Australian Slavonic and East European Studies* 1 (1987): 29–56.

Wollons, Roberta, ed. *Kindergartens and Cultures: The Global Diffusion of an Idea.* New Haven, Conn.: Yale University Press, 2000.

Wood, Elizabeth. *The Baba and the Comrade: Gender and Politics in Revolutionary Russia.* Bloomington: Indiana University Press, 1997.

Zelnik, Reginald. "On the Eve: Life Histories and Identities of Some Revolutionary Workers, 1870–1905." In *Making Workers Soviet: Power, Class, and Identity,* ed. Lewis Siegelbaum and Ronald Grigor Suny. Ithaca, N.Y.: Cornell University Press, 1994.

Index

225